1986
THE RANGERS
REVOLUTION

1986
THE RANGERS REVOLUTION

JEFF HOLMES

First published by Pitch Publishing, 2016

(pitch)

Pitch Publishing
A2 Yeoman Gate
Yeoman Way
Worthing
Sussex
BN13 3QZ
www.pitchpublishing.co.uk

A CIP catalogue record is available for this book from the British Library.

ISBN 978-1-78531-166-6

Typesetting and origination by Pitch Publishing

Printed in India by Replika Press Pvt. Ltd.

Contents

This book is for my
wife, Elaine

Also, for my children,
Derek and Carey, and
grandchildren Josh
and Zac

Acknowledgements

A PROJECT such as this is nigh-on impossible without the help of so many people. To that end, the following have given me invaluable assistance in a variety of ways: Paul Stringer (West Ham United), Andy Hall (Carlisle United), David Mason (Rangers FC), Brian Gallagher, Stan Gordon (Stonefield Tavern, Blantyre), Alex Boyd, Willie Clark, Colin Stewart and Finlay Calum Macaulay.

And a big thank you to Donald R. Findlay QC for a quite magnificent foreword.

Many of the chief protagonists of that era were also only too willing to give up their time either to meet for lunch and chat, or have a conversation over the telephone – so a big thank you to Alex Totten, John MacDonald, Ally Dawson, Colin West, Chris Woods, Ian Ferguson, John Brown, Derek Ferguson, Bobby Russell and Scott Nisbet.

And not forgetting the team at Pitch Publishing, including Paul Camillin, Jane Camillin, Duncan Olner, Graham Hales and all the others who put their heart and soul into making this publication what it is. Thank you.

Publications I found invaluable included *Rangers: The Complete Record* by Robert McElroy and Bob Ferrier; *Rangers: Player by Player*, by the same authors; *Rangers News*; the *Daily Record* and the *Sunday Mail*.

Fifty per cent of the profits from this book will be split equally between the Rangers Former Players Benevolent Club (formerly run by the late Colin Jackson) and the Rangers Youth Development Company – two causes close to my heart.

Introduction

THERE are a couple of reasons I decided to write this book. The most obvious is to mark the 30th anniversary of the arrival of Graeme Souness as player-manager, an appointment that changed the face of Glasgow Rangers and brought back the glory days after almost a decade of living in the shadows of others.

I started watching Rangers in 1970, and as a ten-year-old boy living in Maryhill I often relied on others to get me to and from Ibrox. Many a time I would walk to the match, though, and if there was enough change left in my pocket, I would get the bus home.

The thrill of going to the game on a Saturday afternoon was the most incredible experience for me, and I was glad I had decided not to follow in the footsteps of the rest of the family and support Partick Thistle.

The European Cup Winners' Cup semi-final against Bayern Munich was my first taste of a massive crowd and an equally massive occasion. It was the perfect European night, and I'll never forget the walk home to Maryhill after the game. We were all singing about going to Barcelona for the final. In those days I didn't have the first idea about where Barcelona was, but on the evening of Wednesday 24 May 1972 I was allowed to stay up late and watch the whole match on delayed transmission, scarves tied round both wrists and my woollen tammy on. It was another magical night.

Fourteen years passed, with varying degrees of success on and off the pitch, and we were floundering a bit when David Holmes and his board made the decision to change the entire mind-set at the club. They dismissed Jock Wallace and brought in Graeme Souness. It was mind-blowing.

I was 25 years old and employed by Scottish Television. I was working on a light entertainment show in the studio at Cowcaddens one day when reporter Jim White walked in. 'Jeff,' he called, 'I'm going over to Ibrox on a hush-hush job, wanna come?'

It was the magic word. As soon as Ibrox was mentioned I was off like a shot. I joined the six-man crew and off we went. In the car, Jim let me into a little secret; Rangers had appointed Graeme Souness as their new manager and he was getting the first, and exclusive, interview. He had become big pals with Souness after filming a documentary on the player while he was with Sampdoria. When Souness was offered the job, he called Jim to give him the exclusive. That was the way it worked.

When we arrived at Ibrox, we were met by caretaker boss Alex Totten who told us Souness was going to be around an hour late. Jim and I chose to wait in the Blue Room while the rest of the crew went off for lunch.

Jim might have been in the Blue Room, but I was in heaven!

Just over an hour later, the door opened and Totten showed Souness in. He had this aura about him, and I stood up – almost to attention! Jim did the introductions and said, 'Jeff runs a Rangers supporters' bus and is a lifelong fan.' Souness smiled, shook my hand and the three of us sat down for a chat, while waiting on the other members of the crew to return from their extended lunch break.

Souness said, 'If you don't mind, Jeff, I'll pick your brains a little,' and he asked me lots of questions about the supporters, the club, the team, etc. It was all going pretty well until he asked the million-dollar question. 'How do you think the fans will react if I sign a Catholic?'

Well, he never was one to shirk a tackle!

I grew up a traditional Rangers fan, singing the traditional Rangers songs, and I was very proud of my club's heritage. Like everyone else in the country, I was well aware of Rangers' signing policy, and occasionally it would be mentioned in the press when a journalist either decided it was completely wrong or he wanted to stir things up.

But whenever I'm asked a question I always try to give an honest answer, and I said to our new boss, 'I think it depends on who you sign. If you bring a talented Brazilian or Argentinian to the club, then I don't think too many people will have a problem, but if it's Peter Grant or Mo Johnston...' and the answer tailed off.

He looked at me, smiled, and nodded his head, and a couple of years later, when Johnston was unveiled as a Ranger, I allowed myself a wry smile, a Souness smirk almost, and thought back to that day in the Blue Room.

Jeff Holmes
April 2016

Foreword by Donald R. Findlay QC

I N the spring of 1986, many Rangers supporters were glad to see the back of another season in which they had witnessed Celtic pip Hearts to the league title.

For the eternal optimist, the World Cup in Mexico may have afforded the prospect of some good cheer. After all, Scotland had made it to the finals. The realist readily appreciated that being there was the traditional high point of our international aspirations.

No one, though, would have forecast that a 5ft 4in Argentinian would out-jump the world's best goalkeeper – albeit God had a hand in the matter, so to speak.

Benjamin Franklin famously said, 'In this world nothing can be said to be certain except death and taxes.' Had he been a true visionary, he would have added, 'And another Scottish football season will dawn bringing yet more gloom and doom for the men in Royal Blue.'

These were dark days.

Nine titles in a row for Celtic had been bad enough but to watch championship after championship ending up at Parkhead, Pittodrie and Tannadice was too much to bear, or too much for the Bears. Rangers were in the doldrums and there were more who were truly blue than True Blue. More of the same seemed an inevitability.

However, the darkest hour cometh before the dawn. As a ray of sunshine can brighten even the gloomiest day, as good must ultimately triumph over evil, as the emergence of a hero can raise the downtrodden masses, freeing them from the shackles of slavery – okay, enough of the prosaic.

Graeme Souness arrived on a winged chariot (one last indulgence) from Sampdoria to become the first player-manager of Rangers FC.

For me, the ideal player would be a class act, a hard man and a winner. Such a man strode into Ibrox and things were about to change – they had to change – and change they did.

While full credit is due to Lawrence Marlborough and David Holmes, it was Graeme who not only revitalised Rangers – he was also the driving force behind a revolution in Scottish football.

The old and restrictive wage structure was swept away. He set about reversing the trend of the best Scottish players heading south of the border. Aided by English clubs being excluded from Europe, he was determined to bring the best players into the Scottish game.

While I was, and am convinced, that his best ever signing was Walter Smith as his assistant, I would never have believed, sitting in a half-empty stadium, that I would see Terry Butcher, Gary Stevens, Trevor Steven, Chris Woods, Trevor Francis, Ray Wilkins, Mark Hateley and yes, Mo Johnston play at Ibrox in a Rangers jersey.

Such was the impact he made, the only question on the lips of the Ibrox faithful was, 'Who do you think will be second?'

However, and a tad worryingly, it did not start too well. Defeat at Easter Road and Souness sent off on his debut was not in the script. While Graeme walked off, George McCluskey was carried off. He had the misfortune to be in the wrong place at the wrong time – on the same pitch as Graeme!

However, as the Bard of Avon wrote, all's well that ends well and the championship returned to Ibrox. Yet this was only the opening paragraph in one of the greatest chapters in Rangers' proud history. What was started by Souness was carried on by David Murray and Walter Smith culminating in nine in a row.

If Rangers dominated Scottish football for a decade, other clubs strove manfully to match them, but could never quite get there. Celtic's championship in season 1987/88 briefly bucked the trend but Gough, Goram, McCall, Ferguson, Laudrup, Mikhailichenko, Durrant, Brown, Gascoigne and, of course, the Super One, to name but a few, kept the Blue Flag flying high.

As I look at Scottish football today, I find it distressing to contemplate when (or indeed if) we will again see such talent (and I of course include Mr Larsson) gracing our Premier League.

It was quite a year in 1986. To be but a small part of what flowed from it was an honour and a privilege and something of which I will always be proud and for which I am eternally grateful.

1986.

Cometh the hour.

Cometh the man.

Souness! Souness!! Souness!!!

Prologue

THE month of November 1985 just about sums up the Rangers of that period: two home games, two away. A scrappy 0-0 stalemate against struggling Clydebank at Ibrox in front of just 16,000, followed seven days later by an emphatic 3-0 win over arch rivals Celtic, watched by the obligatory full house.

The final two matches of the month brought road defeats at Hearts and Dundee, with the Light Blues losing three goals each time. It wasn't great, even for those supporters who, with much bravado, insisted the only games that mattered each season were the four against Celtic.

But while Ibrox regulars – and they were becoming fewer – were suffering in silence, plans were well afoot for a spectacular Rangers revolution. Just a couple of days after the 3-0 defeat at Tynecastle, the club appointed a new director. David Holmes was the man entrusted with both looking after the business interests of his employer, the Lawrence Group, AND creating the spark that would awaken a sleeping giant.

However the appointment caused a real stir in the media, with some commentators suggesting a bitter power struggle was looming. At the time, Mr Holmes countered, 'There is absolutely nothing sinister about what has happened. It's all very simple, above board and I'm sure it will benefit Rangers greatly.'

It transpired that the Lawrence Group, with Lawrence Marlborough at the helm, were making a serious bid to become the major stakeholder in Rangers Football Club. In view of the company's long and proud association with the club – Lawrence Marlborough was the great-grandson of previous chairman

John Lawrence – it seemed a natural course to take, although the decision was taken on far more than just sentiment alone. Mr Marlborough, Rangers' major shareholder, met with vice-chairman, Jack Gillespie, and the end result saw the Lawrence Group strengthen its position and links with the club.

At the time, Mr Gillespie owned around 81,000 shares in Rangers. The Vauxhall dealership proprietor had joined the Ibrox board eight years previous and risen to the dizzy heights of vice-chairman. At one point, he had been Rangers' largest single shareholder, but on this occasion he was the man responsible for the deal which would see the club have a single owner with a controlling stake for the first time ever.

Mr Gillespie, who had bought his first Rangers share in 1952, still harboured ambitions of becoming chairman, but while he never quite made it to the top seat, his decision to accept an offer for reputedly 29,000 of his shares turned the structure of the club on its head, and gave Lawrence Marlborough's firm a total holding of 52 per cent.

It was a decision which would herald the dawning of a bright new era for Rangers. It would also see Mr Gillespie marked down as a man of vision, and not just for the part he had played in ensuring Mr Marlborough was able to take charge of the club. He had also been heavily involved in the redevelopment of Ibrox Stadium, and was one of the brains behind the financing of the three new stands and the development of the Club Deck, working to ensure it was done speedily and at the best possible price. The late, great Rangers legend Sandy Jardine insisted Mr Gillespie did it for no reason other than he was 'a real Rangers man'.

Once the new addition to the boardroom came to terms with the way things operated at such a massive club, he knuckled down to ensure Rangers would grow sufficiently to fulfil its huge potential. Mr Holmes promised to keep Mr Marlborough – who was based in Nevada – up to speed with everything that was going on at Ibrox, but insisted he was no 'yes man' for the absent boss. Mr Holmes, who had lived in Falkirk all his life, brought enthusiasm, business know-how and a real hands-on approach to his new job.

He had started his working life as a joiner, before becoming a teacher at Jordanhill Training College. Moving to the Lawrence Group as a training officer in 1968, he worked his way up to the lofty position of managing director, a title he would acquire at Ibrox. But it was his approach to his new position that instantly impressed those around him. He would regularly turn up for work at Ibrox at 7am, and it was often a full 12 hours later before he left. It was this workaholic approach to his new job that helped make him such a success.

And while Mr Holmes may have been a fully paid-up and self-confessed member of the Falkirk Supporters Club, wife Betty, and daughter Lynne – who was to join her father at Ibrox as a marketing executive – were both bona fide Gers fans!

When asked what he could bring to Rangers, Mr Holmes answered, 'I can assure every supporter that I won't be happy until Rangers are a success again. That means regular participation in European competition and one day bringing the premier trophy to Ibrox.

'I will be using all the skills and experience I've picked up with a successful company like the Lawrence Group to augment the talent which is already on the Rangers board. All seven directors want success for the club, and I'm looking forward to the challenge of achieving that success as quickly as possible.'

Mr Holmes might not have been able to oversee the arrival of the European Cup at Ibrox, although the team did come close in the 1992/93 season, but he was true to his word in every other sense, and kick-started a revival that was to see Rangers once again installed to the higher echelons of the game at both home and abroad.

The Rangers Revolution might have taken place in the spring of 1986, but there is no doubt the building blocks were put firmly in place in the winter months of the year previous. The long-suffering days of the Rangers supporter were coming to an end – and what a pleasant journey we were about to embark on.

1

New Year, New Hope

IF 1986 had started off with Rangers in the doldrums, the end of the year would bring lashings of hope and optimism. The contrast was staggering – but there was a long and arduous road to negotiate in between.

The last match of the old year had begun with Ibrox Stadium's underground heating system failing due to a burst pipe – and ended with Rangers being frozen out in the Premier League by table-topping Hearts.

But if the weather was cold on 28 December, the atmosphere inside Ibrox was red hot. Sadly, though, it was the visitors who responded to the occasion best of all and left Rangers fans feeling anything but festive.

The biggest cause for concern was the apparent ease with which Hearts won at Ibrox in the Premier League for only the second time. And, soon after, when the draw was made for the third round of the Scottish Cup, it seemed as though the TV scriptwriters had been working overtime. Hearts at Tynecastle was one of the toughest ties imaginable, and it also meant a mad scramble for the 27,500 available tickets.

But Rangers manager Jock Wallace, never one to shirk a fight, said, 'Hearts are obviously the form team just now, but we aren't scared of them – regardless of where the tie takes place. We will go to Tynecastle looking for a win and it should be a cracking match for the fans.'

Rangers legends Alex MacDonald and Sandy Jardine were in charge of the Edinburgh side and had them challenging at the right end of the table. A tough tie awaited the Light Blues.

Meanwhile, Rangers made the short trip across the city for the traditional Ne'erday Old Firm derby – the 100th league meeting between the sides and the 199th overall – and it wasn't a good day for the blue half of the city.

In Celtic's first attack, Owen Archdeacon sent over a cross which the unmarked Paul McGugan rose to head past Nicky Walker to send the home fans in the near-50,000 crowd wild with delight. Rangers then had three opportunities to equalise but squandered the lot. Davie Cooper jinked past Danny McGrain and delivered a fierce knee-high cross, which beat Pat Bonner, but eluded everyone else – including Ally McCoist.

McCoist then had a shot blocked by Bonner, before Bobby Russell's curling chip rose above the keeper, and appeared to be going in. At the last moment, though, Bonner managed to back-track and claw the ball out from under the bar.

Celtic started to boss the game and doubled their lead four minutes after the break. Paul McStay crossed from the right, Stuart Munro managed to block it, but it fell again for McStay, and his cross was headed home by Brian McClair.

McCoist then sprung Celtic's offside trap but failed to beat Bonner from 14 yards. The victory saw Celtic leapfrog Rangers into fourth place, with the Ibrox side also adrift of leaders Hearts, Aberdeen and Dundee United.

Rangers were crying out for someone to help share the workload up front, but despite John MacDonald finding the net 18 times for the reserves before Christmas, he would spend the biggest part of the season banging them in for the second string.

But if Rangers had got off to a poor start in January, then the rest of the month would bring some much-needed, if somewhat belated, festive cheer to supporters. Just four days into 1986, Dundee arrived at Ibrox on league duty – and the Light Blues hit them for five. The Dens Park side might have been Rangers' bogey team at the time, but there was no sign of any curse on 4 January. And for the fans who braved the blizzard conditions, a return to goalscoring form was just the tonic to provide some much-needed warmth.

Boss Wallace knew his men had to improve on their poor record at Ibrox if they were to sustain any sort of challenge for silverware and there's no doubt he would have slept a lot easier after the match against the men from Tayside. It's doubtful there had ever been a more one-sided match between the sides in the Premier League and had it not been for the excellence of Dundee keeper Bobby Geddes, it could have been double figures.

The Light Blues attacked from the first minute but didn't make the breakthrough until the 25th with McCoist breaking the deadlock to end his mini goal famine – three games without hitting the net. It was just 1-0 at half-time, and after the interval Dundee started to come more into the game, but McCoist grabbed a crucial second direct from a free kick.

The Dark Blues' defence crumbled in the final ten minutes and Gers scored another three, despite being without Davie Cooper as Wallace had somewhat controversially decided to rest him. The legendary boss felt Coop had lost his edge, although his replacement, Ted McMinn, was forced off just four minutes after the break clutching his stomach. He was reported to have vomited blood during the interval.

The following day, Wallace was asked about possible transfer target Mogens Hansen, but insisted he had made no moves for the 29-year-old Danish midfielder. A report in the *Sunday Mail* that the international, who played for Maestved, would be coming to Ibrox for trials was also denied. Wallace said, 'I certainly haven't spoken to the player and neither has anyone else at Ibrox. I know who he is, but I couldn't even tell you which team he plays for.'

Meanwhile, one young Ibrox player who had bought two plane tickets back to his native Canada was delighted when he was told he wouldn't have to use them. Colin Miller had also sold his car and looked at thinning out his possessions after being given the bombshell news that his six-month contract with Rangers wouldn't be renewed. His deal was due to expire on 5 January but the 20-year-old Canadian World Cup star was walking on air when he was handed a reprieve by Jock Wallace.

He said, 'I was totally sick after putting my heart and soul into every day of my spell at Ibrox – but it seemed the number of players at the club had dictated that the boss couldn't keep me. He never questioned my ability and told me constantly I was playing well. So when he broke the news to me, it was pretty hard to take.

'But after the match against Celtic at Parkhead, he took me aside for a chat and, to my delight, we were able to agree to me staying on until the end of the season at least, but with an adjustment to my financial terms. Money is important to any player, but all I am considering at the moment is the chance to prove myself with Rangers and to keep playing competitive football in order to be on the plane with the Canadian squad for the World Cup finals in Mexico.

'My wife Maria and I were all set to head back to Vancouver. The flights were booked and I had reluctantly sold my car, but now nothing else matters and I'm still in with a chance of playing in the World Cup finals.'

Miller had moved with his family from his home in Allanton, North Lanarkshire to Canada at the age of ten, and even back then was a Ranger through and through – thanks to his father Joe.

He said, 'Dad is Rangers daft and I can vaguely remember him taking me and my brother to Ibrox for matches. But even when I went to school in Canada I had football in my blood, particularly Rangers.

'My dad played amateur football with Bonkle and Shotts and I suppose it was always his hope that one of his kids would one day make it to the professional ranks.'

After school, a 17-year-old Miller signed for Toronto Blizzard in 1982 and in the summer of 1983, he returned to Scotland at the request of Jock Wallace, then manager of Motherwell, to train at Fir Park. Wallace wanted to sign him but the player decided to return to Canada to honour his contract with Blizzard.

'In 1984, not long after we had played against Rangers on their world tour, and I had played very well in our 2-0 win, the North American Soccer League collapsed,' said Miller.

'Inex took over the club for a while before Jock Wallace asked me back to Scotland, this time for a trial period at Rangers, on the strength of that display for Toronto in that tour game. Since then I may have faced another contract disaster but now I've got it back and I'm looking forward to the future again.'

It was back to league business for Rangers on Saturday 11 January, with Clydebank the visitors to Ibrox. Just over 12,000 were present but the Gers prevailed in a six-goal thriller, to record their second successive league win for the first time since September – when they also beat the Bankies.

But, perhaps more importantly, they were starting to look capable of finding a consistency at Ibrox, where their title challenge had faltered in past seasons. The fixture against Bankies was switched from Kilbowie to Ibrox, but it was the decision to swap Bobby Russell for Ian Durrant which was to prove decisive.

It was 1-0 at half-time after Jim Gallacher had saved well from McCoist. But he then punched Ted McMinn's cross into the path of Craig Paterson, who shot home from ten yards. The Ibrox skipper then put through his own goal to make it 1-1, and when Bankies took the lead, the sighs from the crowd were audible. Rangers needed something special, although when Bobby Russell was on top form, they didn't come much better. He replaced Durrant on the hour and inspired Rangers to victory by creating all three second-half goals.

But another creative sort who felt he needed a break at the club was wing wizard McMinn. The 23-year-old wide boy had spent most of the season on the bench for the first team but was called into the side against Dundee at Ibrox. McMinn had a terrific first 45 minutes, causing his marker Jim Smith so much bewilderment that Smith was substituted by Dundee boss Archie Knox nine minutes from half-time.

But the Light Blues' ace was forced to leave the field only three minutes into the second half, clutching his stomach after having vomited blood during the interval. Then, after recovering from that in time to play against Clydebank, he discovered his booking against Celtic on New Year's Day had earned him a two-match suspension, which meant he would miss the games against St Mirren and Hearts.

McMinn said, 'I just can't seem to put any sort of run together in the first team this season – things simply aren't working out my way. I was really pleased with how I was playing against Dundee, then Jim Smith caught me in the ribs with a pretty heavy challenge. The club doctor reckons that's what caused me to be so violently sick. I felt really bad, and even though I was determined to play in the second half, I had to give up after a few minutes.'

But the team as a whole was having a much better time of it than the unorthodox winger, and when they grabbed a third successive home victory – a 2-0 win over St Mirren – many of their fans started to believe.

The leaders of the Premier League pack may still have been roaring along at top gear but Rangers were revving up very nicely in the race for the chequered flag. In the most fascinating title battle for years, Hearts continued their remarkable run of success with victory at Pittodrie. Meanwhile, many miles south, at Ibrox, Rangers were overcoming a slightly easier hurdle with a deserved success over the Paisley Saints, but the victory was no less significant and kept the Light Blues in the championship race despite having been written off in many quarters.

After getting off to such a bad start at Parkhead, 1986 was turning out to be pretty good for Rangers and this latest victory was the perfect boost ahead of the Scottish Cup tie against Hearts. The win over Saints couldn't be described as a vintage performance but it was competent enough, especially in the first half when Rangers killed off the game with two goals in half an hour.

After surviving an early scare when Nicky Walker – again in superb form – had leapt well to touch a cute Tony Fitzpatrick chip-shot over the bar, Rangers opened the scoring. Davie Cooper, making a significant contribution on his return to action after his much-publicised two-week lay-off, sent over a swirling corner. Craig Paterson rose above everyone to head the ball down and the sharpest striker in Scotland, Ally McCoist, added another to his tally with a right-foot drive from eight yards.

Super Cooper was the creator of the second, this time with a good cross from the left. Davie McPherson used all his power and height to beat two Saints defenders and send a fine header past the despairing Campbell Money. It was a good solid display with Hugh Burns and Ally Dawson outstanding.

One young Rangers player then switched sports from the green field of Ibrox to the green baize of the snooker table. Billy Davies may not have been much of a threat to his near namesake, Steve, but the talented midfielder was proving himself pretty useful with cue in hand. The Ibrox reserve team skipper was a regular visitor to Bailey's Leisure Centre, near Ibrox, and along with young brother John, the ex-Ranger who moved to Clydebank, Billy entered the club's open snooker tournament.

Up against some better-than-average amateur players, Billy and John won through to the quarter-finals to play each other, with Davies senior clinching a narrow 2-1 win. There was no stopping Billy after that and he made it to the best-of-five frames final, in which he defeated Malky McKay 3-1 to lift the splendid silver trophy.

He said, 'Snooker is a great way of relaxing away from training so to win a competition was a bonus. Now a few of the other players at Ibrox are planning to enter next year to try and take my title from me.'

There was one player, though, who was earning the plaudits of his manager for his sparkling performances on the field. Jock Wallace was a big fan of Bobby Russell, and said, 'I have been a long-time admirer of Bobby ever since I took him for his first senior training session as a full-timer way back in July 1977. You must also remember I signed him after watching him for only 20 minutes in a reserve game, so nobody needs to tell me about the boy's ability.

'However, there is no doubt that until recently he hadn't quite lived up to the standards we all know he is capable of. The last few weeks, though, seem to indicate he is right back on form. But

I'm more delighted for the club because when Bobby's playing well, he is one hell of an asset.'

At that time, Rangers were considering building a Hall of Fame museum at Ibrox – and were looking for help from supporters. The club were hoping to set up the initiative during the close season but needed lots of memorabilia to make it a success. Tom Dawson was the director in charge of the project, which had been gathering pace, but it all ground to a halt when Mr Dawson was ousted from the club during upheaval in the boardroom.

Meanwhile, defender Davie MacKinnon was told he required an operation on his damaged right knee, and was convinced his season was all but over. But the 29-year-old, who sustained the injury on Boxing Day against Celtic reserves, reckoned without a brilliant new medical advance.

MacKinnon picked up the knock while crossing the ball and jarred his foot on the turf. It later transpired that he had damaged a cartilage in his knee. Normally, an operation for such an injury would take around six weeks to recover from, with the player getting back into action sometime after that period, but thanks to the marvels of modern science that was no longer the case, and MacKinnon was operated on with an arthroscope on the Friday night at 5pm. That same evening, he was out of hospital and the micro-surgery was so successful he was back in light training just a fortnight later.

He said, 'It was terrific news when the doctors told me how quickly I would be back in action. I should actually be fit again in time for this weekend, which is quite remarkable. With my contract up at the end of the season, the last thing I wanted was to be out for a long period. Now I can get back into it quickly and try to battle my way back into the first team.

'Obviously it isn't going to be easy to get back into the side with Hugh Burns and Ally Dawson filling the positions in defence I have played in, but I reckon I could do a good job in midfield, too, if necessary and help along young Derek Ferguson and Ian Durrant, who are such promising players.'

Another youngster trying to make his mark at Ibrox was goalkeeper Andy Bruce. The 21-year-old shot-stopper was in his sixth full season as a Rangers player. Signed on a provisional full-time contract in 1980, he was farmed out to leading junior side Linlithgow Rose, and the Edinburgh youngster was tipped as one of Scotland's top goalkeeping prospects.

Since then, he had shown his talent to be worthy of that early praise, winning Scottish caps at schoolboy, youth and under-21 level, but he still hadn't been able to win a regular first-team place at Ibrox. In fact, he had only made 11 senior appearances since making his debut against Southampton back in 1981/82. But none of that bothered him too much and even though his contract was due to expire at the end of the 1985/86 season, he was still keen to stay on at Ibrox.

At the time, he said, 'I have complained in the past, probably a bit too loudly, about a lack of first-team opportunities, but I certainly can't complain about that this season. There is no way I would expect to get into the side with Nicky Walker playing so well. He is having a great time of it and proving just what a fantastic goalkeeper he is.

'Perhaps some people might have thought there was some sort of bitterness from me towards Nicky when I spoke last season of my feelings at not being in the side. Nothing could be further from the truth – we have been good friends for a long time and still are. I hope he continues to play well for a long time.

'That's not to say I don't want that first-team place. Of course I do. But what I'm more immediately concerned with is being guaranteed a game every week, either with the reserves or first team. I know it's a problem at a lot of clubs with three keepers on their books [Peter McCloy was also at Ibrox] but I really feel I must be sure of being able to play 90 minutes every Saturday.'

Bruce was a regular for the reserves and hadn't lost a goal all season until near the end of January, when the Ibrox colts took on Aberdeen's second string. It was top striker Frank McDougall who broke his heart that day, but even the player himself admitted he had no chance with the goal.

One other record Bruce hoped he would never achieve was his 100th match for the reserves – although his next game would notch up the landmark figure. He made his debut for the reserves in an 8-2 win over Albion Rovers in February 1981, and with the score at 8-1, he came flying out to dive at the feet of Rovers striker Stuart Burgess, who caught the keeper in the head with his boot. Bruce received nine stitches and afterwards manager John Greig asked him why he had executed such a daring move, especially as his team was 8-1 up. 'Because he would have scored, Mr Greig,' said a proud young keeper!

But the big match was looming, and it wasn't long before everyone's attention was turning to Tynecastle – and the third round of the Scottish Cup. Prior to the tie, Jock Wallace had overseen 32 Scottish Cup ties and won 23. Rangers had drawn four and lost five on his watch – but this one would arguably be the toughest of the lot.

Since leaving Ibrox, Alex MacDonald and Sandy Jardine had moulded Hearts into a team of genuine championship contenders – and had also turned Tynecastle into something of a fortress.

The Gorgie Road stadium was packed to capacity as the teams took to the field, and at the end of 90 torrid minutes the only expectation this game failed to live up to was the one Rangers had – of winning it.

The determination of the Light Blues to clear the toughest possible hurdle into round four of the cup was immense, yet in a match that had everything which makes cup football so popular with the fans, the Ibrox men could point to a couple of controversial incidents which arguably cost them a chance of progressing – and left their fans screaming with rage.

With Rangers having clawed their way back to 2-2 in a pulsating match, Gary Mackay fouled Derek Ferguson out on the stand-side touchline in the 72nd minute. Fergie showed his inexperience by retaliating and pushing the Hearts player to the ground. In the white hot atmosphere of such an important game his actions deserved no more than a booking but instead the youngster, who was never a dirty player, was shown the red card by referee Tommy Muirhead.

Rangers were left with ten men but appeared to be holding out for a replay at Ibrox when along came flashpoint number two just five minutes from time. As Nicky Walker raced from his line to collect a through ball, he was engulfed amid a number of players from both sides. Suddenly, John Robertson emerged from the pack with the ball and cracked it into the empty net. The Rangers players were furious and Ally Dawson, who had a close-up view of the action, clearly felt Walker had been fouled. But the sweeper, who chased the referee all the way to the centre circle, saw his protest come to nothing and Rangers were out of the cup.

It was tough luck on the Gers, who had been forced to reshuffle their side when Craig Paterson was stretchered off following a clash of heads with Sandy Clark, who also had to leave the field. Rangers managed to settle down, with McPherson moving back into the centre of defence and Russell coming on in midfield. And a minute from half-time they opened the scoring in style.

Hugh Burns ran down the right and played the ball inside to Durrant, who fed Cooper on the left. The winger's swerving cross was superb and McCoist dived to head his 30th goal of the season in all competitions.

It looked good for Rangers at that stage but Hearts turned the tie round in the first ten minutes of the second half. A Mackay corner was cleared by Colin Miller, who then blocked a Kenny Black shot on the line, but he had no chance with a low drive into the opposite corner by Colin McAdam.

Seven minutes later, a Colquhoun corner saw Burns sweep a McAdam effort off the line, but the ball broke back to Colquhoun, and his cross was turned in by Mackay.

Rangers fought back and on 69 minutes they got the goal that seemed certain to earn them a replay. Smith and Levein made a mess of a through ball and Durrant nipped in to head home – but it was too little, too late and Robertson's controversial strike meant Rangers were out of the cup. Surely, though, the battling performance would stand them in good stead for the challenges that lay ahead.

2

Ally's Dons Goal Jinx

ALLY McCoist's goals may have kept Rangers in with a slender chance of winning the title, but the man who would go on to become the club's all-time top goalscorer was still aiming to smash a personal jinx in the Granite City. To that end, the Premier League's top scorer – and without doubt the form striker in Scotland – had the names of Leighton, McLeish and Miller fixed firmly in his mind. That trio made up the spine of the most famous defence in the country – and Aberdeen were the only Premier League side McCoist had failed to score against since his £185,000 move from Sunderland almost three years previously.

But the 23-year-old was enjoying a quite marvellous season and viewed the weekend crunch game against the Dons at Ibrox as the best time to break his duck and complete his top ten of scoring scalps.

He said, 'To be honest, I wouldn't mind playing my worst game of the season as long as we take two points – that's really vital for us. But I'll be looking to keep my good run going and I would love to finally stick one past Jim Leighton.

'I don't really find it any harder playing against Leighton, McLeish and Miller than any other defence, although obviously they are rated as the best in the country. But as far as I'm concerned the Dundee United defence are just as good and I have a good scoring record against them.

'I think it's all a question of how the breaks have gone for me against Aberdeen, although I'm the first to admit I have missed a few chances in these games. In my very first game against them for Rangers, at Ibrox in September 1983, I did everything right before trying to beat Leighton, but hit the post with a shot. They went on to win 2-0 that day so it made a difference.

'And last season when we drew 0-0 at Pittodrie in our first meeting of the season, I should have buried a couple of chances I got in the air. However, those are the kind of opportunities I am now putting away and I'll be going into Saturday's game as confident as I have ever been.'

At the start of the season, Super Ally had set himself a target of 30 league goals. With the Aberdeen game looming, he was well on target to break that barrier – and had re-assessed his goals goal as a result. His recent strike in the 2-0 win over St Mirren at Ibrox had been his 90th first-team goal for Rangers, and his 100th overall in a light blue jersey when the ten he had scored for the reserves were taken into account.

Although his first two seasons could by no means be described as failures, with 36 goals in 1983/84 and then 25 the following term, 1985/86 was turning out to be his most consistent yet. He said, 'I haven't been doing anything differently this season, although I possibly have more confidence to have a go with any half-chance which comes my way, and thankfully, a lot of them are going in.

'Playing alongside Bobby Williamson is a big help too, as he works tremendously hard. I might have scored more goals than Bobby but he deserves just as much of the credit for the unbelievable amount of effort he puts into a match.'

McCoist's success had inevitably seen the media point to him as a possible Scotland candidate for Mexico – but while he remained flattered, he insisted the World Cup was the furthest thing from his mind.

He said, 'A lot of people were commiserating with me about being excluded from the international squad for the Israel game – but I would have been astonished to have been given the nod for the original pool. But I am now delighted to be going to Israel, even if it was only because of call-offs. Of course I want to play for my country and I have as much ambition as anyone to play in the World Cup finals, but all I'm concerned about at the moment is continuing to score goals for Rangers.

'If I can do that, Fergie [Alex Ferguson] won't ignore me, and if I can stick a couple past Aberdeen on Saturday, that would be the best possible way to make him sit up and take notice.'

But it wasn't to be, and even though Rangers managed to take a point from the game, it was Hugh Burns who scored for the Light Blues. Mind you, even 'Shuggy' didn't manage to hog the headlines, as that accolade went to the irrepressible Ted McMinn. The 24-year-old, who confirmed he was an asthmatic, socked it to the Dons despite being in opposition to the formidable Neil Simpson. The gangly player emerged from the contest like the Lone Ranger with the big cigar.

Before the match, McMinn's claim to fame was a goal direct from a corner at Dumbarton and the £100,000 purchase price from hometown club Queen of the South. He was certainly unorthodox and ran like a colt unsteady on its feet, and in the style of Don Kichenbrand, an Ibrox star of the 1950s. These were qualities fans loved in a game being played more and more by robots.

Success was all around McMinn at Ibrox. Five World Cup stars on the pitch – and he was better than any in a stirring 90 minutes. It was the stuff punters love. Like a boxing match with a close call or a top athlete bashing out a world record in the 1,500m.

Mind you, perhaps the Premier League had slipped a little, because for the first time since it started, there was no outstanding title contender. Jock Wallace, who told his players to run at Aberdeen, said, 'If we could pick up some of Aberdeen's poise and discipline, it would do no harm. A bit of consistency would see us right up there as genuine contenders.'

McMinn, a former saw-miller, said, 'I was shattered at the end. When I intercepted a loose pass by Jim Bett and ran nearly the length of the pitch, I thought I'd need an oxygen tent. It's the first time I've played in central midfield for Rangers, although Drew Busby reckoned it was my best position at Queen of the South.'

Joe Miller headed a goal in two minutes and it looked as though Aberdeen would romp to victory. The Dons hadn't won away since their last visit to Ibrox, four months earlier. In the second half, Rangers took over and, apart from Burns equalising, Jim Leighton made the save of the season from Ally McCoist's left-foot shot.

The day after the match, boss Wallace let rip – at the bookmakers who had decided his Rangers side were title also-rans. In fact, he went one step further by tipping his side to win the league, and snarled, 'I think, and so do the players, that the championship is still there to be won.'

The bookies clearly believed otherwise, listing the Ibrox men at a staggering 16/1, but Wallace insisted that was 'rubbish'. Aberdeen and Dundee United were 9/4 favourites, with Celtic at 11/4 and Hearts 4/1.

'Rangers will never give up on anything,' said Wallace. 'On Saturday I thought we were unlucky only to draw. I read that Aberdeen thought they would slaughter us – that will be right! Anybody who thinks Rangers can't still top the lot is a pretty poor judge. We're there, and we're fighting.'

As a result of a tremendous performance against the Dons, the Rangers players were given an extra day off but most of the first-team squad still turned up for voluntary training. Skipper Craig Paterson had the ten stitches removed from the head wound he had suffered during the Scottish Cup defeat at Tynecastle and was able to resume training.

The old adage that football fans have very short memories certainly couldn't have been levelled at the Ibrox faithful. Iain Ferguson, very much out of the first-team picture for so long with Rangers, was a surprise choice of substitute for the match against the Dons. And when he was introduced to the action with 21 minutes to go, Fergie received an ecstatic welcome from the Light Blues' supporters, who made it clear the 23-year-old striker was still tops as far as they were concerned.

He was clearly very pleased at the response he received from the large support – but was quick to point out his situation with Rangers hadn't changed.

He said, 'I still want to leave the club and 21 minutes against Aberdeen doesn't solve the situation which led to myself and Cammy Fraser being put up for sale in the first place. The manager has said some encouraging things about me recently and I know he still rates me highly as a player. There was never any doubt about that.

'Cammy and I were put up for sale because the boss felt our style of play wasn't suited to Rangers. I have never argued with that. In fact, I have never had an argument with Jock Wallace since I signed for Rangers.

'If I hadn't been injured and out for seven weeks after being put on the transfer list, I honestly believe I would be with another club just now. There are still rumours going on about various clubs being interested at the moment. But until anything concrete arrives I want to play for the Rangers first team and score goals, which is what I was bought for. I have certainly never lost any faith in my ability. If I ever did, I would chuck it.

'And I know the fans have faith in me too. To get the kind of reception I enjoyed against Aberdeen after being out for so long was amazing and I can't thank them enough. I have had a terrific relationship with the punters right from the day I signed for the club and I hope it will stay that way whatever happens in the future.'

And while Fergie was still adamant his future lay away from Ibrox, the words of Jock Wallace gave the fans some hope of seeing the player in a Rangers jersey for some time to come.

Wallace said, 'There's a first-team place for anyone who shows me the right form and attitude and Fergie has been doing that recently. He has more than earned the right to challenge for a place in the top squad. He has looked sharp in the reserves and also in training and there's no way he will be kept on the sidelines by me just because he is up for transfer.'

Up until February, Ferguson had scored just one first-team goal and 12 for the reserves. But any talk of transfers was tossed to one side as Wallace was determined to capitalise on a top display against Aberdeen when his side made the short trip to Motherwell to face Gers legend Tommy McLean's bottom markers. However, heavy snow looked like scuppering plans for the match – and McLean was in no hurry to ask Rangers to host the game, despite the benefit of undersoil heating which would have ensured it went ahead.

McLean said, 'At the moment we have two inches of snow on top of a soft pitch. Naturally we don't want to fall any further behind in fixtures, as we have three games to make up already, but if the game is called off it won't be a total disaster.

'Rangers are starting to get results again, so we want them at Fir Park with the chance of a big crowd instead of facing them in maybe the second last game of the season when there might be nothing to play for.'

The game did go ahead but a devastating 1-0 loss saw Rangers' championship challenge hit the skids. After reviving their title tilt with seven points from their previous four matches at Ibrox, they slipped up badly against the lowly Lanarkshire side. And the defeat left them a massive eight points behind leaders Hearts, with only ten matches left to play. Hugh Burns was once again outstanding for Gers but Andy Walker scored the only goal of the game.

Rangers could have no complaints about the result – and Jock Wallace didn't make any excuses. His post-match comments against his old side were short and to the point, 'We were a shadow of the side that played so well against Aberdeen last week. But playing one good game every six weeks is absolutely no good.' There was no doubt about it, inconsistency was killing Rangers.

Jock Wallace might not have admitted as much, but even in February, the Light Blues' season was all but over. It wasn't just the defeat at the hands of struggling Motherwell, but the manner in which they had succumbed to McLean's side.

Mind you, one man bang on form was McMinn. The 'Tin Man', as he was christened by some, was nigh on unplayable on his day – and spoke of how his 'free role' was helping him achieve some devastating results. Oh, and he also touched on the fact that THREE different Aberdeen players had tried to mark him out of the recent battle at Ibrox.

McMinn thrilled the Rangers fans with his perpetual motion and while his praises were sung right through the media afterwards, the player admitted he found it all pretty amusing.

He said, 'I was more or less given a free role in the middle of the park by the gaffer and it worked a treat for me. I just played the way I always do and I was amazed at how rattled Aberdeen were.

'I started off the game with Neil Simpson marking me, then Jim Bett was switched into the middle on to me and I ended up with Billy Stark following me around the pitch. It was quite flattering really and I was very pleased with how I played.'

It was all good news for McMinn after a season which had so far delivered only the frustrations of being in and out of the first team and, when he had been with the senior squad, more often than not he had been used only as a substitute.

But the player had a theory, and said, 'I think the problem has been the gaffer's reluctance to play me and Davie Cooper in the same side. And I didn't do my chances any good when I took over from Coop for the Motherwell game in December while he was on World Cup duty.

'I had an absolute nightmare that day – I was just far too keen to impress. However, I got another chance the following month when the gaffer told Davie to have that two-week break and I did much better in the games against Dundee and Clydebank.

'Then, of course, I was suspended for two games and I was pretty fed up as I thought I would lose my place for a while again. But then the manager gave me the central midfield role and it seemed to work out fine. I played there with Queen of the South a few times and Drew Busby told me he would play me in that position all the time if I wasn't so greedy with the ball! I've got rid of that fault now and feel I could keep a regular place. Dougie Bell helped me tremendously against Aberdeen and, as far as I'm concerned, he was the man of the match – he was terrific.

'Another thing I have improved on is my fitness. When I first came to Ibrox I really struggled to last the 90 minutes, but Coop recommended I run a lot of circuits round the Ibrox track and that helped my stamina considerably.'

But if defenders and punters didn't know what McMinn was going to do next, the Ibrox board certainly had a plan for the future – and it was to make Rangers one of the most successful businesses in the country.

There was no magic wand in the Edmiston Drive boardroom, but the directors had all agreed to run the club on the sound basic principles which have to be followed in any business, regardless of whether you are selling sweets, computers or running a football club. It was important to have sound management and a staff doing their jobs properly.

Liverpool and Manchester United were perfect examples of clubs run on modern business lines, while closer to home there had been a dramatic change in the fortunes of Hearts since a man who knew more about business than football had taken control of the Tynecastle club.

The last man who had treated Rangers as a business, in the true sense of the word, was, coincidentally, the late John Lawrence. He had created a huge building firm before joining the Ibrox board and, in the 1960s, had made a point of stating how he felt Rangers had been hopelessly undervalued and how he had restructured their shares and transformed their financial situation.

Now, in 1986, his nephew, Lawrence Marlborough, had clearly decided Rangers again required 'sorting out' – although in a slightly different way.

He had taken the first steps towards the end of 1985 by arranging to buy a chunk of vice-chairman Jack Gillespie's huge shareholding. That gave the Lawrence Group control of Rangers FC and David Holmes, their managing director, and Hugh Adam, the man behind the successful Rangers Pools, were soon on the Ibrox board alongside chairman John Paton.

Rae Simpson, Jim Robinson and Tom Dawson had resigned from the board, which led to a field day for the press, who likened the goings-on at Ibrox to a TV soap opera. Mind you, if all the people they had tipped as future directors had been given a seat, the wall in Rangers' famous Blue Room would've had to be knocked down to allow them all to sit round a massive table!

They also distastefully suggested that Lawrence Marlborough, based in America, was sitting across the pond pulling the strings of a puppet board, but David Holmes pointed out that business didn't work like that. He insisted the boss of a big company would never install a management team and then do the work for them.

Mr Holmes, a man with a sparkling management record, was clearly handed the task of making the new set-up work. He was also given a certain amount of time to get results since his company had made a huge financial investment in Ibrox and were expecting a return. He and the three other directors were also well aware that the team's supporters were not in a patient mood.

Ex-chairman Rae Simpson's departure no doubt surprised few as at 70 years of age he had enjoyed a long spell in legislation with the Scottish League and SFA. However, Jim Robinson and Tom Dawson were perhaps unfortunate to be in office at the end of an era.

It was becoming ever clearer that the days were over when people became a Rangers director simply because they had gathered a substantial number of shares or because they had played well for the club years earlier.

It was easy to predict that, like any other well-run company, Rangers would only add to the board if they could find individuals whose expertise, experience or flair would be used to make the club more successful. It was true of all successful football outfits that they made few mistakes on the field and even fewer off it. The modern history of football had also shown that when a club's directors started consistently making good decisions they didn't have to wait too long before the players started mirroring those achievements on the field of play.

That's why those close to Rangers, and that multitude who cared so much about such a world-famous team, could say with confidence that Rangers were starting to go places.

Back to the football, though, and Rangers – out of the Scottish Cup – lined up a top-drawer friendly match to fill the vacant weekend. London giants Chelsea were invited up to Ibrox, and readily accepted. The game was due to take place on a Friday night – Valentine's Day – and Jock Wallace was hoping to feel the love with a famous victory.

The match-up gave Rangers fans a chance to see international stars like Kerry Dixon and David Speedie in action. The Chelsea side also included Pat Nevin, Doug Rougvie and Mike Hazard, as well as their exciting front player Paul Canoville. The Rangers and Chelsea fans were known to have a close relationship, particularly in the mid-1980s, when they had gone to great lengths to attend each other's matches.

On the eve of the match, *Rangers News*, the club's official publication, asked readers to help find the best ever Rangers team – a full 13 years before the 'definitive' vote to find the Greatest Ever Ranger. The *News* vote was to include all players who had made an appearance for the club between 1946 and 1986. More than 500 supporters took the time to vote and their favourite team was: Bobby Brown, Sandy Jardine, Eric Caldow, John Greig, Willie Woodburn, Jim Baxter, Willie Waddell, Ian McMillan, Willie Thornton, Ralph Brand and Davie Cooper.

Brown easily landed the number one jersey, polling more than 300 votes as opposed to Peter McCloy's 90. But while the goalie slot was a stick-on, it was a little closer in midfield where McMillan just edged out Bobby Russell, while Thornton held off the challenge of Derek Johnstone and Jimmy Millar up front. Surprisingly, Ally McCoist – in his third season with the Gers – polled just 1.72 per cent of the final vote.

On the domestic front, critics were suggesting the lights may have gone out on Rangers' title challenge – and it certainly seemed that way on the evening of the match against Chelsea when there was a power failure at Ibrox. But nothing could dim what proved to be a sparkling match in front of an appreciative crowd of more than 17,000 who braved the freezing weather. And Rangers' victory was just the tonic the players required ahead of their double header against the so-called 'New Firm' – with both games away from home.

Rangers started the match against Chelsea the brighter of the two and Blues keeper Eddie Niedzwiecki was busy early on saving from Ally McCoist and Iain Ferguson – although he couldn't prevent Rangers taking the lead. A Cooper corner was flicked on by Ferguson to Ally Dawson who chipped the ball towards goal. Derek Johnstone rose to challenge Niedzwiecki, and the ball broke to Paterson at the edge of the box and he hammered it in.

Future Ranger Nigel Spackman equalised with a terrific shot, but if that was a good goal, Rangers' second in the 53rd minute was quite brilliant. The Chelsea defence was ripped apart by a superb one-touch move involving Dougie Bell, Ferguson and McCoist, with Bell supplying the finishing touch from ten yards to record his first goal for the Light Blues.

Nicky Walker then superbly saved a Spackman rocket before Kevin McAllister set up Keith Jones for the equaliser. Sadly, a small section of the crowd almost spoiled a superb atmosphere by booing Chelsea's black midfielder Jones. The Rangers board had posted a message in the club newspaper earlier in the season asking supporters to stop this type of behaviour, but the lesson quite clearly hadn't been learned by some.

It was end-to-end stuff after Chelsea's equaliser but Hugh Burns scored a spectacular winner late on from 25 yards to give Rangers a narrow, but well-deserved, victory.

Attention then switched to off the park, and the continuing saga of the 'Rebel Nine' Scottish clubs.

Their seven-month-long battle for a breakaway league reached its conclusion near the end of February when agreement was finally reached with the League Management Committee.

The package agreed between the two sides meant that no team would be relegated from the Premier League at the end of the 1985/86 season, while the next two campaigns would see a league formation of 12-12-14.

All Scottish League clubs were informed of the proposals and at a special general meeting in Glasgow they were asked to approve the joint decision. Campbell Ogilvie, Rangers' secretary and representative of the Rebel Nine, and league secretary Jim Farry issued a joint statement.

It read, 'At the end of season 1987/88, three clubs will be relegated from the Premier League and one promoted from the First Division. This will restore the present 10-14-14 set-up.'

A compromise package was put before the First and Second Division clubs. The proposals, which were agreed after a meeting of Wallace Mercer (Hearts), John Paton (Rangers) and Jack McGinn (Celtic), were as follows: Two clubs to be promoted from the First Division at the end of this season – but no relegation, which will make the Premier League up to 12 clubs.

At the end of the NEXT season two clubs would be relegated and only one promoted, leaving the Premier League with 11 clubs for a season.

At the end of 1987/88, two clubs would be relegated and one promoted to restore the Premier Division to ten clubs. The format for promotion and relegation would then be one up, one down every season. Makes you wonder exactly why they had bothered changing things in the first place!

Campbell Ogilvie and John Paton weren't the only club representatives hanging around the SFA offices in Park Gardens, as Jock Wallace faced up to his second charge of the season. The SFA's Executive Committee decided the Ibrox manager had a case to answer for his criticism of referee Tommy Muirhead after his club were dumped out of the Scottish Cup by Hearts in January. Big Jock had been critical of Derek Ferguson's sending off, saying, 'I don't know why he was sent off. It was a terrible decision.'

Meanwhile, Ally McCoist was on target as Rangers left Tannadice with a hard-fought 1-1 draw in a Premier League encounter with Dundee United. The result summed up a month which had proved a microcosm of Rangers' entire season – draws against Aberdeen and Dundee United, the top two teams in the league, victory over Chelsea and defeat against bottom side Motherwell.

Cammy Fraser was outstanding against United and when Wallace moved McPherson back and put Derek Johnstone up front, they gave United as good as they got. Once again, Hugh Burns walked off with the man-of-the-match award and was acquiring quite a reputation.

With February drawing to a close, Rangers were set to open the doors to the punters as never before – even though the club was now a closed shop financially. David Holmes explained,

'Rangers belongs to the fans and my company, and our chairman Lawrence Marlborough, have never thought otherwise. We want to give them the best deal, but above all to feel that when they come to Ibrox, the door is never closed to them.

'The customers are important to Rangers. We want them to come to the ground and be treated as reasonable people; to get to know us all and especially the players. We have to maximise Ibrox as a place in every way.

'Rangers must be reorganised and we will use our business acumen to do so. The club can't live in the past, nice as this thought might be. We want Ibrox to be used by the community. It doesn't make sense to have a stadium such as ours, which can be used for other things during the week, lying idle.

'I'd like to see fans having meals at Ibrox and making full use of the place. A winning team is important, we know that, but I want to see all 47,000 seats full and I'd like to see a day when payment can be by computer or in advance so that nobody has any hassle going through the turnstiles.

'I realise this is easy to say and equally simple to dismiss. However, I mean it and so does the company I work for. Lawrence Marlborough has the greatest affection for the club which is why he has become involved. We are not in this to fail or be half-hearted.'

Meanwhile, manager Wallace was in the hunt for new players – and targeted a Northern Ireland international playing in the English Third Division. He was Bournemouth forward Colin Clarke, whose transfer value had multiplied by ten since he was signed for £22,000 from Tranmere Rovers at the end of the 1984/85 season.

Wallace made a special trip to Paris to watch Clarke on his international debut for Northern Ireland in the 0-0 draw against European champions France – but Rangers were facing intense competition for the 23-year-old striker with Spurs manager Peter Shreeve and David Pleat of Luton Town also in the French capital to have a close look at Clarke.

Bournemouth boss Harry Redknapp said, 'I've already had half a dozen top English clubs making inquiries about the lad.

We're not in dire financial straits, but if the offer was right we couldn't stand in his way.'

Clarke grabbed 30 goals for Tranmere and Redknapp said, 'He's scored 24 already this season, and we've not had a particularly good season.'

Clarke said, 'I'm flattered so many clubs are showing an interest. It's the sort of move I hoped would materialise once I got international recognition.'

But former Rangers skipper John McClelland, an international team-mate, warned, 'I've told Colin to think very hard before he makes his decision. If he's confident enough in his ability he should not rush into a move because I'm sure English First Division clubs will still want him.'

3

Alex Totten

ALEX Totten has been in football more years than he cares to remember, and in every capacity going.

His playing career took him from Anfield – where he spent three youthful years under the watchful eye of legendary Liverpool manager, Bill Shankly – to the likes of Dundee, Dunfermline Athletic and hometown club Falkirk.

He has also managed the Bairns, St Johnstone – where he took the Perth side from the bottom division to the top – and Kilmarnock, but the three years he spent at Ibrox as assistant to Jock Wallace will forever remain the pinnacle of a 50-year footballing odyssey.

In fact, the day he received the phone call from big Jock asking him to become his number two is still etched indelibly in his mind, so much so that he can still reel off the date his phone rang – oh, and the time!

He recalled, 'It was 11 November 1983 – at 8am – and Jock asked me to be at Ibrox at 4pm on the Friday. Until then, he asked me to keep it quiet, although I had to tell my dad – who was a massive Rangers fan. He had taken me to Ibrox when I was a kid and I simply loved going there to see all the famous names play.

'The Friday couldn't come quick enough, but when it did, I went there with a whole range of emotions: joy, trepidation, pride etc. The first person I met was Stan the commissionaire, and he said to me, "Hello Mr Totten, Mr Wallace is waiting at the top of the marble staircase."

'I walked into the Blue Room and there was Jock. He had such an aura about him and he said to me, "Great to see you son, you're now a Ranger. Come and meet the directors," and there was Willie Waddell, Rae Simpson etc, and that's when and how it started. I will never forget it.

'But walking through the front door and up the marble staircase was a nerve-wracking experience. It wasn't like working at any other football ground. In fact, it wasn't really like working at a football club at all. That entrance and staircase just scream history and tradition, and make the hairs on your neck stand to attention every time you walk up them.'

In fact, Totten thought so much of the imposing Ibrox entrance that he would park his car inside the stadium and then walk back out the gates at the Broomloan Road end and stroll along Edmiston Drive and in the front door just to remind himself every morning of the wonderful job he had.

The third and final year of Totten's tenure at Ibrox was 1986 and even though all good things have to come to an end at some point, he was gutted when he was finally shown the door. Mind you, like everything Alex Totten has done in his life, he accepted the decision with great dignity.

He said, 'Obviously the board felt Jock and I weren't as successful as they had hoped we would be. David Holmes came in as the new chief executive and he wanted a complete change. When big Jock got the sack, I was asked to take charge of the team for the league match at Clydebank, which I did.

'The following Monday, though, I was invited in to see David Holmes, and I was relieved of my duties there and then along with Stan Anderson and John Hagart. Obviously Graeme Souness had wanted a clean sweep of the backroom, which I had a fair idea might happen.

'I had known David Holmes from my days at Brockville, as he was a Falkirk man, but he told me that he couldn't let sentiment get in the way of what was a tough decision for him. I fully understood and accepted the decision because I didn't know Souness from Adam. I had never met him before and, at the end of the day, I was big Jock's man.

'Naturally I was really disappointed at the club's decision, because when I had initially gone to Ibrox, Jock told me he wanted to try and run the club along the same paternal lines as Liverpool. They'd had the likes of Bill Shankly, Bob Paisley, Joe Fagan and Kenny Dalglish in charge and these guys had all learned from the previous incumbent. They had always enjoyed great continuity, and it was something that was brought up every time the topic of conversation turned to the success Liverpool FC had achieved.

'Jock would always say to me that when he stepped up to be general manager, I would take over as team manager, but sadly that never materialised. In fact, he told my dad the same thing one day while we were all sitting in the manager's office, and you could see the pride welling up in dad's eyes. It was a great shame it didn't happen because to have been manager of Glasgow Rangers would have been such an honour. Having said that, the time I spent at the club was fantastic and it was still a tremendous experience.'

There is one nagging little matter that has remained at the back of Totten's mind though. The question is this: That had the board managed to find millions of pounds for Wallace to spend, instead of Graeme Souness, could things have been different?

He said, 'I would say so, without a doubt, because big Jock had managed at a good level in England and knew the scene and the players down there very well. Everybody knew him from his time at Leicester City and he had made an awful lot of excellent contacts.

'During the three years I was with Jock at Ibrox he spent somewhere in the region of £600,000, whereas when Souness came along, he spent £16m in the same period, so the club had changed beyond belief by then.

'When I was at Ibrox, all the players were on the same basic wage, and it didn't matter if you were Ally McCoist, Davie Cooper or whoever, but the first two big signings Souness made were the England centre-half and goalkeeper, Terry Butcher and Chris Woods, so the scale of the changes were there for all to see. The wages policy also changed, which no doubt made it far easier to attract the big names.

'It would have been interesting to see how Jock and I would have fared with the cash that was made available to Souness. It's something I wonder about from time to time.'

But the decision to bring in the Scotland midfielder as player-manager is credited with not only changing the Rangers Football Club as we knew it, but also the course of Scottish football forever. Totten agrees with that sentiment.

He said, 'I think that move changed our game, without a doubt. When Souness came in he had to make sure Rangers were going to be a big success, and to do that he had to sign quality players, and pay top dollar for the privilege. Then, of course, the other teams had to try and play catch-up, and this is one of the problems with Scottish football, as many clubs were spending money they didn't have just to compete with Rangers. I think that was one of the drawbacks and you can even see signs of it in our game to this day.'

In fact, Totten reckons the off-field problems Rangers faced in 2012 can perhaps be traced back as far as 1986, to the free-spending days of Souness and those who followed. He said, 'I think there is probably a connection there, but the overriding emotion for me in the last couple of years, and as far as Rangers is concerned, is one of great sadness. The situation at my old club is so sad to see. They are a great institution and the fans have been so loyal over the years. The supporters really have backed Rangers to the hilt in their hour of need, which is good to see, but I don't think the problems have fully been erased.

'Let's be honest, Rangers are one of the biggest clubs in the world, not just this country, so to see what has happened to them over the last three or four years has been tough to take. The fans deserve a really good Rangers side competing at the top level and I'm sure if you asked Celtic supporters, many would say the very same thing. They have missed Rangers while they have been out the top flight, not just for the money but also the rivalry the clubs enjoy. You also have to play in a competitive league, because the last thing you want is to be continually walking away with the league championship. We all thrive on competition. It's so important in football.'

He added, 'I've been back to Ibrox many times and I never lose that awe-inspiring feeling I get every time I walk through the front door. There is definitely something endearing and magical about it.

'Regardless of how it all finished for me, I wouldn't have changed it for the world. Not for a minute. When I was managing Falkirk, I had a chance to go to Motherwell as full-time boss, with a five-year contract, and I would have been my own man, but I chose to go to Rangers to be second-in-command to big Jock, and it was one of the best decisions I made in my career. I thoroughly enjoyed my time at Rangers. It was a great experience and I got to work with a great bunch of lads. I also got to see a lot of the world, although possibly the greatest experience was learning from Jock Wallace. That was invaluable and we formed a tremendous bond that remained right up until the great man passed away.

'Rangers are a massive club and I loved every single minute of my time there, but I would like to think that in many ways Jock and I were a success, winning the League Cup twice against Celtic and Dundee United. At a club like Rangers, though, you are always going to be measured by the trophies you bring in.

'The first game after Jock left was against Clydebank, and it was a match that didn't so much dent my professional pride as completely knock it for six. We lost 2-1 at Kilbowie, which was the Bankies' first ever league win over Rangers.

'After the match, I was furious and remember saying to the players, "Managers and coaches are the people in football who get the sack, but players can't escape responsibility either." I felt sorry for our fans. As far as I was concerned, I was looking for a lot more from a Rangers team than I got. Players should always have pride in their own display, no matter the circumstances, but no one else can give them that other than themselves. If Graeme Souness had someone watching – which I'm sure he did – then they should have wanted to show how much it meant to play for Rangers.

'But not many people in the game can look back on their time in football and say they managed to play or work for Glasgow Rangers. I can, and it's something I will always be very proud of.

My last act as an employee of Rangers was to scribble a good luck note to the man who was taking over my office, Walter Smith. Walter and I were good friends and I wanted to wish him all the best. There were certainly no hard feelings on my part.'

4

March: A Vital Month

RANGERS had four incredibly important games in March and Jock Wallace knew that if his team wanted to be playing in Europe the following season, they would have to knuckle down and take points from the matches against Hibs, Dundee, Celtic and Hearts.

One avenue which could have seen the Light Blues take to football fields abroad – certainly for pre-season – was cut off when the Russian FA confirmed they couldn't fit Rangers into their schedule, so Wallace was left looking for other avenues to explore.

The Rangers boss vowed to sit his players down and spell out to them the importance of a club like Rangers being involved in Europe – and also in the latter rounds of the domestic cups. Once again, they were left twiddling their thumbs while eight teams fought out the quarter-finals of the Scottish Cup.

But the Light Blues' boss was making sure his players weren't left moping around and put them through a tough training schedule to prepare them for the important matches that lay ahead.

He said, 'Our next four league fixtures are real testers and I expect the players to rise to the challenge. There is certainly a lot for them to play for – don't let anyone think any differently.

'We've got Hibs at home, Dundee at Dens Park, which are always hard games, then the Old Firm match at Ibrox which provides motivation in itself for the players. Victories in these games would set us up nicely for the trip to Tynecastle to play Hearts and we certainly owe them one after the disappointment of being knocked out of the Scottish Cup.

'As always, it is vital for this club to get into Europe – but even more so now with all the young players in the side. It's very important for lads like Hugh Burns, Derek Ferguson and Ian Durrant to learn their trade in Europe. That's where their future is with Rangers and that's what we are building towards.'

And Rangers strengthened their claims for a Euro place when they beat Hibs 3-1 – although it was perhaps a sign of the times when Wallace described a home attendance of just over 16,000 as a 'good Ibrox crowd'.

He added, 'It's very gratifying that the punters are turning up in such loyal numbers and we know they appreciate everything we are trying to achieve here.'

Meanwhile, Ally McCoist moved one step closer to a place in the Mexico sun with Scotland at the World Cup tournament by firing a stunning hat-trick in the game – and in the process confirmed his mantle as the most potent striker in the Premier League.

McCoist's terrific treble was also a comprehensive answer to those who had been casting doubt on his potential as a genuine candidate for a place at the 'greatest show on earth', and he punched the air more with fury than delight while celebrating his opening goal – as if to tell the doubters to zip it!

After such an impressive showing, there was certainly no doubt Scotland boss Alex Ferguson would find it difficult to ignore the country's top scorer when he got round to naming his final squad of 22.

From Rangers' point of view, it was an extremely encouraging performance, McCoist's hat-trick apart. The team showed tremendous spirit and played a lot of neat football with Ian Durrant giving one of the best individual displays seen at Ibrox throughout the 1985/86 season. Durrant was terrific first in midfield and continued to dictate play even when moving back to sweeper to cover for the injured Ally Dawson.

McCoist scored his first on 12 minutes when Cammy Fraser cleverly headed a clearance into the path of Ted McMinn ten yards outside the penalty area. He neatly chipped the ball to the edge of the box and McCoist didn't need to break stride as he lashed a tremendous half-volley past Alan Rough from 18 yards.

A minute after the break, McCoist bagged number two. Dougie Bell, replacing the injured Derek Johnstone, sent Davie Cooper clear through the middle and with the Hibs defence carved wide open, the winger squared for McCoist to clinically shoot past Rough from ten yards.

And the talented goal-getter completed his hat-trick 17 minutes from time. Rangers were always the dominant force and clinched the points when they were awarded a penalty for handball – and McCoist sent Rough the wrong way.

The downside was that three Gers players picked up bad injuries. Dawson suffered a broken jaw after being struck on the face by the boot of Gordon Hunter, while Johnstone left the field with torn ankle tendons and Craig Paterson a fractured toe on his right foot.

But the action soon switched – once again – to off the park as the club introduced a new face to the boardroom. In the first week of March, Freddie Fletcher became Rangers director number five, with each individual board member given a specific area to look after. Mr Fletcher was put in charge of sales and marketing, while others were handed control of administration, franchising and playing aspects.

When the new change was announced, David Holmes said, 'Mr Fletcher's initiative and enthusiasm will be of great benefit to us.'

He added, 'I feel that giving each director a specific area of responsibility will be far more productive for the club. It is vital the board sets an example for all to follow.'

Fletcher was born and brought up in Greenock and his first interest in football came when he was presented with a season ticket for local team Morton on his seventh birthday.

He went into business on his own after leavir
successfully, and in 1966 began an equally succ.
career when he was elected as a Liberal councillor in ᴄ.
In 1977 he was named as Provost of Inverclyde District Couɴ.
the youngest man ever to hold the post, which he relinquished
in 1980 before retiring from politics four years later.

He was appointed a director of Morton in 1978, where he
gained invaluable experience during his time with the club. His
tenure ended just before he agreed the switch to Rangers, and
Mr Fletcher insisted he learned a lot from the late Hal Stewart.

In November 1983 he joined Treeby, the office supplies
division of the Lawrence Group of Companies. He was managing
director of Treeby as well as being responsible for all marketing
activities at Lawrence.

A dad of three, and based in Broomloan House, he didn't see
being a lifelong Morton supporter as any handicap to the work
he would be doing for Rangers, saying, 'At least I won't have to
buy a different-coloured scarf. But seriously, you only have to
look at Hearts where Wallace Mercer has done such a fine job.
He is a Rangers supporter but you won't find many Hearts fans
complaining. Football is big business now and we have to treat
it as such.'

Canadian star Colin Miller was all but guaranteed a spot on
the plane to Mexico but insisted one of his team-mates should
be joining him. He reckoned Ally Dawson would do a superb
job for Scotland against Denmark, West Germany and Uruguay.

Miller said, 'I lost my place in the team to Ally but I have
nothing but total admiration for him. He has helped me so much
since I came to Ibrox and as far as I'm concerned he is a world-
class defender – and I don't use that phrase without conviction.

'I know he takes a lot of stick from some people but I just
cannot see why. He uses his experience to the benefit of the
younger players around him, his tackling is good and he is
tremendously composed on the ball.

'He is also a very intelligent player, and I tell you this, if I was
the Scotland manager, Ally would be in my squad for Mexico.
He's one of the best players I have ever seen and I can only say

ıt's a tragedy he hasn't been seen by a wider football audience. He's certainly one of the most important players for Rangers moving forward.'

But it was once again time for a long-held Ibrox tradition, the ever-popular Rangers Supporters Association Rally, and the 37th annual bash was heading for a new venue. The big night out was the first to be held at the 'new' Scottish Exhibition Centre – and it proved a great success.

Tickets were sold out a fortnight in advance of the event and the loyal punters who turned up were treated to an evening of excellent entertainment. The ever-popular Mr Abie – a massive Rangers fan – was compere for the night and brought a smile to everyone's face. The laughs continued when Ronnie Dale took to the stage, with the kilted comedian raising plenty of smiles with his own special brand of humour.

He was followed by songstress Valerie Dunbar, always a popular performer at the Rally and she received her usual warm welcome and applause for a beautifully sung set. Next up were husband and wife duo The Spangles, who mixed comedy and song. They warmed the audience up for the evening's star turn, Allan Stewart, the comic who proved himself one of Britain's top impressionists with his starring turn on ITV show *Copycats*.

But the highlight was always the presentation to the guest speaker, and in 1986 it was the turn of Davie McPherson to enjoy the honour. The 22-year-old defender delivered an articulate, if slightly nervy speech, thanking everyone who had helped him in his career and outlining his fierce desire for further glory in the future. And big Mac was well pleased with the set of golf clubs he received as a gift from the Association, presented by Social Convenor Jimmy Clements.

But it was time for another break from the football, and the long-awaited Bailey's Rangers Snooker Classic was in full swing. Cammy Fraser and Billy Davies were red-hot favourites to lift the title but were told to beware Hurricane Hugh Burns!

The tournament was organised by the leisure centre next to Ibrox with the help of the Light Blues reserve skipper Davies.

And when all first-round ties had been completed, it was Burns who caused a major upset in the opening second-round match. The talented defender beat one of the more fancied competitors, Bobby Williamson, and produced some impressive snooker which included a highest break of 18 – and was immediately tipped as an outsider for the title.

The young full-back had received a bye in the first round, as did McCoist, Williamson, Fleck, Fraser and Walker, but the round produced its fair share of shocks, with Philip Knell and Alex Rae striking a blow for the ground staff players, while Burns and Fraser were the first two players into the last eight.

Meanwhile, chairman John Paton admitted Rangers were completely happy with the compromise deal which ended the threat of nine Premier League clubs breaking away from the Scottish League to create a new league structure.

He said, 'As a club we made it clear from the start that we wanted a new set-up within the Scottish League and this is what has been achieved. The balance of power is now with the major clubs who have the largest overheads and who bring most people through the turnstiles. We now have control of our own commercial activities and that was vital as far as we were concerned.

'Future decisions as far as sponsorship and the size of sponsorship deals will be negotiated by the clubs with most at stake as the league's commercial committee will in future consist of five members – all from Premier League clubs.'

The same committee would negotiate all future TV deals, which meant the big clubs would be able to ensure whatever coverage there was going would benefit the team concerned without reducing their revenue.

Mr Paton pointed out, 'If the major clubs felt strongly about something in the past, the League Management Committee would crush them by simply calling a full meeting of all clubs to get a two-thirds majority – but those days are now over.'

Having control of their own commercial activities was so important for Rangers, and would play a massive part in the blueprint being drawn up by the club for future success.

Supporters wondering how the new rules would benefit their club were given a simple answer. Rangers, for instance, like the other big guns, would now be able to fully exploit their commercial potential and with bigger sums coming in from various forms of sponsorship, they would also be in a better position to buy the players they wanted, as well as satisfying star players who may otherwise have been tempted by offers from outside Scotland.

The playing staff apart, improved revenue from the commercial side of the game would also help Scotland's full-time clubs cope with the ever-rising costs of maintaining the team and stadium.

But all that was put on the back burner when Rangers answered the call – like they had done so often throughout their illustrious history – to help celebrate the career of a journeyman player, on this occasion Elgin City star Chico McHardy.

And while the Rangers supporters in the 2,500 crowd at Borough Briggs would no doubt have preferred to see the Light Blues record a big victory, on a cold and wet night up north the Ibrox party weren't too unhappy with the result. One of the main benefits of the exercise was to give the Ibrox first-team men a good workout since they'd had no game the previous Saturday – and they got it. In the second half particularly the Highland League outfit gave the Rangers defenders plenty to think about. Ted McMinn scored for Rangers on 58 minutes but Kellas equalised and the match ended 1-1. Former Elgin keeper Nicky Walker was Rangers' captain for the night.

It was back to league business for the Light Blues mid-March as they chased the final UEFA Cup place. They were once again on their travels, this time to Dens Park, Dundee, for a match against the team trying to wrestle the Euro place from their grasp.

And once again they failed to catch a break from an Edinburgh referee. They had been flying high in the Premier League until they lost at home to Aberdeen in a game during the first half of the season which was best remembered for a couple of controversial decisions by capital ref George Smith. And it was another man from the same city whose penalty decision in 33 minutes allowed Dundee to get the vital winning goal which put them just a point behind the Ibrox men in the Premier League table. It meant the Gers would have to scrap very hard in their remaining matches to be sure of a place in Europe the following season.

Reports suggested Dundee midfielder John Brown had gone to ground easily when challenged by Hugh Burns. It looked a pretty ordinary tackle, but when referee Douglas Downie pointed to the spot the roars from all over the ground indicated that few people agreed with his decision.

A draw would have left Rangers three points clear of Dundee, but that penalty goal put the Dens Park men in a decent position to move into fifth place in the table and into Europe. Rangers, of course, could still pip Dundee in the run-in, but they would have to strike top form as some difficult games lay ahead.

Dundee opened the scoring on 15 minutes, but despite having few chances throughout the 90 minutes, McCoist proved his scoring touch was still there on the half-hour when he took a pass from Robert Fleck and sent a well-placed shot past the keeper.

Just four minutes later Dundee were awarded the hotly-disputed penalty and it became a bad-tempered affair from there on in with Rangers stars Russell, Munro, Fraser, Beattie, McMinn and Cooper all being booked.

But there was some good news off the park for seven of the 40,000 weekly readers of *Rangers News*. These readers were blind, and had a copy in braille sent to them each week. The technical name was a 'Thermoformed' copy and that meant the *News* was transformed into what looked like a loose-leafed book with about 50 pages carrying various stories picked out in braille. Page one had a large embossed reproduction of the Rangers crest.

Rangers News was the first sports paper to be produced in this way – and there was another story behind this marvellous boost for those blind fans, because all the work was done by a group of lags from Perth Prison.

And the readers would have plenty to get excited about while poring over the match report from the latest Old Firm contest, played on Saturday 22 March – as it was an eight-goal corker. For

90 minutes Rangers supporters forgot all about the troubles at their club, the ongoing battle for a UEFA Cup slot and all their other worries, because both sides served up a thriller that was unlikely to disappear from memory any time soon.

Manager Jock Wallace admitted he was delighted with the commitment shown by his players, as were the Rangers fans in the healthy 41,000 crowd. He added, 'I was pleased with what the players showed against Celtic. I have never, ever questioned their commitment, only their inexperience. As far as that goes, they still have a lot to learn but I feel confident we are approaching the side I want to put together for Rangers. They now have another chance to show what they can do when we visit Hearts, but there's no way anything will match what we have just enjoyed with Celtic.'

If anyone doubted the Old Firm was the world's best soccer double act, then the match at Ibrox proved the fact beyond any doubt. This was the game of the season – in fact, probably the most exciting match the Premier League had ever produced.

It had everything – and over 40,000 wet and bedraggled, but ecstatically happy fans giving a united ovation to the players of both teams. And no sets of players had ever deserved the plaudits more after a game which had the pulse racing from start to finish, contained genuine commitment and skilful football in equal measure and quite clearly proved that, as far as excitement and passion were concerned, the Old Firm were still miles ahead of the rest.

There was a shock for Rangers fans before kick-off with Davie Cooper relegated to the bench but it was the Light Blues nonetheless who dominated the opening exchanges. McCoist turned brilliantly after two minutes to force Bonner into a fine save and McMinn might have done better in the 14th minute when he lobbed the ball wide with McCoist and Fleck in better scoring positions.

The Celtic keeper had a scare two minutes later when he let a McCoist header slip through his legs only to retrieve the situation before the ball crossed the line. It was all Rangers but unpredictable was the key word and the Light Blues' fans were stunned when Celtic took the lead with a goal of real quality in the 20th minute.

Paul McStay powered forward from midfield and sprayed a great pass out wide to Owen Archdeacon on the left. The young winger's cross was fluffed by Murdo MacLeod but fell kindly to Mo Johnston who smashed home a fine shot from 12 yards, which gave Nicky Walker no chance.

Rangers fought back well with Cammy Fraser bringing another excellent save out of Bonner, but in the 29th minute Celtic really took the upper hand with a stunning second goal. A McStay free kick found Archdeacon in a dangerous position on the left once more, and this time his low cross was missed by the entire Rangers defence and MacLeod teed the ball up for McClair to shoot past Walker from 16 yards.

Rangers were up against it but three minutes later came the game's only unsavoury moment. Willie McStay had already been cautioned for persistently fouling the dangerous McMinn and referee David Syme had no option but to send him off after another bad foul on the Rangers winger. Past experience of Old Firm contests suggest there is little advantage of playing against ten men but two minutes after McStay's departure Rangers hauled themselves back into the match. Durrant found McCoist on the left-hand side of the penalty area and the striker steadied himself on the byline, looked up and sent a perfect cross to Fraser who powerfully headed home from six yards.

The second half began with Cooper on for McMinn, who hadn't been able to shake off the injury inflicted by McStay, and Rangers must have been hopeful of putting Celtic under pressure. But only two minutes into the half, it was the Parkhead men who were once again two goals to the good. Johnston had time and space to play a nice pass into the penalty area, which Tommy Burns ran on to and fired past Walker and into the corner of the net from 14 yards.

Rangers were now facing a mountainous task but set about it in thrilling fashion and had their fans in sheer ecstasy with a stunning burst of three goals in 12 minutes to roar into the lead.

In the 53rd minute we were treated to the undoubted goal of the season from McCoist. Taking a long clearance from Walker wide on the right, the striker cut inside two Celtic defenders and cracked an astonishing drive into the corner of the net from the edge of the box.

Six minutes later, the Copland Road end went crazy when young Fleck scored the goal he had no doubt dreamed of for years. Hugh Burns fed McPherson – who had a magnificent second half – and he strode forward down the right. His low cross eluded the Celtic defence and Fleck crashed the ball home from close range with the aid of a deflection. The youngster couldn't contain his joy, and performed a somersault in front of the Copland Road.

A further six minutes later and Rangers were in front. A Cooper corner was punched out by Bonner to the edge of the area. Davie MacKinnon headed it straight back over Bonner and the Celtic defence and into the net with Fraser rushing in just to make sure.

At that point, the victory looked secure, but in the 71st minute Celtic equalised with a magnificent goal from MacLeod. The midfield man took a pass from Mo Johnston in his stride and thumped a terrific shot from almost 30 yards into the top-right corner of the net. But even then the drama wasn't over and Bonner denied McCoist a last-gasp winner with a world-class save.

When the final whistle arrived, it was greeted with disappointment from no one with the players warmly congratulating each other after a game which would be remembered for years to come.

In the aftermath of the big game, it was suggested that Fleck was all set to claim a permanent place in the Rangers attack alongside star striker McCoist. That was the verdict of Ibrox boss Jock Wallace after the 20-year-old had turned in a superb 90 minutes against Celtic, which he capped off by scoring Rangers' third goal.

Fleck had been in and out of the team since making his debut against Hearts at Ibrox in April 1984, but according to Wallace, the young Glaswegian was ready to become a regular. Big Jock added, 'I thought Robert had his best game yet in the first team against Celtic and now it's in his own hands to stay as partner to Ally McCoist.

'The reason he played so well was because he used all his strong points to the full. The boy has terrific pace, is very strong and can score goals with both feet. His attitude was first class and if he can keep that up I will have no hesitation in keeping him in the side. His goal will have done his confidence a lot of good too, but he can't afford to become complacent and I'm sure he won't. He has to remember there are players like Bobby Williamson, Iain Ferguson and John MacDonald waiting in the wings for their chance again.'

Fleck was on cloud nine after the match and said, 'I was very pleased with how I played and scoring that goal was a moment I have dreamed about for years. The only disappointment for me was that we didn't win but to even take part in a game like that was brilliant.

'I feel I proved something with my performance and I have to make sure I keep it up. I may never get a better chance to win a regular place in the side so the few matches we have left this season are very important to me.'

Next up for Rangers was Hearts, and they represented a significant barrier to grabbing that much hoped for UEFA Cup spot. But the Tynecastle side were unbeaten since September, and had gone 22 games without losing. Mind you, they still had five games to go to beat Rangers' unbeaten record of 27 league games, a run which took place from 13 December 1975 to 23 October 1976.

The match on Gorgie Road was vital to the club's ambitions, but would ultimately prove once again everything that frustrated the Rangers fans – that their favourites were riddled with inconsistency.

A match report from the game – which ended 3-1 to the home side – read, 'If Hearts go on to win the Premier League, as now seems almost certain, they will fully deserve the honour. But they may look back on Saturday's 90 minutes with a relieved smile for Rangers deserved far better than defeat against the league leaders at Tynecastle.'

Once again, the Light Blues could point to a couple of baffling refereeing decisions which turned the game in the Edinburgh men's favour. The first came five minutes from half-time when McCoist superbly twisted past Craig Levein and slotted a good shot past Henry Smith and into the back of the net. For some inexplicable reason the goal was chopped off, even to the amazement of the Hearts fans who thought McCoist had equalised.

Worse was to follow two minutes into the second half when Hearts increased their lead to 2-0. As Davie McPherson ushered the ball out of play for a goal kick, he was challenged by Hearts skipper Walter Kidd – and the referee promptly awarded a free kick to Hearts. From the kick, Davie MacKinnon handled a Sandy Clark header on the line, Hearts were awarded a penalty and John Robertson slotted the ball home.

It was always going to be an uphill task for Rangers after Hearts had taken the lead in the ninth minute when Robertson ran on to a Kenny Black through ball and sent a cute lob over Walker and into the net. But those two decisions turned the job into a mountainous one for Rangers, who, to their credit, almost salvaged a draw, putting the Hearts defence under mounting pressure in the final period.

Their only reward for that pressure, which was orchestrated by the rejuvenated Cammy Fraser in midfield, was a 66th-minute penalty kick converted by McCoist, his 37th goal of the season, after he had been sandwiched between Brian Whittaker and Clark in the box.

Rangers threw on Bobby Russell and Davie Cooper as they battled furiously for what would have been a valuable point but it was Hearts who summed up the afternoon by having the last word, and Clark shot home in the final minute.

The Ibrox men were facing an extremely difficult task in the closing weeks of the season if they were to grab that elusive UEFA Cup spot. The month of March had come and gone, and the next few weeks would be crucial if Rangers supporters were to have European football to watch the following season. But no one could have foreseen just how crucial the next few weeks would turn out. No one, that is, apart from those in the Rangers boardroom, and a certain gentleman who was enjoying the opportunity to show off his talents in the top flight of Italian football, which was at that time, arguably, the greatest league in the world.

5

Ally Dawson

DURING the last couple of years, we have on more than one occasion had good cause to refer to the 'Rangers Family' as fans far and wide have rallied to support their toiling club in its hour of need.

But there is one former Ibrox stalwart who can lay genuine claim to having come from a bona fide Gers family.

Signed as a prodigious schoolboy by Jock Wallace, Ally Dawson made his first-team debut at the tender age of just 16 – in 1975 – in a pre-season tour of North America. He would go on to lift the Scottish Cup as captain of the most decorated club in the world seven years later. And the talented defender described that moment as 'the high point of my career'.

He said, 'I had grown up a Rangers supporter and my whole family had close connections with the club. In fact, my uncle just retired at the end of 2015, at the age of 80, after giving 50 years' service to Rangers. He worked in many different departments at the club.'

The versatile defender also gave sterling service to the Rangers from 1975 to 1987, and despite suffering horrific injuries such as a fractured skull and a dislocated and fractured jaw, the Johnstone-born defender racked up more than 300 top-team appearances for the Light Blues.

A club legend? Absolutely. Dawson played through the pain barrier many, many times for Rangers, but in his own words, said, 'I was fortunate enough to play for the club I loved and had supported as a boy. It really doesn't get much better than that.'

He added, 'When I was made captain of Rangers it was one of the proudest moments of my life. I had just come through an awful year of injury and was captain when we lifted the Scottish Cup in 1981 – mind you, it came at a price.

'We beat a very good Dundee United side 4-1 in a replay at Hampden, when John MacDonald scored a couple, and that was my moment if nothing else. After playing in the first tie – a 0-0 draw at the national stadium – I was struggling to make it for the replay due to injury, but let's just say I had to get some "special treatment", and it got me through that game.

'Mind you, I ended up missing what was left of the season and the Home Internationals for Scotland. I was forced to withdraw from the national squad, but only because it had meant so much to me to play for Rangers in that Scottish Cup Final replay.

'And it was definitely worth it as walking up the stairs and lifting up the Scottish Cup at Hampden at the age of 23 was just such a phenomenal feeling. If you had asked me when I was 16 or 17 whether I would achieve something like that I would have sworn you were having a laugh.

'I love the club so much and am fortunate that I'm still fit enough to be working with the youth teams, and it's simply fantastic. Mind you, after 12 years with Rangers you're bound to have many highlights – and I have – but leading the club to the Scottish Cup in 1981 is one of my biggest.'

But exactly two decades after that crowning moment, Dawson was again making the headlines when he was inaugurated into the Rangers Hall of Fame – the 97th inductee. In doing so, he followed in the bootsteps of many, many famous names. Moses McNeil, Davie Meiklejohn, John Greig, Davie Cooper and Sandy Jardine: they're all there.

Players such as Chris Woods and Terry Butcher arrived at Ibrox 11 years after Ally Dawson first signed on the dotted line, and the former Scotland international recalls the 'Souness revolution' with great joy. He said, 'I suppose we were all thinking the same, like what's going to happen now that we have a new manager? To be honest, I don't think I realised the scale of the changes that were afoot, maybe none of us did. But Graeme Souness had bags of experience and was finishing off his career abroad and I'm sure he was relishing the opportunity to take over at Ibrox as player-manager, although I think it was something he found very difficult at first. Perhaps that was why he brought Walter Smith in, as he had a lot of experience of the Scottish game.

'We just didn't know what to expect at the time. Graeme wanted to do things his way and one of the first things he introduced was training sessions up at Jordanhill. At that time we still only had the one training pitch over at the Albion, which wasn't really sufficient. It had served its purpose and had its day but the club was growing and we needed more than one pitch to train on.'

Dawson had a head start on his team-mates when Graeme Souness first walked through the front door at Ibrox, as the Renfrewshire man had played alongside him for Scotland, but he doesn't think for a moment it gave him any advantage.

'I wouldn't say it made it any easier for me,' he said. 'When Graeme joined the club, he came in as manager, or head coach, however you want to put it, so that was the difference right from the start. Those of us who knew him, knew right away there needed to be a line drawn as he was now our manager.

'Graeme's arrival came at a time when I was battling back to fitness after fracturing my jaw. I had dislocated and fractured it during a game and had been out for six or seven weeks. He asked if I was fit to play and I said I was. It was the right decision to make because I played the last few games of the season and I was absolutely fine. In fact, I think he made me captain until the end of the season, which was certainly fine by me.

'I think the main difference is that as a player you have to make certain decisions throughout your career, mostly just for yourself, but as a manager, as I later found out, these decisions are different, and far more difficult. And they come with more consequences.'

Dawson added, 'Naturally, Graeme wanted to do things his own way at Rangers, but as players we were all hoping to make a good impression on the new man. Personally I was quite fortunate that even though I was injured, the nature of the injury hadn't prevented me from doing light work. The only thing I was losing at that time was a bit of match fitness. I was still training up to a point. There was no contact in training but it definitely helped me. It wasn't as if I was off limits and still had weeks ahead of me before I could play again, so that definitely worked in my favour and gave me a boost.

'My biggest problem at that time, and with the benefit of hindsight, was that I took a holiday after the season had finished. If I had the decision to make again I would definitely have trained throughout the close season so I was ready to hit the ground running for pre-season. Even though you tell yourself you will do a wee bit to help, it's never enough. Ideally, I should have taken a two-week break after the last game and then got straight back down to working on my fitness, but I didn't. Instead, we went shopping etc, which just didn't do my body any good whatsoever.

'So my problem was I didn't get the new season off to a flying start and Stuart Munro came in and did very well. During that period, Stuart saw off some more than decent players and fully deserved his place in the team.

'For me, though, I was a wee bit behind and it was my own fault. That annoyed me because it was a really important season for everyone at the club. I was always a traditionally slow starter to a season anyway, and told myself I would catch up, but by that time it was too late as far as I was concerned or, more importantly, as far as Graeme was concerned. He had his eye on everyone at that point to see how they were doing, so that's a big regret of mine.'

The following season, 1986/87, Dawson's appearances in the first team were restricted to half a dozen in the Premier League, one in Europe and three in the Scottish League Cup – although one of those came in the final against Celtic, a 2-1 success which brought a fourth winner's medal in that competition. Some 75,000 fans saw goals by Ian Durrant and Davie Cooper give Rangers the trophy, and although the final was played in October, 1986, it was the last big match the Rangers stalwart would play in for his boyhood heroes.

He explained, 'The following close season, when I did leave Ibrox, I went over to Switzerland to see Robert Prytz. He was at Young Boys Berne at the time and even though I was supposed to be on a break, I ended up training with them. I was also trying to get sorted out at a club but they were in the middle of their season so I thought I should get myself fit. Actually, when I came back from Switzerland I probably had one of my better pre-seasons in years, which was quite ironic.

'By then, though, I knew it was time for me to move on from Rangers. There had been a club from Switzerland making noises about signing me but Rangers wanted a fee and that seemed to put them off a bit. I ended up going down to Blackburn Rovers, where I loved it. I had good times at Ewood Park so I had no complaints about the way it panned out for me. Naturally it was very sad to finally leave Ibrox, but I had enjoyed 12 great years at the club so that probably helped with the parting of the ways.

'I enjoyed my time with Blackburn but unfortunately I had a few injuries near the end of my time there. You start picking them up if you aren't playing regularly, but it was just one of those things.'

Rangers will always be Dawson's one and only true footballing love, and he reckons that, with the benefit of hindsight, the arrival of Graeme Souness at Ibrox was certainly the beginning of some major changes at the club.

He said, 'Whether he wanted that, or other people did, it was definitely the start of something really big. He made a lot of massive changes. I mean, who could have foreseen the likes of Terry Butcher, Graham Roberts and Chris Woods coming up to play for Rangers at that time? Terry had just finished at the World Cup, so to get that calibre of player up to Ibrox was exceptional. As good as we all thought we were, I think the calibre of player that came up from down south was the biggest change. But they all settled in very well and we all learned from each other. We all benefitted from the changes Graeme made, myself included.

'I think the truth is Rangers were falling behind a lot of the other top Scottish clubs at the time and changes were necessary. We probably couldn't afford to stand still. Under Jock Wallace, we were a team that could more or less win any game, but couldn't win games week in, week out. We proved that by getting to cup finals etc, but we didn't have the consistency over a period of time in the league.

'The likes of Aberdeen and Dundee United were very strong at that time, but had that not been the case then it might have hidden the fact we were a bit weaker, but that would only have covered up the things that needed to be addressed at Rangers, so it probably was something that was needed, maybe not so drastically, but the club changed so much over the next few years.'

Down the years, many folk have asked the question, that if Jock Wallace had been given more money to spend, could he and assistant Alex Totten have made sufficient changes to get the club back to the top?

Dawson answered, 'Yes, there is definitely merit in that. I think Jock and Totts would have done a good job with a bit more cash to spend. To me, Jock was the best manager I ever worked with – bar none. His man-management skills were fantastic and he definitely got the best out of people.

'Jock and Graeme were very different. Graeme expected people to know a lot more about the game than perhaps we had been taught or were used to. It was just two different styles of management, and for me they were both very good in their own ways. Jock, especially, was a great manager in the mid-to-late 1970s, his teams were very strong and were winning trebles.

'When John Greig took over from Jock, he inherited a very strong team, and was really just a game or so away from winning a treble, but unfortunately one of the most important games was against Celtic. With the exception of one or two young players, who were emerging at that time, it was a fairly experienced team, and I was fortunate enough to play with guys like John MacDonald, Bobby Russell and Davie Cooper. They were the younger ones at that time and were very good.

'The main problem we had during Jock's second spell was that the emergence of the likes of Aberdeen and Dundee United pushed us a bit further down the pecking order. At Rangers, it's not good enough to be second, but when you're being pushed down to the likes of third and fourth, then it definitely becomes a problem.'

If that's the team side of the game, then there is always the personal angle, and Dawson admits being admitted to the Rangers Hall of the Fame was the icing on the cake.

He said, 'There are about three or four things that happen to you in your life which you would describe as life-changing – things you would never, ever want to change. Personal things like getting married and having kids, but when it comes to football, being inaugurated into the Rangers Hall of Fame, along with my first game for the club and playing for Scotland, are these types of moments.

'It is very, very difficult to describe just what it meant to me. When I initially found out I was overcome with sheer pride. I was fortunate to be at Rangers for more than 12 years, after coming through the S-form system for two or three years.

'I still love the club with all my heart and would do anything for them. When I was a player at Rangers the atmosphere around the place was second to none, and I have also been involved in coaching youngsters at the club.

'When I found out I had been nominated for the Hall of Fame, though, it was just such an incredible feeling, but when I actually received the trophy I was gobsmacked. It was a real honour and I was bursting with pride.

'But that's what being a Rangers player does to you!'

6

Beginning Of The End For Big Jock

APRIL 1986. Arguably one of the most consequential months in the history of Glasgow Rangers, and it all started off with speculation rife about the future of Scotland World Cup star Graeme Souness.

Rumours were doing the rounds in the press that the 33-year-old midfielder was set to call time on his stay at Serie A side Sampdoria and move to the UK to become the player-manager – of English First Division side Tottenham Hotspur.

It was suggested in some quarters that Souness could be in charge at White Hart Lane by the start of the new season. Others speculated that he might stay abroad. What seemed certain, though, was that the player had made up his mind to leave Italy, and Genoa, where he had been resident for two years.

The Scotland international was set to lead his country in the forthcoming World Cup in Mexico during the summer and suggested he would make up his mind about his future sooner rather than later – and it was no secret that troubled Spurs, the club he signed for as a teenager before moving to Middlesbrough, were keen on his services.

It was said the success of his former team-mate Kenny Dalglish as player-boss at Anfield had convinced those at top clubs that such a role was well worth considering, and axed Spurs manager Peter Shreeve had hardly set the heather on fire in north London.

Over at Ibrox, Jock Wallace renewed Rangers' Icelandic connection by taking three players from the island to Ibrox ahead of the forthcoming FV Olympia Youth tournament in Stuttgart. The previous season, the Light Blues had full Iceland international striker Ragnar Margeirsson on loan from Keflavik for a spell.

The trio – Olafur Viggosson (16), Ronar Kristensson (16) and Thorstein Halldorsson (18) – would be scrutinised closely by John Hagart and Stan Anderson at the tournament and were hopeful of furthering their careers in Scotland. Wallace had first spotted the lads while manager of Motherwell, and they had come over to play for the Fir Park side's under-15 side, so he was happy to give them a second look in Rangers colours.

But while the Icelandic kids had a chance to impress the second string coaches, Wallace had other things on his mind, like finding a solution to his team's fluctuating on-field performances, so he organised a friendly match for Rangers' free weekend while Scottish Cup fixtures were taking place elsewhere – against Tottenham Hotspur at Ibrox!

One player expecting to play in the glamour match was Cammy Fraser, who had been taken off the transfer list. It was a fitting reward for the midfield player who, along with his fellow buy from Dundee, Iain Ferguson, had been put up for sale by Wallace the previous September. Fraser's form since returning to the first team as a substitute against Aberdeen at Pittodrie in February had been superb. He had subsequently picked up man-of-the-match awards in the games against Dundee United, Celtic and Hearts.

Wallace said, 'I was more than delighted to take Cammy off the transfer list. He is now the player he was when I bought him from Dundee. He simply took far too long to settle into the Ibrox system and for whatever reason, it took time for him to handle the pressures of being a Rangers player.

'But he gets 11 out of ten from me for his attitude in the past few months and the way he has battled back into his present situation. Against Celtic and Hearts in the past few weeks, he has looked every inch the influential midfield player everybody knew he was. Now it's up to him again – he has a great chance to make a name for himself as a Ranger.'

That was something which had looked nothing more than a dream for Fraser at the start of the season but the 28-year-old had shown admirable determination since. Certainly, his form leading up to the Spurs game was beyond argument and there looked to be brighter times ahead for Fraser and Rangers.

Meanwhile, Wallace was expecting a crowd of around 25,000 at Ibrox for the Sunday afternoon match against Spurs, and said, 'This is a marvellous opportunity for my young players to play against top-class opposition.'

Stuart Munro was a doubt but Rangers were set to field Davie Cooper, Derek Ferguson and Dougie Bell from the start. Sadly, though, the players put on their Sunday worst at Ibrox as they slipped tamely to a defeat which had Wallace in a fury. The Light Blues boss was in no mood to mince his words after a dreadful 90 minutes which saw Spurs grab a 2-0 victory without really moving anywhere close to top gear.

Wallace fumed, 'It was an absolute disgrace. We didn't make passes, didn't run and didn't work. We didn't play like a team and you will never win anything like that. It was a terrible performance and makes no sense to me at all. I'm very angry.'

The true blue boss was as confused as the rest of us as to why Rangers had failed to follow up a promising beginning to the match. After five minutes, a Cooper corner was met by Derek Ferguson, only for the youngster's header to be cleared off the line by Danny Thomas for a corner.

A minute later Ally McCoist did well to pierce the Spurs defence and collect a long through ball from midfield. McCoist's cut-back from the byline was met by Iain Ferguson but his shot was well saved by Ray Clemence.

Ferguson came close again in the 32nd minute when he shot just over the bar after good work by Ted McMinn, but there was an immediate setback for the Light Blues two minutes into the second half when Spurs took the lead. Ally Dick, on as a substitute for Tony Galvin, broke from midfield and played the ball to Mark Falco. The striker's shot was parried by sub keeper Peter McCloy and John Chiedozie nipped in to shoot home.

Rangers made an attempt to get back on level terms with Cooper having a good shot well saved by sub keeper Tony Parks, but it was the London side who were running the show now and only a super save from a Paul Allen shot in the 68th minute by Peter McCloy kept Tottenham at bay.

The second goal was only delayed by a minute, however, as from the resultant corner by Chris Waddle, Falco headed the ball on to the back post where Paul Allen shot home from a couple of yards. When the final whistle sounded, it was almost a relief for the fans, those in the crowd of 12,665 who were still inside Ibrox.

But while the fans were quite clearly disappointed, the consequences for Wallace were far more severe. It was the last time he would take charge of his beloved Rangers, although many believe his fate had been sealed long before the match against Spurs and the board of directors had already made their minds up to bring in a new manager.

Just moments after the last supporters were filtering out of the stadium, Wallace was summoned to the boardroom and given the bad news. He was out of a job. It seems he had been let down badly by the players he had put his faith in to restore Rangers to its former glories.

The next morning, assistant Alex Totten was placed in temporary charge of the club after a meeting with chief executive David Holmes.

Meanwhile, tears were shed in the dressing room as the players were told of Wallace's departure. Full-back Stuart Munro came out fighting and said, 'We are the best football team in the Premier League – and the last four weeks of the season will give us a chance to prove that.'

They were bold words from perhaps one of the few players to do himself justice that season, but the league table didn't lie. Munro was angry at the criticism of the team and reckoned Rangers would be able to go some way to silencing the detractors by taking maximum points from their last four Premier League matches.

Those games, of course, were crucial to the Ibrox club's hopes of playing in the UEFA Cup and they were due to kick off with a potentially treacherous trip to Kilbowie to face Clydebank, to be followed by away fixtures at St Mirren and Aberdeen before Motherwell arrived at Ibrox on the last day of the season.

Munro may have seemed a quiet, unassuming character in the way he went about his business so consistently every week on the park, but he was actually brimming with confidence and enthusiasm.

He said at the time, 'People have to start living in the real world as far as Rangers and the Premier League is concerned. Times and styles have changed in Scottish football and we are now adapting to meet the challenge thrown up by the likes of Aberdeen, Dundee United and Hearts.

'We are a very young team and this season has been more successful for the side than anyone is giving us credit for. We have learnt a lot and although the major trophies have all eluded us, we have achieved a fair bit.

'Some of the football we have displayed has been terrific and on our day there really is no team in Scotland to touch us. That is fact as far as I am concerned – not just an opinion! The magic ingredient missing, of course, is consistency. But I think it is just about to be added to the mixture. I honestly believe we can win our last four matches of the season and that would be a terrific boost for next season.

'I personally can't wait for next season. If we fire on all cylinders like I'm sure we will, the rest of the Premier League had better watch out. We have the best squad of players in Scotland – next season we are going to have the best team.'

And Munro was confident Rangers were up to qualifying for the UEFA Cup.

He said, 'On paper we look to have an easier run-in than Dundee with the game at Clydebank on Saturday looking like a certain two points, while they have to go to Easter Road to face Hibs. I fancy us to stick a few past Clydebank but they are very stuffy opponents and we certainly don't want any repeat of our last visit to Kilbowie when we didn't score the winner until the last minute of the match.

'I know we are all desperate to make sure of that European place, and lads like myself who have only had limited European experience know we need to play on that kind of stage. Celtic did us a bit of a favour by beating Dundee last week and now our fate is in our own hands. It will actually be a good experience for us, going into the closing weeks of the season needing points from every game.

'I just hope we turn on our best form in each of the matches and make a few of the people who are far too quick to slag us off shut their mouths.'

It was fighting talk from Munro, and only time would tell whether or not the players could back up the tough words.

Meanwhile, though, there was soon to be a new boss in town...

7

Wallace Out, Souness In

'OUT goes Wallace with a reputed £60,000 handshake – IN comes Souness after a £300,000 deal,' screamed the *Daily Record*'s front page headline. It was, the newspaper said, an 'Ibrox Bombshell'. It was difficult to argue.

It was Tuesday 8 April, just 48 hours after Rangers' apathetic display in the friendly defeat by Spurs and the Gers had named World Cup skipper Graeme Souness as player-manager. It was Scotland's most breathtaking soccer move for years.

Out went Wallace with his golden sweetener – but only two days' warning of the shock announcement. And in had come Souness, 33, leaving behind a beach-side villa at Genoa and the Italian club Sampdoria, a move which cost Rangers in the region of £300,000.

Wallace, 50, was philosophical about the decision to axe him – and the appointment of Souness – and said, 'Good luck to the guy. I have been with four teams but getting the sack is a new experience.'

The chief sportswriter at the *Daily Record* in the mid-1980s was Alex Cameron, and his editorial raised a few eyebrows.

It read, 'Rangers have appointed their first ever player-manager and the man behind the big-thinking enterprise is David Holmes, the tough ex-joiner. Holmes bowled me over when he named Wallace's successor. Although Rangers were expected to set their sights on a Scot, Jim McLean was the hot tip. But earlier in the day it was made clear he would not be leaving Tannadice.

'Souness was expected to go to Tottenham, so this makes the Rangers capture even better. He hasn't played any of his senior football in Scotland, but recognises Rangers as one of the biggest clubs in Europe.

'I predict Souness will have no trouble settling in, although it is a big job to combine management at Ibrox with playing. He is a natural leader and has served under some of the best managers in the business, including Bill Shankly and Bob Paisley at Liverpool. Souness has style and he will bring this with him to Ibrox. He would never travel second class and will expect Rangers to act in the same way.

'Rangers needed new ideas and a completely new deal. The supporters made it clear they were heartily sick at the club's last AGM when shouting broke out all over the hall.

'Souness is a player of tremendous authority and fearless with it. I mean no disrespect to Jock Wallace when I say he will shake up the dressing room as it has never been done before. But he will do it fairly. He is a players' man. In fact, he will not forget he is one himself. The World Cup skipper can't start at Ibrox until after 27 April, when the Italian season finishes. He will have total authority – and Holmes will see to it that he gets every assistance possible from the board.

'Souness was last night delighted at the prospect of coming to Scotland for the first time as a player, and even though he will be 34 on 6 May I reckon he has at least two good years left to make his imprint before deciding to sit matches out wearing a collar and tie. Rangers have done well.'

One man who admitted he was as proud as punch at the move was Souness's dad, Jimmy, who revealed how his son had supported Rangers from the slopes of Ibrox Park when just a schoolboy.

Jimmy Souness, 66, of Saughton Mains, Edinburgh, had a phonecall from Graeme telling him he was the new boss at

Ibrox, and said, 'This is a great continuation of his career and it's especially so because he is back in Scotland with a great club with proud traditions.'

Asked how he thought his son would cope with the pressures of being Rangers boss and captain of Scotland, Jimmy, a retired glazier, said, 'He is such a competitor and will take everything in his stride. He has always tried to be a winner – and I hope he will be a real winner with Rangers. My only regret is that my wife isn't here to share this moment. She died two years ago.'

Souness was stepping into a job where failure wasn't an option. He was well aware that supporters would look beyond his film star looks and jet-set lifestyle and demand an almost instant change in the club's fortunes.

In Souness, Rangers had acquired a world-class footballer – the captain of his country. His qualities as a footballer stretched to cinemascope proportions, but even he would have admitted that going into management at that particular stage in his career was like taking a step into the unknown. There was no doubt whatsoever Souness would very much be his own man. Not only did he apply uncompromising attitudes on the field, he also didn't suffer fools gladly. His make-up was such that he combined arrogance with elegance and while he was likely to lead from the front, his position was in the middle of the park.

Controversy had followed Souness since he first broke on to the senior football scene as a kid with Spurs and Scotland's youth team. In fact, he walked out on the White Hart Lane side and went back to Edinburgh homesick.

It was then he made what proved to be the most important move in his career. Later on he would say, 'I joined Middlesbrough as a raw 19-year-old. Big Jack Charlton signed me and was to prove one of the biggest influences on my attitude to football. He told me I'd better get a grip or I'd disappear out of the game. It was the fright I needed.'

But the man who impressed Souness most as a manager was Jock Stein. His death after the World Cup qualifying match at Cardiff against Wales saw Souness in tears outside the dressing room.

He said, 'My regard for Jock Stein was immense. Personally I couldn't fathom the criticisms of him as Scotland manager.'

But then Souness – who revealed in 1985 that he was a Hearts *and* Rangers supporter as a youngster, and spoke of playing in the Scottish Premier League – had himself come in for stick from fans. He said, 'There are some supporters who say Kenny [Dalglish] and I never play for our country the way we play for our club. I can't accept that.'

It was thought by some that Souness might employ the 'Paisley Pattern', which had been so successful at Liverpool. He said, 'I discovered in my first season at Liverpool why they finish fresher than all the other sides in the English First Division. It's because they do less training than their rivals.'

Of Bob Paisley, another father figure manager Souness respected, he said, 'Praise from him was like a snowstorm in the Sahara. Nobody messed him about.'

It was also a well-documented fact that nobody messed Souness about on or off the field. He had been accused of being dirty as opposed to hard – but did anyone ever say it to his face!

Souness relished a challenge, and took one head on when he accepted the top job at Ibrox, despite the job being turned down by two of Scotland's top managers of the period – Alex Ferguson and Jim McLean.

But as a player, Souness was used to winning at the highest level, and Gers fans were eagerly anticipating that they might be in for some of the same.

Souness admitted he'd had other offers – one almost certainly from Spurs. He said, 'I don't want to sound corny. I've avoided this all my playing career, but I have to say Manchester United are the only club bigger than Rangers.

'The last time I saw Rangers was when I played against them for Liverpool at the opening of the new stadium in December 1981. However, I've been told they have good players and I hope my experience on the pitch will be helpful to them. Of course there will be changes and it's up to me to make the right ones. I'm sure nobody will interpret this as a criticism of my predecessor.

'The playing part of the job will not be a problem. Management is new to me, though, and I'll have to take advice, but I'll make it work. When I heard about the Rangers job there was no way I was staying in Italy. It was too good a chance to pass up.'

Six months before accepting the job, Souness recalled saying, 'The man who turns Rangers round is really made.'

But the one Ibrox tradition he insisted he would not be following meant the trademark moustache was safe! The Ibrox side's last major signing, Dougie Bell, had been forced to remove his on Jock Wallace's orders after his transfer from Aberdeen. But Souness dismissed any suggestions his razors would be working overtime when he joked, 'It's in the contract what happens to my moustache.'

Souness was speaking as he sat for the first time in the imposing manager's office at the top of the marble staircase. On the wall was a framed picture of the European Cup Winners' Cup side of 1972, with the details of the matches inscribed as 'The Great Campaign'.

The new boss was due to get a first look at his team in action in their final league game of the season against Motherwell at Ibrox on Saturday 3 May, with another chance the following week when they were scheduled to face Celtic at Ibrox in the Glasgow Cup Final, but he insisted he wouldn't play in these games. 'It would defeat the object as I want to see the players in action,' he said.

After his flying visit to Glasgow, Souness was forced to return to Italy to play in Sampdoria's last three league games and he admitted, 'It's a crazy situation and I'm not happy about it, but mathematically we could still go down, as we need one point from three games. Mind you, they're three easy ones – against Juventus, Napoli and Inter Milan!'

Souness revealed he would ask two top names to assist him in looking over Rangers' team, with one of them almost certain to be his former Liverpool boss Bob Paisley.

He said, 'A place like Ibrox motivates me, and when the job was offered there was only one answer. My priority now is

Rangers FC, but of course I will go to the World Cup finals if I'm selected, and I hope to be still playing for Scotland next season. I intend turning out for Rangers in every game and feel that barring injury I can still play on for another two seasons.'

And it was inevitable he would be forced to face 'that' question in his first press conference as manager of Glasgow Rangers.

'What is your stand on signing a Catholic?' Souness was asked.

He answered, 'How could I possibly have taken the job if they had said to me I couldn't sign a Catholic? I'm married to one – how could I have taken the job and then gone home and faced my wife?

'It was made very plain to me that there was no longer sectarianism at Ibrox. I wouldn't have taken the job had it been any different.'

A couple of journalists mentioned this might have been said many times before without being implemented, to which David Holmes answered, 'If I had gone to negotiate with Graeme and started off by telling a lie, he wouldn't be here – and I don't think I would be either.'

Souness's wife Danielle was at the family's luxury home on the shores of the Mediterranean in Genoa while her husband was signing his contract. The 30-year-old said, 'I'm absolutely delighted.'

Danielle had married Graeme in 1980 after her first marriage had ended in divorce. She insisted religious differences had never been a problem in their relationship, and said, 'We are both Christians. My being a Catholic has never posed any problems for us. We don't even discuss it.'

But she agreed the religious issue at Ibrox was one her husband would obviously face when he took over, and admitted she had known about the possibility of Graeme's switch to Rangers for a couple of weeks.

She said, 'He was approached with the offer and he was delighted. But we have been very happy living in Italy for the past two years. We have a lovely home provided by Sampdoria. It is a large flat in a large house with huge gardens running down to the sea. This has been a wonderful climate to live in. We will be sorry to leave the country and the friends we have made – but it is a wonderful opportunity for Graeme.'

Danielle and Graeme met when he played for Liverpool – her birthplace. At that time she was working as a personal assistant to her father, millionaire stores tycoon Austin Wilson, who eventually moved to Majorca.

She added, 'I will not be returning for some time yet. Graeme will be settling in first at Ibrox and then we will look for a home.'

Meanwhile, the SFA gave the green light for the Glasgow Cup Final to be played the night before the Scottish Cup Final. The Rangers–Celtic game at Ibrox was due to take place less than 24 hours before Aberdeen and Hearts faced off in the national showpiece match.

SFA secretary Ernie Walker said, 'I feel the attraction of Aberdeen v Hearts is so great that an Old Firm game the night before will have no effect.'

Mind you, had Souness decided to play, there would be a guaranteed 45,000 at Ibrox – and not many more for the televised final next day. Many felt the Scottish Cup Final shouldn't be opposed in this way, and that as the biggest single club game, it deserved to be treated as such. There were even calls for the 'out-of-date' Glasgow association to be disbanded.

And while on the subject of the importance of football, the late Bill Shankly also said, 'There is only one job worse than being a manager, and that's being a debt collector in Glasgow!' Graeme Souness was about to find that out for himself. As Rangers' new manager he was about to pick up all the debts this slumbering giant of a club owed its fans, and they hadn't lifted a championship flag since 1978.

But Souness promised nothing more than his total commitment, and was set to bring all the habits of success to Ibrox. However, it was believed his greater value to Rangers would be as a player than as a manager in the forthcoming season.

The Rangers team needed organisation, and Souness was just the figurehead to bring calm and composure to a midfield already brimming with talent. They had lost too many games they should have won, scrambled draws from games which lacked quality and showed little promise.

It was suggested there had been no inspiration or direction to their play since John Greig hung up his boots in 1978. Rangers were, indeed, the perfect example of that established axiom – good teams always have good captains.

So the midfield majesty of Souness would be important to them. His natural, instinctive organisation of players around him and his intimidating qualities were certain to be vital. Like John Greig, George Young and others before him, Souness was a real leader of men on the field.

8

Entering A New Era

RANGERS may have rocked Scottish football – and beyond – with the left-field appointment of Graeme Souness, but one man was left to fill the vacuum created by Jock Wallace's departure, and Souness's eventual arrival, and pick up the pieces at a club in limbo.

Alex Totten, Wallace's assistant, had emerged as the 'forgotten man' while all the headlines revolved around Souness, his likely number two Walter Smith, and Totten's ex-boss Wallace.

Totten knew success in the last four Premier League matches would mean European football for Rangers – but the sack for him! It was an almost unique situation for the man who had been at the club more than two and a half years.

At the time, he said, 'No one has actually said I'm going at the end of the season, but I've been long enough in the game to recognise when the writing is on the wall. When I took over as manager of Falkirk, I insisted on Gregor Abel being my number two, and obviously Graeme Souness will want his own man.

'Walter Smith has been mentioned in newspapers and on radio. As it happens, he's a friend of mine and I think he'll do a great job if he comes to Rangers. But it's still a strange position to be in. I love this club and no way would I say anything against them. However, it looks like my time is nearly up here. That doesn't mean I won't do my utmost to ensure Rangers get that place in Europe

'This week has been a traumatic time for myself and the family, but I must assure Rangers fans that now that I know where I'm going I feel more positive. I have no question marks over my own ability. I joined Rangers as a successful manager in my own right – and actually turned down the Motherwell and Dunfermline jobs before moving to Ibrox. I've loved every moment of my time at the club and feel I've gained tremendous experience.'

What upset Totten – not unnaturally – was the fact that so much speculation was taking place about Graeme Souness's deputy at a time when he was being asked to perform a mini-miracle and take the team into Europe. One was given the impression Totten may have preferred to have left along with his boss, but he was man enough to take on the task in hand and do his best to try to get Rangers that UEFA Cup spot.

David Holmes, Rangers' main man, denied Totten had one foot out the Ibrox door when he said, 'I've spoken to Alex personally and while it's not a situation I like, he is still an employee of the company. He's in charge until Graeme Souness takes over officially, and if Graeme chooses another deputy, then that's a decision he will make, but I can only admire Alex Totten's attitude. Remember, I only want the best for Rangers FC.'

Mind you, Totten didn't enhance Davie Cooper's chances as an automatic pick for Scotland's World Cup squad when he dropped the wing king for the next match – at his former club Clydebank.

Totten explained, 'I've picked the team I think will do a job at Kilbowie. Davie Cooper is listed with Bobby Russell and Robert Fleck, and two of these three will be substitutes.'

Cooper hadn't performed to anything near his capability in the previous match – against Spurs at Ibrox – and Totten declared candidly, 'He didn't do anything other than have one shot in the second half. That's why he's not playing against Clydebank.'

Back at outside-left was John MacDonald, who had been linked with a move to Luton Town prior to the game. He was handed his place because Totten rated him 'one of the best pros' at Ibrox.

'I've always thought John is one of the best six-yard-box players in Scotland. That's what I'm looking for against Clydebank.'

Totten convened a meeting with all 34 players at Ibrox the day before the match, and explained his own position, before underlining the importance of his players getting the club into Europe. 'They owe it to themselves and to the fans who have backed them to be ambitious,' he said. Rangers were without five first-team players – injured pair Craig Paterson and Derek Johnstone, plus suspended trio Stuart Beattie, Cammy Fraser and Ally Dawson.

But all the planning and team talks in the world failed to inspire lacklustre Rangers and they crashed to defeat against the worst side in the Premier League. It was a bitter disappointment for fans still on a high after the appointment of Souness. The 2-1 loss left the Light Blues fifth in the table, one point ahead of Dundee, with both teams having three games left.

To be honest, Souness would have choked on his spaghetti when he heard the result. Even in his absence he expected Rangers to make short work of a Clydebank team languishing at the foot of the table. The Ibrox men were, after all, supposed to be chasing a place in Europe, but on this showing the best chance Souness had of playing on the continent the following season was to stay in Italy!

Quite simply, Clydebank had taken Rangers apart in a breathtaking first half. They were well organised at the back and full of running with every player responding to the brilliant midfield play of Gerry McCabe. Rangers, by comparison, were pedestrian, lacking in flair and imagination. McCabe, ironically playing a Souness-style role, was the architect of both Clydebank goals, scored by Conroy and Bain in the first half-hour. Ian Durrant scored a consolation for the Gers in the second half.

But there was better news for the Light Blues a couple of days after the painful defeat when Souness got his man – and lifelong Rangers fan Walter Smith left Dundee United to take up the position of assistant manager at Ibrox.

It was a badly kept secret that the 38-year-old was a wanted man in Govan – but Smith, who was also Scotland's assistant boss, was delighted to make the move. Rangers had held back while Dundee United, with whom Smith was ending a 20-year association, were still chasing honours, but Hearts' 3-0 win over United at Tynecastle ten days previous had set the wheels in motion.

But as Smith was checking in at his new workplace, three men appointed by Wallace were saying a sad farewell to the club. Totten, reserve-team coach John Hagart and youth-team coach Stan Anderson were all released from their contracts.

Totten had been appointed first-team coach by Wallace in November 1983, with Hagart arriving at the club the following week to take charge of the second XI. Anderson's unique association with the Light Blues saw him join on three separate occasions. He had a short spell as a midfielder on the playing staff in the 1960s before being freed. He joined the coaching staff for the first time in 1970, left to manage Clyde, where he was dismissed in 1977, and two years later re-joined the coaching staff under John Greig. He was appointed youth coach by Wallace.

Totten said, 'I wish Walter Smith all the best. He takes over my room and I left him a good luck note on his desk. The other coaches and myself were told we were leaving on Monday night but I'm not going to say anything against Rangers. For me, they will always be the greatest club in the world and I reckon I've gained from my experience with them.'

Souness and Smith may have been creating all the headlines with their moves to Ibrox, but one Ranger managed to go from 10 Downing Street to the Blue Room at Ibrox, all within the space of three hours.

That was the hectic programme faced by chief executive David Holmes when he found himself in the presence of two very famous world leaders. At Downing Street he had Prime Minister Margaret Thatcher, and Sir Stanley Rous, former president of FIFA, for company. In the Blue Room, he completed the signing of his two top men, Souness and Smith.

It was a very successful day for the dynamic boss who was doing a fantastic job of getting Rangers back on top with his detailed planning, the same way he did as managing director of the Lawrence Group.

At Downing Street, Holmes presented the Prime Minister and Sir Stanley with portraits of Alan Morton, the former Rangers and Scotland international left-winger who became a director of the club after his playing days had ended. Sir Stanley was delighted to receive such a wonderful gift to mark his 91st birthday since he was a personal friend of Alan Morton.

There were three Cabinet ministers present at the Downing Street reception; John MacGregor, George Younger and Malcolm Rifkind. And also there was Ken Friar, managing director of Arsenal, with whom Rangers had enjoyed a long association.

Sir Stanley spoke of the magic of the Wembley Wizards, especially the Wee Blue Devil, Alan Morton. In 1928, Sir Stanley was linesman at Wembley when Scotland defeated England 5-1. He said, 'It was one of Scotland's greatest ever performances. Every player was outstanding and I can never forget the brilliant work of Alan Morton. He became a personal friend and we had a long friendship after his playing days were over. He was a great credit to football.

'The night before Scotland played England, their captain, Jimmy McMullan of Manchester City, told his players just to go to bed and pray for rain the next day. The heavens opened and the rain teemed down. And before the match started, Jimmy, who began his career with Denny Hibs, the team that produced Sir Matt Busby and Rangers legend Jimmy Smith, told his boys, "Just go out and play your natural game." They did just that and the memories of that great triumph have lived on.'

Sir Stanley added, 'When the games were played in Scotland, it was always an English referee who was in charge with Scots officials at the line, and at Wembley, the roles were reversed.'

The Prime Minister also spoke of her own wee blue devil John MacGregor, who went to the same Dykehead primary school in Shotts as Jack Gillespie, vice-chairman of Rangers.

Meanwhile, Smith revealed how he had finally arrived at the club he was perhaps always destined to join. Smith's earliest memories of the beautiful game were as a four-year-old being taken by his grandfather from his Carmyle home to watch Rangers.

He explained, 'My grandfather was a founder member of the local Rangers supporters' club and after that first time he took me to Ibrox, I was a Rangers fan for life.'

Like every young fan of the club, Smith dreamed of wearing the light blue jersey one day but although he was to enjoy a distinguished, if unglamorous playing career, playing for Rangers would elude him.

He began in amateur football with Bishopbriggs before being picked up by Ashfield. His spell there lasted just four months when Dundee United manager Jerry Kerr signed the 18-year-old defender in October 1966. That was the start of a 20-year association with the Tannadice club broken only for a year and a half when he signed for Dumbarton in September 1975 for £10,000. He would return to United in January 1977 at a reduced fee of £4,000.

In March 1982 he was appointed assistant manager by Jim McLean after a spell on the club's coaching staff. He said, 'Jim always encouraged his players to think about the game and he asked me to take charge of the reserves for a while which I enjoyed greatly. It all really started from there.'

In June of 1982, Smith tasted his first international coaching experience when he was assistant to Andy Roxburgh and the Scottish under-18 side, which won the European Championships in Finland.

Jock Stein put him in charge of the under-21s in September 1984 and a year later he was appointed number two in the senior set-up by Alex Ferguson.

There are many football folk who influenced Smith's thinking and approach to the game – Dougie Smith, Doug Houston and Jimmy Millar being just three he talks of. Millar, a former idol of the Rangers fans, went to United in the later stages of his career and playing in the reserves proved a big help to the younger players at Tannadice of whom Smith was one.

But there's no doubt the biggest influence of all on Smith was the man who transformed United from an also-ran to a trophy-winning side – Jim McLean. Smith said, 'I have enjoyed a close working relationship with Jim and I will always be grateful for what he has done for me. I would certainly not have left Tannadice to be assistant at any club other than Rangers.'

Life was just about to get hectic for the Smith family – Walter, wife Ethel, and sons Neil, who was nine at the time, and six-year-old Steven, who settled in Helensburgh after leaving the north-east.

Smith and Souness also had the World Cup finals in Mexico to look forward to, but Rangers' new assistant boss insisted it wasn't too much to cope with. He said, 'There will be no problems. Neither Graeme or myself will have a holiday, there will be work done with Rangers and we will give everything for Scotland during the build-up and the actual finals. There is no question of a conflict of interests.'

While on a flying visit to Glasgow, Souness explained why he had appointed Smith as his assistant. He spoke highly of the man whom he had worked under in the Scotland side for just over six months, but who would now be working under him. He said, 'There's no surprise that Walter has arrived here. He is a man with a big name in Scotland and he possesses a tremendous knowledge of the Scottish game with which, admittedly, I am unfamiliar.

'I am certain we couldn't have picked a better man for the job – he has all the credentials this club are looking for. When with the Scottish squads, I have been really impressed with his relationship with the players and that was a very important factor when offering him the job.

'I also asked other people in the game about Walter and every one of them gave me a glowing report. I am sure he will do a tremendous job here. The two of us have already discussed the players we would like to have at Ibrox and we have made inquiries – but there is a limit to the amount of money we can spend at the moment.

'That's why it is so important we qualify for Europe. If we can get a good run in the UEFA Cup and also perform well at domestic level, the big crowds will turn up and that means more money will be available to buy quality players.'

Getting Smith was also a coup for Souness as several clubs had sounded him out about being their number one.

Smith said, 'I am a great admirer of Graeme Souness and I think he will benefit the game as a whole – he will be the best player in the country. His leadership qualities, both on and off the field, will be invaluable for Rangers and I'm delighted to be working alongside him.'

McLean was naturally disappointed to lose his man, but said, 'Our loss is Rangers' gain. I have nothing but admiration and respect for what Walter achieved with United in recent years. We could never have bought what he gave to this club. We were very fortunate to have him here.'

On Saturday 19 April, Rangers made the short journey along the M8 to Paisley for a meeting with St Mirren at Love Street. It was a game the Light Blues should have been capable of winning – but once again they came up short, and the road to Europe was looking rather rocky after the 2-1 loss. As if defeat by an injury-hit Saints side wasn't bad enough, Dundee won convincingly at home to Motherwell to take the initiative in the run-in. Rangers' task was clear.

They had to win at Pittodrie and again at home to Motherwell the following week – and hope Dundee slipped up against either Celtic or Hearts.

But while the Gers faltered in Paisley, Saints were well worth their win and despite a battling second-half fightback from Rangers, Smith would be able to tell Souness the task they were facing was a huge one.

The home side took the lead in the 14th minute and the goal came as no surprise since they had enjoyed all the early pressure. Peter Mackie's cross fell for defender Steve Clarke, and although his shot was well blocked by Peter McCloy, the veteran keeper could do nothing to stop Frank McGarvey steering the loose ball into the net.

Rangers' attempts to get back into the match were all too easily frustrated by Saints, although McCoist saw a fine volley fly inches over the bar on the half-hour. But three minutes later the Light Blues were in real trouble when the home side made it

2-0. The Rangers defence failed to deal with another cross and Billy Abercromby shot past McCloy.

Four minutes into the second half, Saints were awarded a soft penalty. McGarvey clearly handled before colliding innocuously with Stuart Munro but the referee pointed to the spot. However, justice was done when McGarvey blasted the ball high over the bar and a minute later Ally Dawson scored to bring Rangers back into the game. John MacDonald broke forward and played the ball inside to Dawson who had moved forward in support. He side-stepped a defender before crashing a terrific shot into the net from 20 yards.

Rangers tried hard to rescue a point but Campbell Money produced fine saves from McCoist and McPherson before the end. Smith was in the dug-out and Joe Fagan was also in the crowd, with the ex-Liverpool boss offering an independent viewpoint for Souness.

The top five in the table were set to qualify for Europe but this defeat left Rangers sixth in the ten-team league, a point behind Dundee but with a superior goal difference.

Hearts were top and Celtic third, a point behind Dundee United but with a game in hand. But there was some cheer for Rangers after the game when goalscorer Dawson was called into the Scotland squad for the friendly against Holland in Eindhoven after the pool was hit by withdrawals. It was a well-deserved call-up for Dawson.

Despite being perplexed by what he had just watched, Smith made it clear there would be no panic or wholesale changes to the playing staff at the club. He said, 'Since we have come in, there has been a lot of talk about needing something like six new players – but I don't think that's necessary.

'It has been my opinion for some time that there are good football players at Rangers and that opinion was strengthened during my first few days' training with them. Obviously when a new manager comes to any club, he wants to bring in some new faces, but Graeme and I agree that we must be fair to the players who are already here and most of them will be offered the opportunity to show us what they can do.

'That means most players whose contracts are up will at least be put on short-term deals for next season to give them the chance to prove themselves.'

He added, 'We must qualify for Europe. Rangers are a European club and the players realise how important it is to us in every way to be competing at that level every season. I believe you have to be optimistic in this game and I'm confident we will make it – but it's not going to be easy.

'Our next match is at Aberdeen and as everyone knows that has been a very difficult place to get a result in recent years. But this is the kind of match Rangers should go into with confidence and with no fears and the players have the chance now to set a new trend for the future. There are no limits here. This club is the biggest in Scotland, if not Britain, and there is every incentive for everyone to do well. It's a marvellous challenge and I'm looking forward to it.'

One thing Smith did announce, though, was that the players would be returning to Ibrox earlier than ever for pre-season training. Souness and Smith had abandoned plans for a holiday in the summer and were keen to have as much time as possible with the squad before the start of the 1986/87 season – and that meant pre-season for the Light Blues would kick off on Monday 7 July – and the following week the first-team squad would head to mainland Europe for a fortnight.

Preparations for the trip were in the very early stages but Spain and West Germany were two possible destinations.

Souness said, 'I want a full week of training with the players before we go away for a fortnight. It's vital our preparations for the new season are as thorough as possible. At the moment, there are no precise details about any trip abroad but even if we can't arrange any actual games, we will still be travelling to get the squad together for several days.'

But Souness also reiterated the importance of the remainder of the current season for Rangers, and said, 'It may start to sound boring and repetitive but I don't care how many times I say it – qualifying for the UEFA Cup is our top priority right now. This Saturday presents the players with a big test when they travel to

Pittodrie but they can do themselves and the club a big favour by getting the right result against Aberdeen.'

But there was bad news for one Gers star – skipper Craig Paterson – when it was announced that he needed an operation, but he hoped it would finally end his sickening run of injuries. The big defender was scheduled to have a growth removed from the back of his troublesome right ankle and although the season was over, Paterson was expected to be fighting fit in time for pre-season training.

And Souness moved to make another addition to his backroom team when he enlisted the help of former Dundee and Coventry City manager Donald Mackay, a team-mate of Smith during his playing days at Dundee United. Mackay was brought in to look after the players for a couple of weeks with both Smith and Souness involved in Scotland's World Cup build-up.

Smith said, 'It is purely a short-term agreement and Donald knows that. He has been good enough to agree to assist us for the next few weeks and we are very grateful.'

Mackay, who quit as Coventry boss after a defeat by Liverpool, said, 'I'm in a bit of limbo at the moment and I'm delighted to help Walter out.'

Off the park, club secretary Campbell Ogilvie announced that new season ticket deals for Ibrox were in the pipeline. The Rover season ticket was to be scrapped and a much fairer type of season ticket was set to take its place.

The club had encountered administrative problems with the Rover, and had received complaints from some fans that the ticket didn't guarantee them a seat at Ibrox for some bigger games. Steps were being taken to rectify the situation, so that when a supporter bought the new ticket, they would specify there and then whether they wanted to sit in the Copland Road stand or the front or rear of the Govan stand. Whichever area was chosen, they would then be guaranteed a seat in that section of the ground for the remainder of the season.

The new deal replacing the Rover was just part of a new package put together by Rangers in anticipation of bigger crowds for the Souness era.

Ogilvie said, 'The details of the whole package are still being finalised but we hope to be able to announce them within the next week or so. We are confident we have put together the best possible deal for supporters considering the fact there will be four more Premier League games at Ibrox next season.'

Ogilvie also announced prices for the forthcoming Glasgow Cup Final between Rangers and Celtic at Ibrox on Friday 9 May, which was to be all-ticket. These were: Govan Stand: £3.50 (Rear) and £3 (Front), Enclosure £2. Changed days!

But it was time for Rangers to head north for the vital Premier League match at Pittodrie, where high-flying Aberdeen lay in wait. The Light Blues desperately needed something from the game – and they got it.

Smith's men gave their UEFA Cup hopes a much-needed shot in the arm with a determined, stylish performance against the Dons, and secured a point in a thrilling 1-1 draw. In fact, Rangers were unlucky not to win the match with the amount of chances they created, but Ted McMinn's magnificent 50th-minute goal looked to have sealed a European place for Rangers. With Dundee losing to Celtic, victory against Motherwell would see the Gers clinch fifth place.

After Aberdeen had opened brightly, Rangers created the first clear-cut opportunity in the 15th minute. Davie Cooper did well to dispossess Willie Miller inside the Dons' penalty area but McCoist miscued the winger's cross.

Super Cooper was looking every inch the player for the big occasion and he was providing plenty of hope for the big travelling support in the 17,000 crowd. But Derek Ferguson was certainly the unluckiest player on the field, as he had two goals disallowed – apparently for offside decisions against Hugh Burns and McCoist.

But Rangers were determined to break down Aberdeen and in the 50th minute their hard work paid off. McMinn, who had a terrific second half, collected a loose ball by Robertson inside the Rangers half, and embarked on a stunning solo run which saw him evade several tackles before crashing a super shot high into the net from just inside the box.

John Hewitt's equaliser, seven minutes later, meant a share of the spoils, but at least Rangers' European fate was now in their own hands. Victory against Motherwell at Ibrox – Souness's first official match in charge of the club – would officially clinch that UEFA Cup slot.

After the 1-1 draw at Pittodrie, Smith said, 'The difference from the previous week at Love Street was night and day and the performance was very pleasing. I was really quite amazed at the transformation.'

While several fringe players were trying to play their way into the new management team's plans, one player who seemed assured of a place was wing wizard Cooper.

Smith said, 'Davie is a special player who does things with a football naturally that ordinary players find difficult, if not impossible to do. His talent is not in question – but Davie needs to be confident. It was clear that his confidence had gone down in recent months along with the rest of the Rangers team.'

9

John MacDonald

IF Davie Cooper was Rangers' talisman, John MacDonald was the supporter who lived the dream. But not only did he fulfil a long-held ambition by playing for his boyhood heroes – he also scored more than 100 goals for the first team.

Mind you, MacDonald and his goals almost never made it to Ibrox. He revealed how he was all set to join Ipswich Town when Rangers pulled out all the stops at the 11th hour to get him to Govan, even turning up at his school in a bid to persuade the talented teenager to sign on the dotted line.

MacDonald lived in Maryhill until he was five, when the family moved to the outskirts of the city to Drumchapel. There, he attended Kingsridge Secondary School, which proved something of a football scout's dream by producing talent such as Gregor Stevens, Alex Miller and Danny McGrain.

MacDonald had something the others lacked; he was a natural-born goalscorer and soon had many teams craving his services. He joined Rangers in 1978, remaining at Ibrox for eight years, before moving on to the likes of Barnsley, Scarborough and Airdrie.

He said, 'We stayed just along the road from Firhill so my dad used to take me to see Partick Thistle most weeks. We went there because it was handy, but once we moved home, and dad didn't want to go to the football anymore, I started going to the games with my mates. They were all Rangers fans and as I was a bit older by then, I was allowed to go with them to Ibrox.'

But MacDonald will never forget the day he signed for Rangers, and insisted it was the proudest moment of his footballing life. He said, 'I was just 17 at the time and when I signed my name on that contract I was delighted – but it took a while to get there, mind you.

'I had been going down to Ipswich every time we had a school holiday. Their chief scout Ron Day had come up for one of the schoolboy internationals when I was 13 and showed great interest in me so I started making the trip south regularly with a few of the other young Scottish players. Guys like Alan Brazil and I would meet up at the station and go down for the holiday weekends. I loved it, and the only thing I could see myself doing at that time was signing for Ipswich Town and playing my football at Portman Road.'

Rangers simply weren't in the frame, and even though MacDonald attended a Glasgow school, it was the Suffolk side who still seemed clear favourites to land his signature.

He said, 'As a young boy, the only team that had showed an interest in me was Ipswich, but when you get older, and start taking notice of things a wee bit more, I realised there were scouts from other clubs coming to my matches. That was when Rangers came to the fore. George Runciman was a Rangers scout at the time and he started coming to watch me quite regularly, and would report back to Lawrie Cummings, who was their chief scout. Eventually, Mr Cummings came up to my school, and one day I found myself sitting in front of both him and my headmaster, when Mr Cummings said to me, "So you would love to sign for Rangers, John?" I felt under a wee bit of pressure and said yes, but when I got home that night I spoke to my dad about it for a while. I told him the Rangers scout was coming up to the school the next day to sign me, and he asked if it was what I really wanted. To be honest, it wasn't, and I said to my dad that I wanted to go to Ipswich.

'The following day, the scout came up to the school as planned but was clearly unhappy when I told him I'd changed my mind. He reminded me that I'd said it in front of the headmaster, but my dad was with me this time so I felt a bit more confident. Mr

Cummings then changed tack and started saying we could give you this for signing, and expenses etc. I was only 14 so I agreed and signed there and then!

'I suppose there was a slight regret that I didn't go to Ipswich because they had looked after me so well, and I liked it down there. In fact, after I chose Ibrox, I received a really nice letter from Bobby Robson, who was their manager at the time, and he said, "We're disappointed you've decided to go to Rangers but if there are any problems in the future we would love to talk to you." It was a really nice gesture, especially from someone with such a high standing in the game, and I still have that letter to this day.'

MacDonald added, 'The good thing about those days was that there were no pro-youth teams and I was still able to play for the school, which was great, because I really enjoyed playing for the school team and in the schoolboy internationals. I feel that's what is lacking a bit at the moment. The pro-youth teams don't allow their youngsters to play for their school teams, so they don't ever get to experience the international scene, which is such a pity.'

MacDonald was called up by Rangers at 17, and it was the start of an eight-year love affair with the Light Blues – something that has continued to this day. He made his league debut for Rangers against Hearts at Tynecastle in a feisty five-goal thriller in February 1979. He made one other appearance that season in a 1-0 win over Partick Thistle in the penultimate game of the season – his competitive Ibrox debut.

He also played in Glasgow Cup ties against the Jags and Celtic that term – the latter a 3-1 final win – and showed genuine predatory instincts by scoring in both games. He was immediately marked down as one for the future.

He recalled, 'I would probably have preferred to have gone to Ibrox a year earlier, because I had outgrown school. I was persuaded to stay on and take my Highers but wasn't really interested in school and just wanted to play football.

'Jock Wallace had left by that time and John Greig had taken over. In fact, I was Greig's first signing. I signed pre-season and he took me up to Inverness for a friendly and I got on as a sub. It was a great experience and while I didn't score, we won 6-2. Billy Urquhart scored in that game – and we signed him right after it!

'I had good times under John Greig. He was there five years and we got to the Scottish Cup Final every year, which was quite a feat. He could have won the treble in his first year had it not been for one game against Celtic. He never managed to win the league, which was probably his downfall.

'As a player, I didn't win the league either, but I took part in seven cup finals – four Scottish Cups and three League Cups – and won three of the seven, which wasn't bad. I also managed to score in a few of them. Anywhere else and it would have been seen as a success but at Rangers you're obviously expected to win the league. The likes of Dundee United, Aberdeen and Celtic were all vying for titles at that time, so it was a tough period for us.

'I think John Greig perhaps made too many changes too soon, and got rid of a lot of the guys he had played with. Guys likes Alex MacDonald and Gordon Smith moved on, as did a few others, but I still thoroughly enjoyed my time working under John and I had a lot of great friends at the club.'

Jock Wallace left Motherwell to replace Greig, and the former Gers boss's return to Ibrox didn't exactly prove to be the best of times for the young striker. In fact, MacDonald feels he perhaps wasn't given enough of a chance during Wallace's second coming.

He said, 'I was in and out of the team under big Jock. There were a couple of occasions when he took not well and had to go into hospital, and I was brought back into the team by his assistant Alex Totten – and I think I scored in every single game. When Jock returned, I would be in and out of the team again, so it was a really frustrating time for me.

'And then when Jock got the sack, and before Graeme Souness was available to take over, Alex Totten was once again put in temporary charge and he started playing me again.

'One thing that sticks in my mind from big Jock's days were the times we would head up to, say, Aberdeen, the night before a game. We would be staying overnight and Jock's favourite meal was a mixed grill. A load of us would tuck into a big plateful of steak, chops, chicken etc. It was excellent, although funny how you seem to remember things like that!

'Walter Smith then came in because Souness was still involved with Sampdoria until the end of the season and I played in the first game against St Mirren, which we lost 2-1. Unfortunately, I then got injured in training, a back injury, so that was it for me. I was also due to go into hospital that summer for an operation on my clavicle, which kept popping out.

'When it came to pre-season training, I was way behind and not really involved. They had just released 11 players and I was on month-to-month contracts at the time, although I was offered a one-year deal. But I was watching the calibre of player coming through the door and decided that I wasn't going to get a game.

'I was then called up to Souness's office and he said, "Your contract's up in two weeks, if you want I can just release you and you can go and find another club," so that gave me a fortnight to look about and see what was out there.'

MacDonald ended up at Charlton for a couple of months and while it proved a successful spell, the timing was all wrong. His next move, though, would prove an even bigger success, and see him make more money than he had ever done at Rangers.

He explained, 'It was a good time for Charlton, and their supporters, as we beat the likes of Chelsea away, and Everton at home, so we had some big scalps. I was playing in these games, but the timing wasn't great for me. My wife was going to move down to London, but she was pregnant at the time, and it was expensive.

'I then got a phonecall from Allan Clarke – the old Leeds United striker. He was manager at Barnsley and I went down there and played a couple of trial games. I did well and he wanted to sign me. I got on really well with Allan so I signed for two years and thoroughly enjoyed it there. Former Celtic player Jim Dobbin was also at the club and we became good pals.

'In fact, I even made some money, as they were paying me more than Rangers! Imagine that, they were bottom of the Second Division and my basic wage was higher than at Ibrox. I started thinking, "Why did I stay so long at Rangers?" I suppose it was a case of loyalty. Let's be honest, I was a Rangers supporter as a kid, and I just loved the club – so that's why I stayed!

'I loved Rangers so much and even when Souness told me I could go, I was walking over to the car park, head bowed, tears welling up in my eyes, thinking, "That's it, it's all over." It was the end of a very personal and important era for me.'

But it doesn't even take the benefit of hindsight for MacDonald to know that Rangers had to change. They weren't even playing second fiddle to Celtic during the 1985/86 season. At one point they were closer to bottom spot than top.

He said, 'There is no doubt the club had to move forward, and it did so for the better. It is probably the best thing that has happened to Rangers in my lifetime. David Holmes came in and just changed everything. Souness also arrived and did a fantastic job. Not all of his signings were great but I don't think there are any managers in the history of the game who have a 100 per cent signing success rate. But the likes of Terry Butcher, Chris Woods, Graham Roberts and Richard Gough helped transform the club.

'Even when I was down in Barnsley, I was still a Rangers supporter, in fact, that's something that will never change. It's in the blood and that's that. I still go to all the home matches to this day.

'Looking back, the first I realised that Graeme Souness was to be our new manager was when I saw it on the telly. There were a lot of names getting mentioned as potential new managers, but Souness was one of the biggest around.

'Training was fantastic under him as he introduced a lot of the stuff he had learned in Italy. It was new to us so it helped freshen things up. We also had double sessions throughout pre-season, and would have pasta between them for lunch.

'Pasta was fine by me, but I couldn't eat it before matches. I was always really nervous before games and would usually just have soup, as it was easier to get up. I remember before one cup final and we were lining up to meet the dignitaries. They were about three players away from me when all of a sudden I was sick, and there wasn't a thing I could do about it.

'Even after my goal in the Drybrough Cup Final I was as sick as a dog. I was sitting behind the goal and Alex MacDonald was saying to me, "That's the way wee man, get it all up." Mind you, once the games started I was usually fine.

'Most of the changes Graeme Souness introduced were subtle, and they worked, but I think one of the few mistakes he made was bringing Phil Boersma in as the new physio. That said, he didn't make many mistakes.

'One thing I didn't enjoy, though, was the way many of the older players who weren't in Souness's plans were banished to the away dressing room. We had to change in there for training and I don't think it did anything to help morale at the club.

'Personally, I used to mix with a lot of the younger players anyway, so it wasn't a big issue for me. The likes of myself, Derek Ferguson, Ian Durrant and Robert Fleck would enjoy going for a businessmen's lunch to a Chinese restaurant every Friday.'

MacDonald had more or less resigned himself to the fact he was leaving Rangers – although he admits to being pleased that they allowed him to go on a free transfer, as he recalled that hadn't always been the plan.

He explained, 'I was pleased that if I was leaving, I was getting a free. When Jock was the manager, the club wanted £70,000 for me, so getting a free made it easier to find a new team. When I was leaving, our coach Donald Mackay talked me into going down to Leicester City but they had a player that was very similar, and I thought it a bit strange I had even been asked to go down there.

'When I eventually signed for Barnsley, I was given a decent signing-on fee. The exact figure shall remain a secret but let's just say it was a bit more than the £250 I got when I signed for Rangers! In all the years I was at Ibrox that was the only signing-on fee I ever received from the club.

'But I had a ball at Ibrox and it makes me very proud that I managed to score more than 100 goals for Rangers. Okay, so a few of them were in friendlies, but I managed 106 goals in 270 games, which isn't too bad a return all things considered.'

Down the years, we've read of players saying that once they leave Rangers, everything else seems like an anti-climax.

MacDonald agrees, and said, 'Once you walk out that magnificent front door at Ibrox everything else does seem like a step down the ladder, wherever you go, unless it's somewhere like Manchester United. Mind you, even when Archie Knox left Man United to go up to Rangers, Alex Ferguson said Rangers were paying him more than the Old Trafford side had been. But when I was at Rangers, we were all on the same basic wage. It was £300 across the board until Souness came.

'But it wasn't just the extra money I enjoyed at Barnsley. I really loved my time at the club. Barnsley is a great wee town with great people, and most of the players lived on the outskirts, in a small village called Ardsley. I stayed near Paul McGugan and Owen Archdeacon, the two former Celtic players. In fact big Paul stayed with me for a few months until he got his own place sorted. We were away from the heat of the Old Firm and got on really well – but we still managed to fit in some great Glasgow banter.

'Our house was built on an old mine, and any time there were any structural faults, due to the mines, we just called someone up and they came and fixed it, or decorated for us. It was a fantastic arrangement!

'When I left Barnsley, I went to Scarborough, which was a big mistake on my part. Allan Clarke had just been sacked and I had just signed a new contract with Barnsley, but Scarborough got in touch and told me they wanted to sign me. I told them what I wanted and, to be fair, they came up with it. I decided to head up the east coast to Scarborough's McCain Stadium. They were in the Fourth Division at that time. I stayed there for a year but they told me they couldn't afford me after that.

'I remember my wife phoning Barnsley to get a hold of me one day, and someone at the club saying, "Oh, John's away for signing talks to Scarborough." There were no mobile phones in those days so I didn't get a chance to tell her.

'But for all I enjoyed my whole career, when I was playing down in England I was still always interested to see how things were going back up the road at Ibrox. Graeme Souness seemed to be doing a fine job. His introduction to Scottish football completely changed the game up here but even then he didn't really crack it in Europe.

'He changed Scottish football, though, as it meant Celtic had to step up to the plate, which they did. And in a way that was a pity because it prevented us from doing ten in a row! That was a great shame, because it would have taken a bit of beating.

'From a personal point of view, though, I still enjoy going to the football and get that special feeling every time I walk through the front door at Ibrox – even to this day!'

10

Bobby Russell

ON the day Bobby Russell made his Rangers debut – Saturday 13 August 1977 – Showaddywaddy were at number three in the charts with the smash hit single 'You Got What It Takes'. It wouldn't be too long until we discovered that here was one teenage Glaswegian who certainly had what it takes to carve out a successful football career.

Plucked from the relative obscurity of Shettleston Juniors, Russell went on to become one of the finest midfielders of his generation and won seven major honours with the Light Blues. Sadly, his time at Rangers came to an abrupt end when he was moved on following a problematic knee injury – although he found a second wind at Motherwell and had five enjoyable years at Fir Park.

He said, 'I only played two games under Graeme Souness; the first game of the season and then against Tampere in Finland in the second leg of the UEFA Cup first round, and then I was out for seven months with an injury. That was the beginning of the end for me.'

Long before that, though, Russell had rubber-stamped his place in Rangers' history by proving his class time and time again in the famous light blue jersey. It almost seems the travesty of the 20th century that his international appearances were limited to just a few caps for the Scotland under-21 side!

But when the midfield ace was plying his trade in the juniors at Greenfield Park, he always hoped that one day he would get a move up to the seniors – although he didn't think it would happen to a couple of Shettleston players at the same time.

He explained, 'I knew from reading the sports pages in the papers that Rangers were interested in me. At that time, Joe Coyle was playing for Shettleston as well and there was interest from Celtic for him. With the two of us under the microscope, we used to see wee bits and pieces in the paper about the Old Firm supposedly keeping tabs on us.

'Mind you, around that time I also had a chance to go to Clydebank. I had a trial with them on the Saturday afternoon, and then a run-out with Rangers the following midweek, and the funny thing was that both matches were against Dundee United reserves. I know Clydebank wanted to sign me but I had promised Rangers scout Lawrie Cummings that I would have a trial with them. Rangers then offered me a contract so there was absolutely no decision to make – I was going to Ibrox!

'In fact, I bumped into the Clydebank chairman, Jack Steedman, a couple of years ago and he said to me, "I know you went to Rangers for more money," and I told him nothing could have been further from the truth. I said to him, "Rangers offered me a signing-on fee of £250, and you offered me £1,500, so it definitely wasn't about the money!"

'When it came to choosing between Clydebank and Rangers, I knew exactly what I wanted to do, and my decision certainly wasn't based on money.'

But despite being well aware that Rangers were watching him in games for Shettleston, Russell insists there was no extra pressure on his youthful shoulders.

He said, 'I knew through the stories in the press that Rangers were coming to watch me but I was only 18 or 19 years of age so it wasn't exactly a heavy burden on my mind. When you're that age, it's a case of what will be will be. It's sort of out of your control so you tend not to overthink things.

'But I was playing for Shettleston one afternoon when I saw this man coming towards me. He was real old school and had a Crombie coat and trilby hat on. It was Lawrie Cummings and he approached me before the kick-off. He introduced himself as

Rangers' chief scout and asked if I would like a trial, and it took me all of one second to say yes! It was then that I started to get excited.

'When I signed for Rangers, I more or less went straight into the first team and we won a treble in my first season – and how do you better that? Well, we nearly did, as we had a great run in Europe the following season AND we should have won the treble again, but all the games seemed to catch up with us and it drifted away. Basically I could have started with back-to-back trebles, but unfortunately we lost the deciding game to Celtic at Parkhead.'

Although he no doubt worked as hard as the next guy, Russell always came across as one of the most naturally gifted players of his generation; the Scottish midfielder who wouldn't have looked out of place in the current Barcelona side, but there is one moment in particular which probably defines his career.

Wednesday 1 November 1978. PSV Eindhoven v Rangers in a European Cup tie in the Phillips Stadium; the arena in which the Dutch masters had never lost a European game – until Russell and co arrived for the second-round, second-leg match. The first game at Ibrox had ended goalless and with just a few minutes of the game in Eindhoven remaining, it was 2-2, when Tommy McLean picked up the ball in his own half, out wide. Moments later, Russell began a lung-bursting run from the edge of his own box, received a pinpoint pass and ran on to bend the ball round the goalkeeper and into the back of the net. Rangers were in the quarter-finals, and knocking out PSV – the UEFA Cup holders – was one of the club's greatest results on the continent.

Russell said, 'I suppose I will forever be associated with that game. Nobody gave us a chance in Eindhoven but we turned in a great performance that night. Mind you, we were one goal down after about 20 seconds, so perhaps those who thought we would fail were about to be proved right. But we did very well to come back and win, although a lot of that was down to the experience we had in the team. I'm convinced that helped get us through.

'Alex MacDonald scored a great goal that night, and then Derek Johnstone managed to get his head to a free kick and knock it in, and of course my goal was just the icing on the cake.

Whenever I do hospitality at Ibrox, people often talk about that goal and some will joke and say, "Where would you be without that goal?" I suppose the answer is I managed to score another 46 for Rangers!

'But back to the goal in Eindhoven and I bet John Greig, who was manager at the time, was pulling his hair out wondering what I was doing charging forward like that because there was only a few minutes to go and a 2-2 draw was good enough to see us through to the next round on the away goals rule.

'People have asked why I done it, but you don't know, it's just something you either do or don't. You try and reflect and go through the movements leading up to the goal, but I think it was basically because Tommy McLean had the ball. Had it been anyone else, like Tam Forsyth for example, and no disrespect to the big man, I wouldn't have made the run because the chances of him playing the pass perfectly would have been a wee bit non-existent, but wee Tam could put the ball on a sixpence. That probably helped make my mind up, as well as seeing the PSV defence running out.

'But you also do something like that instinctively, because you can't afford to think about these things too long. Mind you, when the ball went in, all the pressure on us was lifted, so it was worth the gamble.'

Russell enjoyed playing under John Greig and his successor, Jock Wallace. But he believes it was inconsistency that played a part in the latter's eventual downfall.

He said, 'Initially, when Jock came back the second time, there was an upturn in our fortunes, and he got the belief back into the team and we were going great. On our day we were capable of beating anyone, but it was a lack of consistency that was our problem. We were losing and drawing games we shouldn't have, where wins would have had us up there challenging for the league.

'Apart from winning the league in my first season, and then going close the season after, we were never really in contention for the eight seasons that followed. And because we were capable of beating anyone in a one-off game, we probably became known as a cup team, which isn't really good enough at a big club like Rangers.'

But when Graeme Souness arrived at Ibrox, Russell admitted it sent a massive tremor rippling through the game north of the border. He knew there and then that everything was about to change.

He said, 'When Souness took over it was a big, big shock. I first heard the murmurs about him coming when we were in at Ibrox getting ready to go and play in a reserve match at Kilbowie. The rumour was doing the rounds that Souness was upstairs, and that he was to be the next manager, but we just all thought there was no chance of it happening.

'But it happened all right, and when it did it was a bit like taking the team into the unknown. The first thing we all started thinking was that there would be massive changes, and if I remember correctly the World Cup was taking place that close season. I was a good friend of Davie Cooper's and he told me that Walter Smith had been asking him a lot of questions about the players already at Ibrox, and I know Davie recommended to Walter that he kept me on.

'But it was a big change for all the players who were already there, as all of a sudden we were wearing flip-flops in the changing room and eating pasta for lunch! Some of the boys then started coming in with wee bags containing shampoo and Brylcreem etc, so it was definitely changed days, but it was certainly a more professional way to go about our business.

'I think the timing of the change was probably right, but did the change need to be so dramatic? I'm not so sure. Money and wages started to spiral out of control, and I don't know if that was altogether a good thing.

'In hindsight I suppose it's easy enough saying now that perhaps it wasn't the best way to go about things, but it happened and it changed Scottish football, although we might still be suffering the consequences.

'After I left to go to Motherwell, I heard rumours that certain players were on £30k a week, tax free, and all that kind of stuff. Now I don't know if it was true, but it was certainly doing the rounds at the time. If it's true, or even almost true, then it's unbelievable – and unsustainable.'

Russell added, 'Graeme Souness was absolutely fine with me. I only played a couple of games under him and when I was coming back from injury, I hurt my knee again and my contract was about due up. He told me to go and see a specialist, see how it was, and then go and negotiate terms with another club and he would give me a free transfer, so I was happy with that and it worked out fine. I went to Motherwell and had five good years, so to get five years with the chronic knee condition I had was a bonus for me.

'When I first went to Fir Park I was keen to do well, but not to prove Souness or anyone else wrong. The only person I wanted to prove anything to was myself. I wanted to get myself to a decent level of fitness and knew that if I did that, I could still play a bit.

'When I was 21 I tore my cruciate knee ligaments, which was a career-threatening injury, and in those days they opened you up and took away the offending cartilage or ligaments and that was that. I was told at the time not to play on, because my knee was so unstable. I wasn't having that, though, and I worked hard to build up the muscle. One thing I had in my favour was that I wasn't carrying much weight. I think had I been carrying another stone-and-a-half then I would have been struggling big time.

'But something like that makes you work harder and you do things you probably wouldn't normally do, like take on extra training. A lot of people don't know about the knee problem when I was 21 because the club didn't broadcast it at the time.

'I suffered the injury against Fortuna Dusseldorf in 1979. I was out for eight weeks and when I made my comeback, I managed about four or five games before it went again. Overall I've had about five or six operations on it.

'I used to play in charity matches but I don't now because I can hardly walk for about a week after it. It's just not worth it to me. Inside your head you still think you should be doing the things you did 30 years ago but the legs simply don't work the same, so you're kidding yourself on. So there definitely comes a time when you can't even take part in bounce games, but I'm okay with that.'

Russell will forever be remembered for his time with Rangers, although he admits when the time came to walk away from Rangers for the final time, it was incredibly hard – although one thing made it just that bit easier.

He explained, 'I knew it would be tough, because Rangers had been a massive part of my life. But if the truth be told, I wasn't completely happy there at the end. I wasn't quoted. I knew I wasn't wanted anymore because when I was making my way back from the injury, Motherwell came in for me and the club accepted their approach. I couldn't agree personal terms but that was the moment I realised Rangers didn't want me at Ibrox anymore, and if you're not wanted then it's time to leave.

'But I didn't leave with a sour taste in my mouth, or with any bad feeling, which was important. I went to Motherwell and I enjoyed it. I struggled a wee bit at the start but then with the help of the physio John Hart, I started getting my fitness levels back, and started acupuncture on my knee, which made a big difference.

'I went through a period where I was doing really well and the knee was holding up, but like everything else it eventually catches up with you, although when it did, the timing was lousy. It was just before the Scottish Cup Final of 1991, and it was all down to wear and tear, but I missed out on the cup final because of it, and that's a major regret because I had played in every round leading up to the final.

'Having already won the Scottish Cup and League Cup with Rangers, it was slightly different with Motherwell, because it was a big thing for the town. It was also a major achievement for the club and people lined the streets to watch the open-top bus go past, but I missed out on all that which was very disappointing. Still, I had a great career, with far more high points than low ones.'

11

Squeezing Into Europe

RANGERS ended their poorest Premier League season on a high note when they beat Motherwell on the first Saturday of May to clinch a UEFA Cup place. It had been a long time coming but Davie McPherson and Ally McCoist got the goals that mattered in what was anything but a stylish display against the Fir Park side.

Mind you, Graeme Souness would have been satisfied, if hardly ecstatic, about the first match under his management and it was clear from the reception he received before the game that the fans had great faith in him.

The Light Blues were certain to start the new season with new faces on show but against Motherwell it was the old guard that got the job done, and made up for a lacklustre campaign in the process.

Apart from a good Nicky Walker save from Reilly, and a Wright shot cleared off the line by Stuart Munro, Rangers had all the first-half pressure, although just when it seemed likely the teams would go in level at half-time, Souness's men broke the deadlock. In the 44th minute, Ian Durrant played a short corner to Hugh Burns and when the full-back's low cross arrived in the penalty area, McPherson was on hand to steer it home from ten yards.

Rangers needed a second goal – and got it in the 65th minute from the penalty spot. McCoist stepped up to score, and although Ally Maxwell got a hand to his shot, he couldn't prevent McCoist firing home his 38th goal of the season.

And as well as the victory, Rangers also proved just why they were still the top club in Scotland. While the Premier League title was being decided at Love Street and Dens Park, Rangers pulled the biggest crowd of the day for their match against the lowly Steelmen. The 21,500 attendance was attracted by two factors – Souness's first match in charge and the battle to get into Europe.

Souness said, 'We are quite simply delighted to qualify for Europe. Big gates at big ties generate more cash for me to bring quality players to the club. It was nice to start off with a victory and I intend there to be many more at Ibrox in the years to come.'

There was one match remaining, the Glasgow Cup Final, and the new player-manager was given some kind of idea of what the Old Firm meant in Glasgow when he took in the reserve equivalent at Ibrox along with 4,000 others. No other second-string fixture in the country would have attracted such a crowd.

Ibrox officials were also expecting a decent crowd for the Glasgow Cup tie, the final match of the season. If truth be told, the competition had lost much of its prestige in the 1980s, but there was still a beautiful piece of silverware up for grabs, and it was one that each of the 22 players was desperate to get his hands on. Both managers also showed they meant business by naming strong line-ups for the fixture.

As Souness settled into the famous manager's office, he said, 'I'm aware that this tournament is hardly the most important around but that doesn't concern me. My club will be playing and any team I am in charge of will play to win no matter the occasion.

'Apart from being my first Old Firm match, an experience which I'm told will be something special, it's also another chance for me to see the players in action and learn more about the staff I have here at the club – and that's important to me.

'I know our fans will be out in good numbers and I'll be expecting the players to end the season on a winning note. No one had better underestimate the value or importance of the 90 minutes.'

Previously, the fans themselves had lost interest in the Glasgow Cup and the 1985 final between Rangers and Queen's Park at Hampden – which ended 5-0 to the Gers – had attracted just 3,584 spectators. However, ten times that figure were expected, with Rangers bidding to win the trophy for a third consecutive year. The last Old Firm final had been three years previous – there was no competition in 1984 – when a Sandy Clark goal saw Rangers win 1-0.

Souness was well aware of the controversy the timing of the Glasgow Cup Final had attracted, but said, 'I would never want to upstage the Scottish Cup Final, that's for sure. I understand its importance and would not try to devalue the occasion for Hearts and Aberdeen. That's why I'm not making any decision about whether or not I'll play in the Friday night game.'

On the morning of the final, Souness dropped a bombshell on his playing staff – and took the first major steps towards building his own Rangers team. Four players were given free transfers with a further two put up for sale. Derek Johnstone, Davie MacKinnon, Billy Davies and Andy Bruce were the players to receive frees, while John MacDonald and Dougie Bell were made available for transfer.

The longest-serving player on the list was Derek Johnstone. The 32-year-old defender, who originally made his mark as a striker, signed for the club in 1970 and again in 1985 after a spell with Chelsea.

MacKinnon, 29, was signed from Partick Thistle for £30,000 in 1982 while Davies, 21, joined from school, as did 21-year-old goalkeeper Andy Bruce.

MacDonald had been at Ibrox eight seasons and signed in 1978. He had scored 106 first-team goals. Dougie Bell moved from Aberdeen at the start of the season for £125,000.

Souness said, 'There is the possibility of one more player being given a free and possibly two more on the transfer list. I am still making enquiries to bring new players to the club as soon as possible.'

But a few hours after his announcement, the players still at the club showed they were behind the new manager as they turned in a cracking display against Old Firm rivals Celtic.

The man with the golden boots, Ally McCoist, made sure Rangers ended 1985/86 in silver style with a magnificent hat-trick in front of a noisy 40,000-plus crowd. McCoist took his Old Firm goals tally to 11 in 13 matches – a record that stood comparison with any player from any era. In the process, he pushed his total for the season over the 40 mark and also his overall Rangers tally to 102 goals – in just three seasons.

It took McCoist just eight minutes to open the scoring in a superb match – and it was his 100th Gers goal. Ian Durrant made a great run through the middle of the park and played the ball out to Hugh Burns on the right. The full-back's low cross eluded the Celtic defence and McCoist stepped in to send Latchford the wrong way from close range.

It was a pulsating match but just when it looked like Rangers were in control Celtic equalised in the 38th minute. Mo Johnston cleverly dummied a through ball from Roy Aitken and the ball ran into the path of Brian McClair, who shot low past Nicky Walker from ten yards.

The second half was more even although Rangers held the edge on chances created. And in the 77th minute they regained their lead. Derek Ferguson played the ball to Cammy Fraser whose pass into the area caught the Celtic defence attempting to play offside. McCoist nipped in to send a shot trickling past Latchford and into the net. It seemed that would be enough to keep the cup at Ibrox but eight minutes from time Johnston stepped in when Walker could only parry an 18-yard shot from Murdo MacLeod and equalised for Celtic.

The 30 minutes of extra time were strength-sapping in the extreme, but in the 97th minute came a goal of genuine quality fit to win any competition. MacKinnon played the ball into the path of McCoist, who sent a superb screaming drive blazing past Latchford and into the net from 20 yards.

Rangers could not have asked for a better finale to their season and Souness for a more successful start to his time at Ibrox.

Mind you, despite scoring 41 goals, McCoist accumulated the miserable total of four points in the annual *Rangers News* Man of the Match competition. Ian Durrant was the clear winner with 26 points, with Hugh Burns second on 16.

Sadly, the Old Firm hat-trick wasn't enough to claim a World Cup place for McCoist, although there was better news for his team-mate Davie Cooper. The 30-year-old was named in the Scotland squad for the Mexico competition and said, 'I'm very pleased that after being involved in the qualifying stages I am now going to be on the plane for the finals. It is probably the last chance I will have of playing in a World Cup and I'm looking forward to it. The manager has had to leave out a lot of good players but I'm just glad my name is on the list.'

The other Rangers player in the squad was Graeme Souness.

With the final fixture of the season taken care of, Rangers were quick to announce plans for a new youth initiative – a first for the Ibrox club. The John Lawrence Group, who were now in complete control of the club, were organising the scheme which was set to follow the pattern of the government's Youth Training Scheme, but which promised to be far more expansive.

Between eight and 12 boys, aged from 16 to 18, were to be part of the initiative where football training at Ibrox under Souness and Walter Smith would be the priority. Lawrence Group personnel officer Ian Elgey, who was masterminding the operation, explained just what type of activities and training the boys would have open to them.

He said, 'At the moment, young boys at football clubs do not fill all of their time during a working week – this scheme will change that and should appeal to both the boys themselves and their parents.

'We have a wide knowledge and experience of training young boys on apprenticeships and the Rangers lads will be able to learn a trade in joinery, bricklaying, accountancy and micro-computers to name just four skills.

'We have to face the reality that not all of these young players are going to make the grade, but with this scheme, if they don't reach the top, they will have an alternative career to take them into their young adult lives. The final details are still being worked on but it will be the first of its kind and the boys will be better rewarded financially than they would be on a normal YTS scheme.'

The choice of which players would be taken on to the scheme was still being sorted out by Walter Smith, prior to him leaving for Mexico, but it was likely that Rangers Boys Club stars like Alex McEwan and John Spencer were candidates.

Meanwhile, Rangers lost yet another player when striker Eric Ferguson joined Dunfermline Athletic. The 21-year-old, who signed for the Light Blues from Gairdoch United in 1982, had been at Southampton on loan but had returned and was now set to play in the First Division with the newly-promoted Pars.

But as one forward left through the revolving door, McCoist put a big smile on the faces of the Rangers support when he put pen to paper and signed a new four-year deal. The 23-year-old striker, the Premier League's top scorer in 1985/86, signed a contract that would keep him at the club until at least the end of the 1989/90 campaign.

Another player offered a new contract by Souness was veteran goalkeeper Peter McCloy, and the Ayrshireman admitted he was excited about the new challenge. The 39-year-old penned a two-year deal with the club, which included a clause saying he would only play in an emergency.

McCloy's primary function would be to work with the Ibrox coaching team, with special responsibility for the keepers, and he was tasked with passing on all his experience to help the men battling for the number one jersey.

The big keeper was part of the side that had won the European Cup Winners' Cup at Barcelona in 1972, and he had also gained experience coaching junior clubs, but knew his new brief would be different from anything else he had ever done.

Speaking in 1986, he said, 'I will be working with all the players alongside the rest of the management and coaching staff, getting them to the kind of fitness we want, but my main role will be to work with the goalkeepers and I feel I have the ability and experience to do a good job.

'Goalkeeping isn't really something you can teach someone. It's something the player already has, and every keeper is an individual, built differently and with his own techniques. It will be my job to hone the abilities of the individual keeper and get him spot-on in terms of attitude so that he can do the best job possible in a Rangers jersey.

'As well as working with the keepers on the full-time staff at Ibrox, I hope to look at all the younger players, S-forms and the like. It's at a young age that goalkeepers can be helped most and as it's hard to pick out who is a good goalkeeper, it is important to catch them young.

'It really is a smashing opportunity for me and I'm relishing the challenge of working with the club next season because I am sure it is going to be a terrific one for Rangers.'

McCloy was delighted at being given the opportunity to stay on at Ibrox and felt it was the best way for him to prepare for a possible managerial career of his own in the future.

He said, 'I think this is the right way to break into the management/coaching game. I would have thought about any offer from outside Ibrox before, but when Graeme offered me the chance of a two-year contract and this type of responsibility, I had no hesitation. I have had a word with Nicky Walker and he knows I'll be trying hard to improve his game and to brush up on any weaknesses he may have.'

With the advent of the close season, the inevitable rumour mill switched to overdrive as supporters tried to second guess the manager's moves in the transfer market, but one of the questions on their lips was who would start the 1986/87 term as skipper?

It was one of the first questions requiring an answer on Souness's arrival back from the World Cup in Mexico. The season just finished had seen a number of different players lead the side, owing to the unfortunate injury jinx which had haunted Craig Paterson, who was appointed club captain by Jock Wallace back in September 1984.

Paterson had just signed a new one-year contract with the club and said, 'I wouldn't be at all surprised if Graeme Souness decided to appoint his own man. I enjoy the role and the responsibility it holds but it would be quite understandable for any new manager to name a new captain. I would be disappointed to lose the job and delighted if I kept it, but the main priority for me is to get back playing every week and convince the gaffer that I should be his first-choice centre-half.

'The operation I've had on my ankle was hopefully the last I will need. I could have played at the end of the season but there seemed little point as I was just one booking away from a long suspension. Now my ankle feels brand new and hopefully I will be able to make a fresh start next season. I know I have to prove myself and to be honest, I would have accepted a three-month contract offer – but I now have a year to show my worth and I fully intend to do that – whether I'm captain of the team or not.'

And it wasn't long before supporters had their first big signing to ponder – and the man who was happy to become a Light Blue was Watford striker Colin West. The centre-forward flew out to the continent for a holiday to celebrate the completion of the 'biggest move' of his career, but before leaving, the 23-year-old spelled out just why he could be an asset to Rangers in partnership with McCoist, a player he was once again delighted to be teaming up with.

The tall, powerful striker – who was clearly very proud and pleased to be Souness's first major signing – was in no doubt as to what the qualities were that prompted the Ibrox boss into snapping him up from Vicarage Road for £180,000.

He said, 'I haven't got the greatest goalscoring record in Britain but I know I can be an asset to any side. I'm good in the air and I can use both feet and I'm really looking forward to teaming up with Ally McCoist again. Unfortunately the pair of us were hardly ever in the team together at Sunderland but when we were we both felt the potential was there to develop a really good understanding. From the look of things, Ally doesn't need much help but I'll be looking to play my part in him scoring even more goals for Rangers next season.'

McCoist said, 'Colin is a very robust, strong player, quite different from my own style but I'm sure the Rangers fans will really appreciate him. I'm hopeful we can complement each other next season. We might have been guilty of lacking height in the attack but that won't be a problem now with the arrival of Colin. I'm sure the punters are in for a very pleasant surprise.'

Colin was born in Wallsend and brought up in the north-east of England and his Geordie accent was sure to sound as alien in the Ibrox dressing room as the dulcet tones of Irishman John McClelland. But while he had no Scottish connections at all, he insisted he simply couldn't wait to play for Souness at Ibrox.

He said, 'I obviously knew about the club as a youngster from TV and magazines but playing alongside Ally at Sunderland and then big John McClelland at Watford, I soon knew just how special Rangers were. When I saw the stadium last Friday, coming in for my medical, I was really impressed and the atmosphere about the place is really something else.

'I have signed for three years but quite honestly I would have signed for longer if I had been given the chance. However, I'll just have to prove myself in the time I've been given.'

While at Sunderland, West made 121 appearances and scored 31 goals. With Watford, he managed 23 goals in 55 games.

West had been Watford's top scorer the previous season with 16 goals, and had travelled south to meet Graeme Souness at a hotel near Gatwick Airport to clinch the deal before the Scotland squad jetted out to the World Cup.

After signing his first player, Souness said, 'I've been studying the make-up of other Scottish teams and Hearts have been successful with a powerful striker like Sandy Clark. West is also big and powerful and Ally McCoist will get a lot more room with him around.'

He added, 'I'll be in daily touch with Ibrox while we're in America, but once we get to Mexico the World Cup will be my only priority. Nobody need worry about my neglecting either of my jobs. I will give 100 per cent to both.

'There are lots of things to be done at Ibrox. Promises which have been made will be fulfilled. The names of players we're inquiring about indicate the standard we have in mind.'

Before joining him on the plane to Mexico, assistant boss Walter Smith had been busy mapping out the duo's plans for revolutionising Rangers. It had been a hectic start to their spell at Ibrox, what with the wins over Motherwell and Celtic, which had helped clinch a UEFA Cup place, and brought silverware to the club in the shape of the Glasgow Cup.

Next up there were the free transfers to decide on, the re-signings of McCoist and McCloy, for different reasons, and the first new signing of the close season – Colin West – to tie up.

When 38-year-old Smith had made his first public appearance as a Rangers employee at a press conference, already kitted out in club blazer and tie, you could see the pride in his eyes. He admitted the decision to leave Tannadice had been among the toughest of his life, and revealed how his first appearance at Ibrox had been as a four-year-old, when his grandfather had taken him to see the Rangers play.

There was no doubt Walter Smith was going to enjoy being the assistant manager of Glasgow Rangers – but first there was the 'little' matter of the World Cup.

In the middle of May, Rangers – and Souness – made the rest of Scottish football sit up and take notice when they were linked with a move to bring England's World Cup goalkeeper to Glasgow.

'Gers Want Shilton' was the headline causing the sensation. Rangers had made enquiries about the world's number one keeper, England international Peter Shilton. The 36-year-old Southampton star was with his national squad undergoing altitude training in America before the World Cup when the story broke.

He was just the latest in a long line of star names to be linked with the club since Souness had been appointed player-manager.

David Holmes said, 'It's true we have made an enquiry about Shilton, but he's only one of about half a dozen players in a similar situation. The whole business is getting out of hand, and it's at the stage we're frightened to ask about anyone because it's blown up into an instant bid.'

According to one newspaper report, Souness had promised his team would sign three star names before the start of the new season, and had already had two bids turned down for Dundee United's Richard Gough.

Meanwhile, in Colorado Springs, Shilton said, 'I don't know anything about this and, anyway, my thoughts are concentrated entirely on the World Cup.'

Shilton, the most capped England keeper of all time, had also skippered his country, and manager Bobby Robson said, 'He's the best in the world. Put together his stature, presence, professionalism and his appetite for work and that's why he's tops.'

The keeper, first capped for England in 1970, had signed a contract the previous season that would keep him at Southampton until he was 40. If Rangers were to be successful, they would have to pay Southampton a transfer fee and would also have to better Shilton's wages at The Dell, estimated at £3,000 a week.

But as the Light Blues continued to be linked with all and sundry, deposed boss Jock Wallace was all set to clinch one of the top jobs in Spanish football. Seville had narrowed down their search for a new boss to just two: Wallace or Don Howe. The Spanish club confirmed either one or the other would be their new manager. Howe had just been sacked by Arsenal, while Wallace was reported to have all but sealed a lucrative contract with the Spanish side.

The top sports reporter of the day was the *Daily Record*'s Alex Cameron, and while out in Mexico for the World Cup, he managed to grab a sit-down chat with Souness. The results made interesting reading.

In his column the next day, Cameron revealed that Rangers were set to sign a top World Cup star. He added, 'The hint to me was that the mystery man could be Roberto Falcao, the elegant Brazilian midfielder who plays for Roma. Before going off to sunbathe at the poolside of the hotel, Souness said his plans for Rangers were to sign a top defender, which was his priority – but the chances of Richard Gough filling this role is becoming "less and less" and he is checking elsewhere.

'Graeme also said he wanted to fix up a big-name foreigner who would be involved in the World Cup in Mexico – and I reckon that man is Falcao!'

He added, 'When the name is announced after the World Cup, you will realise why it couldn't be mentioned now. He is a foreigner, but not an Irishman or Englishman, currently playing in Italy. It isn't Michel Platini or Maradona. However, he is a big name.'

It all made for very interesting reading, and was indicative of just how Souness had upped the ante at Rangers.

But with May drawing to a close, the final piece of news concerned Wallace, who did indeed see off the challenge of Howe to land the Seville job, an appointment which reportedly came with an annual salary of £55,000 – with that figure rising by £10,000 a year if he proved a success.

12

John 'Bomber' Brown

JOHN Brown was a manager's dream: the wholehearted footballer who could play a bit and was equally at home in midfield or defence. He filled the former role at both Hamilton Accies and Dundee with aplomb, and it was as a result of his goalscoring prowess – and his reluctance to pull out of tackles against tough guy Graeme Souness – that he earned a dream move to Rangers.

But that was only half the battle. Keeping his place in a star-studded line-up, crammed full of international players, was the big test – and, boy, how he passed with flying colours.

Mind you, Bomber gave Rangers supporters a few headaches before finally ending up in Govan.

He said, 'I did have a particularly good scoring record against Rangers, which I think was down to the fact I was a Rangers supporter and was always keen to impress. I go back to 1985 when Jock Wallace was the manager and I definitely wanted to catch his eye, and it just came about that I got a few chances to score goals – and I took them.'

Brown admits it pained him to see the troubled times Rangers were enduring in 1986, with both the Light Blues and Dundee vying for fifth place in the table, and a spot in the following term's UEFA Cup.

He said, 'At that time, the Rangers were going through a tough period on the park. I was playing for Dundee and I wanted to do well there to get the opportunity to play at a higher level, and from big Jock in '85, through to Graeme Souness and Walter Smith, I thought to myself, "Keep playing the way you're playing in these games and it might just happen."

'Thankfully I managed to do that for Dundee on a consistent basis, although I always seemed to do well against Rangers – and it was also the team I seemed to score against more often as well.

'And then there were the battles I had when coming up against Graeme Souness in the middle of the park. Don't get me wrong, I relished them, but took a few kidney punches from him, rough tackles as well, but I could dish it out too and I think he liked that. Graeme had a big reputation but I wasn't for shrinking when we went toe-to-toe. I think that played a big part in getting me to Ibrox.

'He told me after I joined Rangers in 1988 that he would have signed me 18 months earlier, but Walter had put him off because of the cartilage and knee problems I'd suffered in my early years. If you work it out, that would have been just after he had signed up at Rangers – but I got there eventually.'

Bomber added, 'Even though I was a Dundee player, the appointment of Graeme Souness really excited me. I looked up to him like you couldn't imagine. Three European Cups, English league titles, FA Cups, the list went on and on. Liverpool were a top, top team at that time with guys like Ian Rush, Kenny Dalglish and Alan Hansen, and Souness was one of the best. So to see him coming to Scotland was like a breath of fresh air.

'And he was bringing in all these top English international players. They had the ban because of the Heysel disaster and the English teams weren't allowed to play in Europe as a result, but all these top guys were coming to Scotland and it made it even better playing against Rangers because of the talent they had. Doing well against them was so much more of a challenge, but it was also fantastic to see Rangers take such a bold step.'

Around 18 months after Souness arrived in Scotland, Brown was a Rangers player. All those hours of toil for Accies and Dundee had paid off, and the goalscoring midfielder was on his way to Ibrox.

Bomber described it as 'the best day of my football life without a doubt'. He added, 'I was brought up a Rangers supporter and my family all followed the team, so to get the opportunity to run out at Ibrox as a Rangers player, be involved in so many games and in a period where we went on to do nine in a row was just fantastic.

'I managed to play my part in eight out of the nine title wins and that is an achievement I will always be very proud of. It was a fantastic time to be a Rangers player. I enjoyed coming into my work every day and being on the training field with Graeme Souness and Walter Smith was a great experience.

'The two of them worked very well together. While Walter was looking after the tactics and sorting out the formations, Souness was getting inside your head and indulging in a bit of man-management.

'I signed for Rangers as a midfield player and the gaffer would say things like, "You're making say ten runs and they're expecting it from you all the time, but if you just do, say, four or five, then they won't always be expecting it, and there will be a better chance of catching them off-guard," so it was wee things like that he was very good at picking up on.

'I joined Rangers two weeks short of my 26th birthday and I feel as though that was when I started to get coached. It was such an important part of my football education.'

Unlike these days, when there is a large percentage of players from around the globe plying their trade on the football fields of Scotland, the Rangers of that period was more or less made up of home-grown players – until Souness arrived and laid down a cross-border marker with our friends from England.

And these weren't just any old players making a comfortable living turning out for second-tier sides, they were the real deal. But Brown insisted there was no conflict with the English guys, far from it – apart from on a Friday, that is, when the battle lines of Bannockburn were redrawn and a 're-enactment' took place on the football field.

He explained, 'We got on very well with the English lads, there were no problems at all, apart from a Friday, when we had the weekly five-a-sides, the Scottish versus the English. It was very competitive – even if we were playing in an Old Firm game the next day – and it would be a case of shinguards on and full steam ahead. It was great and we all got stuck in, without really thinking that someone could get injured before the big game the following day, because that would tell the manager who was ready for action.

'To be honest, it's like any sport. The coaches look at how you're training, what levels you're at, and they are building up to the weekend. That was always the case and the gaffer knew exactly who would come flying out the traps on the Saturday afternoon.

'Souness always told us we were fitter than any other team in Scotland, better players, and even though he said it might take us 70 or 80 minutes to break down the opposition, he always backed us to do so and let us know that our talent would eventually win us the game. To be fair to him he was spot on the majority of times. And then Walter carried that on when Souness left for Liverpool.

'But I can say with hand on heart that Souness's training was the hardest I ever encountered at any time in my career. For the full six-to-eight-week pre-season schedule, he battered us. He ran us into the ground and then it was competitive five-, seven- and 11-a-side football. We didn't ever do crossing or finishing drills, where we thought we might have added goals to certain areas. He wanted us playing competitive football all the time, and that's why he was so successful as a player and a manager with Rangers.'

Brown played such a huge part in many of Rangers' title and cup wins, but never was his determination to take part in a single game more evident than in 1991, when he took painkillers just to make it out on to the pitch for the title decider against Aberdeen at Ibrox. Two goals from Mark Hateley might have won the championship that afternoon, and they will forever be etched into the psyche of every Rangers follower, but the effort made by Bomber – just to take part – was also a major factor.

That's why it broke his heart to see his beloved Rangers slip into what seemed like terminal decline in 2012, and that's why he famously stood on the steps outside the front door at Ibrox Stadium not long after the meltdown and blasted the new board for the way they had mis-managed his club.

That is the level of passion this man has for Rangers Football Club. He was willing to put himself – and his reputation – on the line for the future of the greatest club in the world, and thankfully it paid off – with the help of a large section of the Rangers support.

But when looking back to the mid-1980s, he firmly believes it was such an important period for the club – and for the game in this country.

He said, 'I think the summer of 1986 was definitely one of the most important times in the history of Scottish football. One major change was the restructuring of players' wages. Players at Rangers and Celtic weren't on a great deal of money. All the money was in England at the time so the arrival of Souness, and the changes he implemented, reversed that trend, and Rangers shelled out the money to get the top players in – and that was to the benefit of everyone in Scottish football even to this day, although a lot of people tend to forget that. Graeme Souness was actually responsible for changing every footballer's wage packet in the country.'

Brown added, 'When I was at Dundee I sensed a real dislike for Rangers within Scottish football. Players that I played with who were Rangers supporters didn't seem to perform at the same level when it came to playing Celtic as the Celtic fans in our team – like Jim Duffy and Tosh McKinlay – did when we played Rangers.

'It's just a fact of life that Rangers are the top club in Scotland and that there is a lot of jealousy around, even within those who run the game in this country, and I include organisations like the SFA in that. I'll be honest and say that when Graeme Souness told me that, it really opened my eyes.

'It takes a very special breed of player to be able to handle the pressure of playing for such a top club. One thing Souness also said when he signed me was, "Never turn your back on the ball, because if you're not having a good game and you do that, I'll sell you." He told me to take the ball 100 times and give it away 100 times but always to have the courage to at least show for it.

'One thing you can say about Souness is that he was right up for a fight 100 per cent of the time, whether that was in training sessions or during games. He demanded 100 per cent commitment from Monday to Friday. He wanted that in every session and that's what I loved about him. You knew you had to bring your A game every day of the week, so that was special, but these were important times.

'It makes me very proud that I played for such a great club like Rangers, but even more so when I look back at the success we achieved. It was phenomenal, and the nine-in-a-row years were obviously incredible in their own right. I played for the Rangers and I loved every moment.'

13

Ticket To Success

THE 1986 World Cup in Mexico is probably best remembered for Diego Maradona's 'Hand of God' goal during Argentina's tussle with England in the quarter-finals of the competition in the iconic Azteca Stadium.

There's no doubt Maradona punched the ball into the net, just as Peter Shilton came out to claim the cross. But if that goal should have been ruled out, Maradona's second was simply sublime, when he picked up the ball in his own half and proceeded to dribble past half the England team, including central defender Terry Butcher.

Meanwhile, Scotland failed to make it out of Group E after being drawn alongside the mighty West Germans, Uruguay and Denmark.

It was the Danes who surprised everyone by topping the section with maximum points, with Scotland's only point coming via a goalless draw with the South Americans. During that game, Uruguay's Jose Batista was sent off inside the first minute for a shocking foul on Gordon Strachan, an unwanted World Cup record that still stands to this day.

So while Graeme Souness, Davie Cooper and Walter Smith were representing the Scots on the other side of the world, staff at Ibrox were getting ready for what was shaping up to be one of the biggest seasons in Rangers' 114-year history.

First of all, the demand for season tickets was, to quote a club official, 'astonishing'. Since the tickets for the 1986/87 season had gone on sale the ticket office had hardly been able to keep up with the quite unprecedented demand.

In 1985/86 a total of 3,000 tickets had been sold for the entire season; night and day from recent times since the club slipped into administration, when sales of between 30,000 and 40,000 have regularly been clocked up. But this was the mid-1980s, times were different, and perhaps season tickets weren't as trendy – or within reach – as they now are.

To give you an idea of how times have changed, the club made 3,000 season tickets available for the 1986/87 season, but the mouth-watering prospect of seeing Souness in a Rangers jersey had persuaded an 'incredible' 1,600 supporters to snap up season books more than two months before the start of the new campaign.

Secretary Campbell Ogilvie admitted the interest created by the arrival of Souness was something new for the Ibrox staff and said, 'To have sold over 50 per cent of our available season tickets already is quite incredible – I would advise those wanting to buy tickets to get them now to avoid disappointment.'

The prices for the in-demand briefs were: Enclosure £50 and Copland Road £65. The club had decided to discontinue the trouble-hit Rover ticket.

Next up for staff was a concert by one of the world's biggest pop groups – Simple Minds. The stadium played host to almost 60,000 fans as the combo returned to their native city for what was generally regarded as one of the biggest and best concerts to be held in Scotland in 1986.

The Copland, Broomloan and Govan stands were filled by fans, as was the pitch – which had been covered in matting to protect it – on the Friday and Saturday night as fans watched their idols on a specially constructed stage, which filled a large part of the Main Stand. Perhaps Simple Minds dedicated their hit 'Promised you a Miracle' to the supporters buoyed by the arrival of Souness!

There's an old line, invariably produced by Rangers diehards, 'There's only one team in Scotland worth watching other than the Light Blues – and that's Rangers reserves!'

Well, the big news during the close season was that there would soon be TWO teams worth watching in Scotland other than Rangers. Although no final decision had been taken, and nothing was due to be announced until Souness had finished his stint with Scotland and was back behind his Ibrox desk, it was on the cards the Light Blues would be fielding a THIRD team in the forthcoming season.

The costs of running a third team were expected to be quite significant when taken over a full season, but had to be measured against some very obvious advantages. It was thought a top club like Rangers should be operating with a squad far in excess of 22 signed players, although that was something which could lead to player unrest on matchdays, because even on days when the league side and the reserves were both in action there would still be quite a number of players sitting kicking their heels in frustration in the stand, and it was believed a third team would sort out the problem.

Meanwhile, in the middle of June, the most exciting young talent in Scottish football signed a two-year professional contract with Rangers. John Spencer, due to celebrate his 16th birthday on 11 September, was asked to report for pre-season training on 7 July with the rest of the Rangers squad. The brilliant youngster revealed how his immediate aim was to make his reserve-team debut, and said, 'I'm absolutely overjoyed. A full-time contract was exactly what I wanted and I just can't wait to join the rest of the players at pre-season training.

'I could have gone on for another season with the boys club at under-16 level but feel I'm ready to step up a grade and I'm really excited about next season. I've heard the transition to reserve football is hard and I'm not thinking any other way. But my aim is to be a regular in the second team before the end of the season.'

Spencer's superb campaign had ended in fantastic style when he helped win two major trophies for two different teams. On the Saturday afternoon, he scored in the Paisley & District Schoolboys team's win over Central Region in the Scottish Cup Final for under-15 schoolboys. Incidentally, Spencer's Rangers team-mate Mark Grossman was also in the Paisley side and he too scored.

And just 48 hours later, Spencer scored a fantastic goal in the final of the Foxbar Youth Tournament which was enough to win the competition for Rangers Boys Club.

His marvellous skills had been highlighted throughout the season by his outstanding form for the Scottish under-15 schoolboys and there's no doubt that if Rangers hadn't stepped in to secure his signature, many other top clubs would have been knocking at his door.

But for this determined young man, there was only one club he wanted to play for, and he said, 'It has always been my only dream and aim to play for Rangers one day and now I'm a step closer to achieving that.'

From the young to the 'slightly older' and there was also a special award in store for arguably Rangers' greatest ever penalty taker. South African winger Johnny Hubbard was recognised by the SFA for his services to the grassroots game in Scotland and became just the fifth man to receive the national award – which was presented at the SFA's Inverclyde coaching courses – for services to the game.

Alex Ferguson, Jim McLean and former Airdrie and St Mirren boss Wilson Humphries were three of the four other figures to have received the prize when Hubbard stepped up to receive his award.

He was certainly joining illustrious company. The Gers great, who also played for Bury and Ayr United, was presented with a silver plaque and a watch at Inverclyde in the presence of the Scottish squad backroom team.

Since hanging up his boots, Hubbard had been involved in coaching youngsters and also ran a prestigious five-a-side tournament in Ayr – which, at one time, was the biggest in Britain – for young players, and which, in 1986, was won by the Rangers Supporters Association Boys Club.

Ross Mathie, a member of the SFA coaching staff, said, 'People used to be excited about watching Johnny in action and his contribution to the game over a number of years deserves to be recognised. He made an art of penalty taking and was the first player to "pass" the ball into the net from the spot.'

Hubbard was signed by Rangers in 1949 and went on to play 258 games for the first team in which he scored 116 goals before his transfer to Bury in 1959.

In a close season full of surprises, there was another in store for fans when chief executive David Holmes announced that Ibrox would belong to them in the forthcoming campaign. He made it clear everything possible would be done to make supporting Rangers a pleasure, and added, 'If we can create a successful football team then it will improve the quality of the supporters' experience, and it also applies off the field of play.'

Rangers were also in talks with Strathclyde Regional Council to obtain ground on which a bus park could be constructed within walking distance of Ibrox, in anticipation of even more supporters' coaches heading to Govan. In fact, the Light Blues were eventually intending to control the travel arrangements of their many supporters' clubs, who came from far and wide, providing them with a pre-arranged package of entertainment before each game.

One player on the move was flame-haired defender Davie MacKinnon, who had been given a free transfer. The 29-year-old, who could also play in the middle of the park, signed for First Division Airdrie. MacKinnon made 169 first-team appearances for Rangers after being signed by John Greig in 1982 but with the emergence of Hugh Burns, he was replaced in the right-back role although he never let the club down in either the centre of defence or in midfield.

Meanwhile, the Rangers Pools, arguably the club's biggest source of income, announced a staggering new record profit in its figures for the 1985/86 season. Despite the fact the country's economy continued to struggle, the Pools made a healthy profit of £1,184,330 – all of which was transferred to the Rangers Development Fund. That meant the Pools had donated close on £12 million to the development fund in the 22 years of its existence.

The primary aim of the fund was to pay for the new Ibrox Stadium and Pools managing director Hugh Adam, also a

Rangers director at the time, said, 'There is still around £2m to be paid on the stadium but these super new figures from the Pools mean Rangers can run the club on a sound, modern footing. No one at Rangers has to worry about looking over their shoulder to see how Ibrox will be paid for. I should think the stadium will be completely paid off by the end of the 1988/89 season.'

If one man knew whether or not Graeme Souness might make a success of his management career, it was his former Liverpool team-mate Bruce Grobbelaar. And he reckoned his old Merseyside buddy was made for management – wherever he went.

The Clown Prince of Keepers knew Souness as well as anyone from their days together at Anfield and the extrovert Zimbabwean likened him to Kenny Dalglish in many ways and was confident he could emulate the success already achieved by the then Liverpool player-manager.

Grobbelaar said, 'He can be arrogant and cutting but he has the total respect of everyone who plays alongside or under him. He is an outstanding captain and his appointment at Liverpool was a stroke of genius by Bob Paisley.

'Graeme has an incredible will to win which dominates him. He wants to be the best so badly that the feeling infects those around him. He also has a fierce loyalty to the club he is playing for as he showed when he went off to Sampdoria and inspired them to their highest-ever league position and their first-ever Italian Cup win.

'This attitude means there are no favourites with Graeme and if his best mates have to be dropped for the good of the team then that is exactly what will happen.'

With June about to fizzle out, and their enquiries for Peter Shilton heading in the same direction, Rangers were still searching for a top-class goalkeeper. So, if you can't get your hands on the England number one, who you gonna call? That's right, his deputy – and that's exactly what Souness did.

Chris Woods was a wanted man on Edmiston Drive and the dream was one step closer to reality when the Ibrox side agreed a goalkeeping record £600,000 fee with Norwich City – newly promoted to the English First Division.

Woods, understudy to Shilton at the World Cup, arrived home from Mexico with the rest of Bobby Robson's squad following the defeat to Argentina, and the 26-year-old went straight to Carrow Road for talks with City manager Ken Brown and chairman Robert Chase about his future.

Just before heading inside for the meeting, all he would say was, 'I should be a bit clearer about my future after I've spoken to Ken and Robert.'

There was a possible fly in the ointment, though, and it came in the shape of London giants Chelsea, who were scheduled to play Norwich at Stamford Bridge on the opening day of the English season.

But a couple of days after arriving home from Mexico, Woods, born in Boston, Lincolnshire, said, 'I would certainly consider a move to Rangers. They are one of the biggest clubs in Britain, a side who have been sleeping giants for too long.

'I don't believe it would harm my England chances if I moved to Scotland. After all, it's nearer for Bobby Robson to get to Glasgow to watch a player than it is to Italy. There is also the platform of European football which must be an attraction for any player. Mind you, I suppose I have to consider how Rangers fans would take to an Englishman!'

It wouldn't be too long until we found out.

14

Colin West

COLIN West turned out for Sunderland and Watford before joining the Graeme Souness revolution at Ibrox. Afterwards, he would go on to play for the likes of Sheffield Wednesday and West Bromwich Albion – but it's his time in a Glasgow Rangers shirt that he remembers with great fondness.

In a career spanning just over two decades, more than 700 matches and almost 200 first-team goals, it's incredible that the fair-haired centre-forward should think so much of his spell in light blue, considering he played so few games. Mind you, that was due more to a horrendous injury suffered in a Skol Cup tie at East Fife than any great lack of talent or graft.

When Souness took over the Ibrox reins in the spring of 1986, West was exactly what a new-look Rangers side would require with his robust style sure to rough up the many tough Scottish defences doing the rounds at the time. It was also hoped that West's no-nonsense attitude to the game would help create some extra leg room for strike partner Ally McCoist to further exercise his effective eye for goal.

But it was the will of Souness that his new signing, who was 23 at the time,·would bring more than just a physical presence to Rangers – as he had just ended the season with 16 goals, and as Watford's leading scorer in the top flight of English football. It had been a successful campaign for the Hornets, who finished mid-table in the First Division.

Towards the end of the season, Watford made the relatively short journey of around 25 miles to posh Kensington to play Chelsea, and it was in the players' lounge after the game that West first learned of Souness's interest in him.

He said, 'Graeme had apparently come to watch me at Watford against Manchester United. At the time I didn't know he was there but we beat them 5-1 and I scored in the game.

'With just a few games of the season left, we played Chelsea away, and he was definitely at that game. You wouldn't believe it but we also won that game 5-1 and I scored again. He asked Chelsea player David Speedie to have a chat with me in the players' bar after the game. David and Graeme were Scotland team-mates at the time, so it was probably quite normal, but it was the first I knew of Rangers' interest in me.

'To be fair, both Manchester United and Chelsea weren't as good then as they are now, and we were playing really well at that time, but when I eventually spoke to Graeme he said I would do well in Scotland and likened me to Sandy Clark. He said I was a similar type of player to Sandy.'

West added, 'The first thing I did when I realised Rangers were interested was speak to my dad, my wife etc. I was just delighted that a club of that size and stature were keen on signing me, and the fact they had a figurehead like Graeme Souness was another plus that excited me straight away.

'I was really enjoying playing at Watford, because we were doing well in the English First Division and the manager, Graham Taylor, was an absolute dream to work for. He was such an organised guy and just wanted everyone to enjoy their football. To be honest, I didn't see myself moving from Vicarage Road for a long time.'

But West admits to having mixed feelings when the call from Ibrox came through officially. The initial contact from Speedie had given him the heads-up but there was still some doubt in his mind. And there was also the issue of moving from the English top flight to Scotland. West said, 'There was an issue and there wasn't, for the simple reason that if Graeme Souness is interested in you and wants to buy you, and for the career he had, then it had to be a win-win situation. It was still tough to leave Watford but I also knew it would give me experience of playing in European football further down the line, which it did, so in the end it was a bit of a no-brainer really.'

He added, 'There is no doubt Rangers were a bigger club than both Sunderland and Watford. The tradition and standing of Rangers was massive, and the potential they had to get a crowd up at Ibrox was another major factor. It was a phenomenal club, and that was something I would soon learn.

'People often ask if 1986 was a turning point for the club. I'm not sure if I sensed that something quite as big was happening but I spoke to a lot of people before making the move, and *they* all seemed to think Rangers were on the cusp of something massive. Of course, we now know that 1986 was such a big transitional year for the club.

'They were pushing on relentlessly and getting better and better with each passing season, but I kind of sensed that when Graeme went there. I knew he wasn't the type of person who would want to rest on his laurels. He wanted to prove himself as a player-manager and you could see that the guy just had so much desire and passion to further his career.

'He had just returned from the World Cup in Mexico and still had such a high profile – and he had only one thing in his mind and that was to enhance that.

'On a personal level, I thoroughly enjoyed working under Graeme. He was excellent for me. What probably helped was that when I was at Watford, the club was renowned for its players being unbelievably fit. The bulk of the work Graham Taylor had us doing was fitness-based, because even though we had some very good individuals, we probably weren't the most talented team in the league. But as a group we knew our positions, how to close the ball down and where it would go when our midfielders got a hold of it. We played really high-tempo football.

'I was really fit, so when I went to play in Scotland, the first pre-season that we did, I remember there was myself, Terry Butcher and Graeme Souness virtually at the front of every training session, running-wise and just about everything else.

'I remember it vividly because I'd just had my first child and my wife hadn't moved up to Scotland at the time, as we were in the process of selling our house down south. I recall the boss letting me off some weekends because my fitness was right up there and he didn't mind me missing the odd session. He knew that missing a few wouldn't impact on my fitness so he gave me extra time to go and see my missus and the little one at the start, and that was something I really appreciated.

'Graeme's training was good because he had brought a lot of exercises and stuff back from his time in Italy and it was things I hadn't seen before. Some of the exercises we did at Rangers had these little add-ons that Graeme introduced, and while they weren't any more complicated, they did help, because they got you a better stretch, and were far better for your muscles. It's also good for the players to keep things fresh.

'He was working more on proper warm-ups and cool-downs. That sort of thing was just starting to get big in this country then, although I know it might sound a bit crazy to players these days. Mind you, I would love to have been playing nowadays, given all the benefits there are to players health-wise.'

West had mixed fortunes during his spell in Scotland, and after a promising start, the dark clouds were circling when Rangers headed for the east coast and a Skol Cup tie against East Fife at Methil. It signalled the beginning of the end for the popular striker.

He explained, 'I started the season at Rangers and got a couple of goals, although I'm not sure of the whole games to goals ratio, but then I got the injury quite early on in the League Cup tie at East Fife, and it damaged my knee really bad. I was in plaster for a while but I tried to get over that. The problem was it had been a nasty ligament injury, with the ligament coming clean off the bone.

'I worked hard to get back to full fitness because I was desperate to get back into the team, but because Rangers were such a big club, and we were trying to push forward all the time, the manager had brought some new players in so I had a fight on my hands to get my place back.

'I just wanted to play football but there was no doubt I had fallen behind in the pecking order. Not long after, I heard of Feyenoord's interest in me, and was told Sheffield Wednesday were also keen to take me to Hillsborough. They had been after me before I signed for Rangers, so it started me thinking. I was interested in a move to Wednesday because I felt it probably represented my best chance of getting a regular game again.

'I absolutely loved it in Scotland but the only reason I left was to get playing more often. I was only getting on every now and again at Rangers, and was a substitute more often than not. You know, it doesn't matter how well you've done beforehand, it still takes you a while to get back up to speed after a serious injury, and with other players doing so well, and the team winning, the manager was hardly going to change a successful team. I can understand it more now as a coach, because the last thing you want to do is change things when you're winning.

'Getting the injury was just bad luck, and who knows how things might have turned out otherwise, but I made a lot of good friends at Rangers. I already knew Ally McCoist really well as I had been at Roker Park with him previously, while all the English lads got on really well because it was all quite unique at first. Out of the home-grown lads I probably got on best with Ally Dawson, as well as Ian Durrant and Derek Ferguson.

'Graham Roberts was also a good pal of mine when he came up, and we have remained good friends ever since. When we played in England, Graham and I had some real tussles, in fact, I reckon they were more "battles" than tussles. It's amazing that he ended up a team-mate in Scotland, and again when we both played for West Brom for a few years. In fact, he stayed in my house for six months when we were at West Brom. He ended up at The Hawthorns a wee while after I'd signed for them – which was quite scary!

'In my earlier days, when I was at Sunderland and Watford, and he was at Spurs, we used to smash each other to bits, but there was always a terrific mutual respect there and we would sit after games chatting for ages. We still get on really well to this day.'

West revealed how he still looks out for the Rangers result every weekend and reckons that even though his time at Ibrox was quite brief, he will always have an affinity with the club.

He said, 'I've said it countless times in the past that Rangers are a fantastic club, and they treated me really well. I will never say anything other than good things about Glasgow Rangers. And as for the supporters, well they are just unbelievable.

'In fact, I really felt for those supporters when the club hit some tough times in 2012. Sadly, I think it's something that happens quite a lot in football these days, where people have dreams, but I have to say that when I was at Ibrox, there was no way I could feel anything other than positivity.

'The money being spent on bringing in better quality players was making the club stronger, which was proved as we won the title in my first season. In my second season, we lost it, but after that Rangers went on that terrific run of nine successive titles, which proves exactly how strong the club was at that time.

'We had lots of good players on the field and we were getting big crowds in and if you're keeping everything bubbling over, then you must be doing something right.

'I'm not too sure of the ins and outs further down the line but perhaps the trouble started when there were the payments going into the different bank accounts. Mind you, I do have a laugh and a joke with mates when they say that I must have been getting lots of money paid into my bank accounts as well. I can assure you it wasn't happening like that for me! We might have played in a lot of big European games etc, but it wasn't the case as far as I was concerned.'

But West is adamant it wasn't all about the money when he put pen to paper for the club.

He said, 'When I was part of the first wave of signings from England under Graeme Souness, it was about far more than just the money.

'There was definitely the lure of playing for such a massive club, and the different culture that we would all experience, and not forgetting the pull of the manager, who was a massive name in the game at that time.

'Financially, I was getting more money than I had been on at Watford, but it wasn't a great deal more, and nothing at all like some of the top players are being paid these days. It was better money, but it was more the pull of the football club that did it for me.'

Like most things in life, West has mixed feelings about the way his time at Rangers drew to a close, although he insists that was nothing to do with the club. So, would he change anything – or just leave be?

He said, 'Yes and no. I loved playing for Rangers and they gave me some great experiences in football. My time in Scotland also gave me a good footballing background in terms of how physical it was, which is something I never shied away from in my career. I always enjoyed getting into tussles.

'Injury-wise, though, I would have to say yes, I would definitely have changed that. I got a really bad one up at Rangers, and sadly it knocked five or six months off my career. Going to Rangers was certainly worth it, but I just wish I had never picked up that injury, because you never know where your career could have gone up in Glasgow.

'I also enjoyed living in Scotland and seeing a lot of the country. I'm from the north-east of England, which isn't too far from Scotland. I always got on well with people away from the football club, and enjoyed going out in Glasgow and the west of Scotland, and I have stayed friends with a lot of them.

'There was just such a really good atmosphere at Ibrox, and we had players like Jimmy Nicholl, who I knew very well. Players like that made it special. In fact, if I was asked to sum up Rangers, I would say it was like a real, proper family club.'

15

Another Top Name
Checks In

RANGERS fans waking up on the morning of 1 July were
given the great news that top goalkeeper Chris Woods had
signed for their club. It was a real boost for supporters
ahead of the pre-season tour of West Germany.

From his home in the tiny village of Framlingham Earl, near
Norwich, Woods said, 'I'm glad it has all been sorted out and the
uncertainty over my future has ended. I'm delighted to be joining
Rangers, one of the big names in European football.' The talented
keeper became the first full England international to sign for a Scottish club since Joe Baker was capped while he was with Hibs in 1960.

Rangers smashed the world record transfer fee for a
goalkeeper when they paid £600,000 to Norwich for Woods,
the previous record being the £560,000 paid by West Ham to
QPR for Phil Parkes in 1979. The English international, who
was understudy to Peter Shilton, was one of the early targets for
Souness and his experience and class were sure to be a big asset
for Rangers.

The 26-year-old former Nottingham Forest and Queens Park
Rangers number one was delighted with the move to Ibrox and
viewed Rangers as one of the 'top six clubs in Britain'.

At the time, he added, 'This is a terrific move for me in every
sense. I am as fiercely ambitious as Rangers and their manager

Graeme Souness matches my own ambitions. I am looking forward to being part of a successful team which wins a lot of honours. You only have to look around Ibrox to see the potential and ingredients are all there – it's now up to the players to make Rangers the best.'

Souness was clearly delighted with the capture of Woods, but he also had a message for Nicky Walker, Rangers' first-choice keeper the previous season. He said, 'Chris is one of the country's top goalkeepers and has learnt from the best teacher possible in Peter Shilton. But we need two top-quality keepers and I hope Nicky will stay as I'm sure he could learn and improve his game working with Chris.'

However, Souness did not rule out the possibility of an offer for Walker being accepted amid rumours of interest from Seville manager Jock Wallace.

But while one player was checking in to Ibrox, another looked to be on the way out. Joining the open-to-offers list was young striker Robert Fleck. The 20-year-old was placed alongside John MacDonald and Dougie Bell on the transfer list by Souness.

Meanwhile, Walker and striker Bobby Williamson turned up at Ibrox for their first day at training knowing their football futures were almost certain to lie elsewhere. Souness, set to supervise his first official training session, had already spent almost £800,000 strengthening their particular areas. He had forked out £600,000 for Woods and £180,000 for Colin West.

Walker, who played 42 first-team games the season before, was aware of the potential interest from Wallace and Seville, who had just sold their first-choice keeper, while Williamson, a £100,000 capture from Clydebank three years previous, was Rangers' second-highest scorer in season 1985/86, although he was more than 20 goals behind Ally McCoist. St Mirren had already failed in a bid to take Williamson to Love Street. While the clubs had agreed a deal, the striker – with a year left on his contract – knocked back the Paisley offer.

And there was widespread speculation in England that Souness – quoted as having £2m to spend – was ready to move for either Terry Butcher or Liverpool defender Mark Lawrenson.

But the revolving door was in full swing again when Avi Cohen grabbed a seat on the team bus that left for the tour of Germany, where he was hoping to win himself a full-time contract. Souness confirmed the possibility that Cohen could be his next signing, and said, 'Avi is a quality player. At Liverpool he was unfortunate that both Alan Hansen and Mark Lawrenson occupied the central defensive positions. But he would have been an automatic choice for any other top club in England. Avi's 29 and has been capped over 40 times for Israel.

'But it's not only a question of me wanting to sign him as him wanting to come – for he has a successful business in Tel Aviv plus a wife and two kids to consider. The next few weeks will determine what happens for both the player and the club.'

Asked if signing Cohen would complete the Ibrox facelift, Souness said, 'No. I'm in the fortunate position that if a quality player becomes available and I think he's value for money, I can sign him.'

But the one player who Souness couldn't get to Ibrox despite having a seemingly elastic cheque book was his World Cup colleague Richard Gough of Dundee United.

Souness admitted that a third attempt to sign Gough had been turned down, 'It was an improved offer, although things can always change in football.'

The busy player-manager added, 'There is also some pruning to be done,' and confirmed that Dougie Bell, who cost £175,000, and Iain Ferguson [£200,000] were available for transfer. As the players headed for their morning training session, Ferguson was preparing to fly to Germany for trials.

On the general transfer front, Souness said, 'Rangers have subsidised this area of Scottish football far too long by buying players and then selling them on for a quarter of the price. That will no longer be the case.'

The full playing squad bound for Germany was: Chris Woods, Nicky Walker, Stuart Munro, Ally Dawson, Hugh Burns, Avi Cohen, Davie McPherson, Ian Durrant, Craig Paterson, Derek Ferguson, Bobby Russell, Ted McMinn, Cammy Fraser, Ally McCoist, Colin West, Bobby Williamson and Davie Cooper.

The Light Blues were initially scheduled to play three matches on the continent, the first two against amateur sides, with a game against Cologne in Koblenz rounding off the trip, but a fourth game was added just before they left.

When the squad left Glasgow, Souness admitted he was delighted with how pre-season training was going, and said, 'The boys have done really well and I'm more than happy with the fitness levels of the squad. It shows me they are as determined as I am to bring success to the club. We have had two excellent weeks working out at Jordanhill and now we are starting the serious work on the field in West Germany.

'The opening matches will be against smaller opposition and will give me the chance to try out a few things before we face Cologne, which should be a good test. All 18 of the players I have taken know they are fighting for a place in the first team for the start of the season – but that doesn't mean the players left behind are out of contention.

'I have been given money to spend and if quality players who I admire become available, you can be sure I will try and bring them to Rangers. We haven't finished yet on the transfer front.'

The Graeme Souness era began in earnest in West Germany and the results and line-ups were as follows:

Sunday 20 July – SG Union Solingen 0 Rangers 2 (McCoist 5, 50). Team: Woods, Dawson, Munro, Souness, Paterson, McPherson, D Ferguson, Durrant, McCoist, West, Cooper.

Tuesday 22 July – TSV Battenberg 1 Rangers 1 (West 50). Team: Woods, Dawson, Munro, Fraser, Paterson, McPherson, Russell, West, Williamson, Durrant, McMinn.

Wednesday 23 July – SV Heidingsfeld 0 Rangers 1 (McPherson 65). Team: Walker, Burns, Munro, Dawson, McPherson, Fraser, Russell, Durrant, McCoist, Williamson, McMinn.

Friday 25 July – Cologne 2 Rangers 0. Team: Woods, Dawson, Munro, Souness, McPherson, D Ferguson, Russell, West, McCoist, Durrant, Cooper.

The lengths some supporters go to in order to watch Rangers in action has been well documented in the past, but one fan who watched the team in all four matches in West Germany provided much amusement. Known only as 'Davy', the punter left the Royal Air Force a few months before the tour and was making some sort of living in a town on the Dutch border. But what made Davy unique was that he cycled to all Rangers' tour matches, although goodness only knows what the German people made of Davy pedalling across the country in his Rangers top and scarf!

Around 25 fans followed Rangers on all four tour matches although that number was more than doubled in the final game against Cologne. For player-boss Graeme Souness, the trip provided not just an opportunity to get to know his players better but to meet with some of Rangers' most loyal supporters.

But there was disappointment for Cohen as he was unable to take part in any of the matches because his work permit had failed to come through in time. The Israeli international skipper, though, fitted in well in training sessions and enjoyed the time away with the rest of the Rangers players. And to make him feel right at home, he encountered a group of his countrymen at one of the tour games!

Of pre-season training, Colin West – who played in three of the four tour matches – said, 'It was certainly a bit different from pre-season with either Sunderland or Watford and the exercises the boss picked up in Italy certainly test you. But apart from all the running in the early stages I have enjoyed the training and feel as fit as I ever have.'

Meanwhile, Derek Johnstone, given a free by Gers, was announced as the new player-coach at Partick Thistle, who had been rejuvenated by the financial intervention of Chelsea supremo Ken Bates. And there was also joy for Alex Totten, who took over the managerial reins at Dumbarton.

One player who had three months to prove himself, and convince Souness he was worth an extended full-time contract with the Gers, was Colin Miller. The 21-year-old defender had returned from the World Cup finals, where he was in the Canadian squad but unfortunately failed to make an appearance.

He said, 'I played at right-back in the warm-up games against Mexico and Wales and everyone told me I played really well

– but the boss Tony Walters obviously took a different view. It was still a great experience to be at the finals and I learnt a thing or two.

'Now though it's back to trying to establish myself at Ibrox and as I only have a three-month contract at the moment, things are still as insecure as ever. However I have been enjoying the training and hope to show the manager and his coaching staff I'm worth keeping.'

West left for West Germany already celebrating one great event. During the close season, on 25 June, his wife gave birth to a healthy boy, the couple's first child, Jack, and he was looking forward to a top West German side visiting Ibrox.

West said, 'I can't wait for the friendly match against Bayern Munich at Ibrox and playing in front of a big crowd. The stadium is impressive enough when it is empty but I can't wait to see what it is like when it's full.'

Rangers were set to take a trip into the cold unknown of Finland after the UEFA Cup first round draw in Geneva paired the Light Blues with Ilves Tampere – a club that had appeared in European competition only once before.

It was the first time Rangers had been drawn against opposition from Finland, and although they were strong favourites to progress, Souness said, 'You can't take any team lightly in Europe nowadays and we have all seen the great strides made by Scandinavian countries in recent years.

'Obviously we will hope to give ourselves a comfortable cushion for the second leg, but it will be no use going at Tampere like a bull at a gate.'

Woods had made a good impression on everyone during the pre-season tour of West Germany – although it seemed one man in particular was thoroughly impressed. Mind you, the real test was due to begin for the giant English goalkeeper when Rangers began the semi-serious stuff against Tottenham Hotspur and then Bayern Munich.

Walker said, 'Without any disrespect to any other keepers in Scotland, Chris will be far and away the best in the Premier League this season. He has got everything a keeper needs.'

But while many believed a top-class English custodian would find it easy to look the part in Scotland, Woods didn't share that opinion, and said, 'In England there are always the jokes going round about Scottish goalkeepers and if one of them makes a mistake it is shown on television down south. But although the standard of keeping in England is probably as good as anywhere in the world, if not the best, the goalies there still make mistakes but perhaps without the same spotlight being put on them.

'I have to be very honest and say I know very little of Scottish goalkeepers apart from Jim Leighton – and I thought he was superb for Scotland in Mexico. I don't know just how safe his place in the Scotland team is or if there are many people challenging him, but I have heard good things about guys like Henry Smith and Alan Rough.

'One of the things I'm looking forward to in the Premier League is finding out all about the standard of Scottish goalkeepers and I don't think for a minute it is going to be easy for me to come into the game here and look good.'

Woods, however, did have tremendous confidence and belief in his own ability – something he had clearly picked up from the great Peter Shilton.

He said, 'One thing I learned from Peter was the importance of never being complacent and I always set myself some kind of target before the start of every new season. This time, I am looking to keep clean sheets in 20 of our 44 league matches and hopefully more than that if I can.

'It's going to be a very big season for me with the challenge of adapting to the game in Scotland with Rangers and hopefully being involved with England too in the European qualifying games.'

Meanwhile, Donald Mackay, who was told he was only a temporary appointment back in April, soon found himself as the permanent reserve-team coach – and the fact he was a good friend of Walter Smith had nothing to do with it.

Confirming that, Mackay said, 'I came to the club to help out an old friend, there was certainly no way that my subsequent appointment was pre-planned. When I arrived I did my best in looking after the players, something I have obviously done well enough to impress Graeme and Walter.'

The move definitely excited Mackay, but he immediately knocked back the theory that winning trophies with the reserves was his most important function.

He said, 'I see a great future for the club, there's a buzz about the place. Exciting times lie ahead but Rome wasn't built in a day. The prospects are bright though and I can only help to build on that.

'Obviously trophies are vital but if I can help supply Graeme with a few players for the top squad then I'll feel happy. My own personal view is that clubs are only as strong as the youth players they can produce.'

The next part of David Holmes's masterplan was to increase revenue off the field, and the chief executive had visions of Rangers becoming a major force in European football. To achieve this, they needed to double their money.

Holmes set a £1m revenue target from commercial enterprises in the coming season – more than twice the amount pulled in from off-field activities throughout the whole of season 1985/86. But while some of the ideas he came up with might be treated as the norm these days, they were slightly alien to Scottish football 30 years ago.

Included in the Rangers plan were: an exclusive matchday lunch club at up to £95 a head; making the Blue Room available for outside companies to host conferences – at a price, naturally; a new sponsorship deal in which companies or individuals could sponsor the match kit for a player of their choice at £500 a season; the appointment for the first time of a marketing executive – and that job went to 23-year-old business studies graduate Lynne Holmes, daughter of David.

But the main weapon in the hunt for that extra £500,000 was to be a quality restaurant and executive lounge to cater for 240 guests on matchdays. Corporate guests would view the games from a specially-reserved section of the stand. Membership was to be made available to companies with the resources to book a table for six or ten guests for a season, taking in league, Skol Cup,

Scottish Cup and European ties at the cost of between £60 and £85 per head, per game.

One of the first instances of the club using hospitality to bring in revenue came at the end of the 1950s. It was the well-patronised Members' Club, which cost individual supporters the princely sum of £15 per season. For that, around 80 members received one of the best seats in the Main Stand and use of an exclusive lounge.

The Members' Club attracted some well-known faces, such as iconic comedian Lex McLean and impresario Ross Bowie, manager of the Alexander Brothers and owner of a number of popular city-centre clubs. The members enjoyed pre- and post-match hospitality, but nothing like we associate with today's extravagant suites and lounges. For the original members, it was tea, coffee, soft drinks and pies. Changed days indeed.

David Holmes said, 'We pay overheads 52 weeks of the year so we must use our facilities to the fullest. We have to take the club forward, and while we hope to do well in the league and Europe, that takes cash. An ambitious club like Rangers cannot exist solely on income from a home game every second Saturday.'

The fans were also set to benefit from two new electronic scoreboards which they could use to send their own messages between adverts before the game and again at half-time.

Meanwhile, though, a storm was brewing, and it didn't look like it would go away any time soon. The BBC was desperate to secure live television coverage of the first Rangers v Celtic clash of the new season, but its request was an action replay of the plan which had led to a bitter row the previous season and brought Scottish football to the brink of disaster.

It was the Beeb's intention to have the all-ticket match at Ibrox – scheduled for Saturday 30 August – switched to the Friday or Sunday to avoid a clash with the other weekly fixtures. But it was only set to fully reveal its plans AFTER the new £600,000 two-year TV contract had been signed with the Scottish Football League at the end of July. The deal would allow the BBC one live league match and STV a live fourth-round Scottish Cup tie along with the normal weekly offering of recorded highlights.

League secretary Jim Farry said, 'We are now just waiting for people to return from holiday and then we will dot the i's and cross the t's. We hope everything will be signed this coming week.'

Once the contract was signed the TV companies would then have the right to televise live any game of their choice. Not surprisingly, the BBC was looking for the Old Firm game, in which it hoped Graeme Souness would play a part.

But the fears that it would all end up the same unmitigated disaster as 12 months previous were very real. On that occasion, a deal had been struck but left unsigned, and STV announced it was to cover the Rangers v Celtic match at Ibrox on Sunday 17 November. Both clubs refused to play on any date other than the original one and the subsequent row almost finished the Scottish League for good.

This time, though, after some hard negotiations by all concerned parties, a deal was agreed and the clubs agreed to 'play the game' on Sunday 31 August, with live TV cameras in attendance. The Old Firm were united in their opposition to live TV but opted to compromise for the Ibrox fixture.

Rangers chairman John Paton said, 'Our feelings are still the same, but television is not going to go away, so we have compromised.'

His Celtic counterpart Tom Devlin added, 'I told Rangers we would prefer a Sunday game rather than playing on a Friday night, but I'm totally against live TV coverage of games in Scotland. Scottish football is a spectator sport and should not be mucked about to satisfy TV.' Prophetic words indeed.

Ironically it was the suggestion of an Old Firm clash on a Sunday at Ibrox in November 1985 that had led to the bitter row that blacked out TV soccer for most of the previous season. The Scottish League had agreed to a deal with the television companies, but the deal remained unsigned.

Scottish Television insisted on covering the Rangers v Celtic game but Rangers said 'no' and were backed by Celtic and the rest of the Premier League clubs, except one – Clydebank. The rebel clubs threatened to form a breakaway league, and recorded highlights of matches returned only towards the end of the season.

But a new £600,000, two-year TV contract was signed by the Scottish League prior to the beginning of the 1986/87 campaign – peace had finally broken out.

And in the Ibrox dressing room, Souness was again trying to talk Nicky Walker into staying on at Rangers – so he could pick up some tips from £600,000 keeper Chris Woods.

Souness said, 'I want Nicky to remain a Rangers player. He can learn a lot from Woods, just like *he* has done from Peter Shilton.' But Walker's Rangers future remained uncertain.

Meanwhile, work had been continuing apace in the new executive dining suite at Ibrox, and there was only one person to open the new facilities – goal-hungry striker Ally McCoist! Chef-for-the-day Ally approved the grub, but admitted his real hunger was for the start of the new season – and all because of his new boss.

'The man oozes class in everything he does,' said the 23-year-old, who hit 32 goals in 45 games the previous season. 'I know the boss took a bit of stick about his fitness during the World Cup match with West Germany, but he's already shown that he's fitter than most of us. He's in tremendous condition. It's obvious he's looked after himself throughout his entire career.

'The whole place is buzzing at the moment. We all know we've got to make a good start to the season to start filling Ibrox. But this early, the signs are good.'

Already Souness had made big changes around Ibrox. The players arrived for training to find tea and juice waiting for them. They were banned from walking around the floor barefoot, and had all been issued with flip-flops to protect their feet from possible infection.

Souness said, 'It is common sense for players to protect their main asset – their feet. Why risk infection or injury from nails, glass or whatever may be lying about the floor?'

Lunch was now served inside the ground when there were double training sessions, and the training gear was changed for every session and neatly laid out on the dressing-room benches.

McCoist smiled, 'We're really getting the star treatment. In fact, we are being spoiled a wee bit.'

He added, 'I'm looking forward to playing alongside Colin West. He's a big powerful lad and I wouldn't like to play against him.

'The boss has been telling us to take more time on the ball, but be sharp in everything we do. He's been showing us how in our five-a-side training where he seems to win himself a lot of time on the ball.'

Things were definitely heating up in anticipation of the new season, and Souness's new-look Rangers took to the pitch in Scotland for the first time when they travelled through to Brockville for a pre-season challenge match. But while the weather was quite horrible, with the heavens descending upon the Central Scotland town, the attraction of Rangers was plain for all to see. Astonishingly, almost 8,000 fans braved the lashing rain and cold to see the Light Blues in action against the Premier League new boys.

The Ibrox side was a mixture of probable and possible first-team starters who took the 90 minutes very seriously indeed and recorded a comfortable if not dazzling 3-1 victory. The first half was enjoyable enough, with Rangers producing some intelligent attacking football with players like Bobby Russell, Cammy Fraser and Bobby Williamson doing themselves no harm at all under the watchful eye of Souness.

Rangers opened the scoring in spectacular fashion after eight minutes. Dougie Bell and Russell began a sweeping move which ended with Fraser playing a neat one-two with Williamson before smashing home from 18 yards. The second goal arrived in the 33rd minute via a cross from Ted McMinn which was headed home by Williamson.

Williamson scored again on 53, but Peter Hetherston pulled one back from the penalty spot after Avi Cohen was adjudged to have fouled McGuire, when the offence looked no worse than obstruction. The Rangers team was: McCloy, Dawson, Munro, McPherson, Cohen, Fraser, Russell, Bell, Fleck, Williamson, McMinn. Subs: Derek Ferguson, Nisbet, Burns and Paterson (not used).

16

Chris Woods

IT'S said that Chris Woods kept more clean sheets for Glasgow Rangers than all of the city's hospitals put together – and perhaps it isn't too far away from the truth.

When Rangers first showed an interest in taking the talented keeper from Norwich City to Ibrox, they weren't alone. A host of clubs – including Chelsea – were interested, but the England international chose a move to Scotland, and it wouldn't be too long before he was putting up the shutters with alarming regularity.

From November 1986 to January 1987 Woods set a British record of 1,196 consecutive minutes of competitive football without conceding a goal. That's just four minutes shy of 20 hours. His record finally came to an end in that infamous Scottish Cup tie at home to Hamilton Accies, and *that* goal by Adrian Sprott. It was a phenomenal run, and it's a record – claims Woods – that still stands to this day.

But let's start at the beginning, and the moment Rangers beat off some stiff competition to land the imposing 26-year-old Lincolnshire-born keeper.

Woods recalled, 'It wasn't really that difficult a decision to choose Rangers over the others. I'd spoken to Graeme Souness after the England v Scotland game at Wembley [the Rous Cup match which ended 2-1 for England, with both Terry Butcher and Souness on the scoresheet] and he put everything to me. Once I had a good think about it I didn't really have any second thoughts. My mind was made up pretty quickly.

'He told me all about Rangers and the fact that the club was a sleeping giant. I knew a bit about the Old Firm but with all due respect, I didn't realise just how big a club Rangers really were, so to actually get there and be a part of it all really was something special.'

At the time, Norwich had just won the English Second Division title and were due to take their place at the top table. The Canaries had one of the best defensive records in the league and Woods had played a vital role in ensuring his team finished the season seven points ahead of second-placed Charlton Athletic.

Norwich, the Addicks and Wimbledon were all promoted to the First Division but Woods soon had other things on his mind as he was named in the England squad for the impending World Cup finals in Mexico. But when he finally agreed to join Rangers, did he find it difficult leaving a club that had just won promotion to the top flight of English football? After all, he had just spent six years with the Norfolk side.

He said, 'I thoroughly enjoyed my years at Norwich. I had some really good times there but they were a smaller club and going to Rangers was a real eye-opener for me. Mind you, I didn't realise the intensity of being at a club the size of Rangers until I got up to Glasgow. The supporters would come up to you in the street and talk to you non-stop about their club. It was so far-removed from what I had been used to. It was probably only then I realised what Rangers meant to so many people, and the great expectation there was on the players to win things.'

But Woods quickly slipped into the groove and when Ally McCoist, Davie Cooper and Ian Durrant scored against Hearts in late November 1986, it not only helped erase the painful memories of the previous midweek's exit from the UEFA Cup at the hands of Borussia Munchengladbach, but also kick-started a run of games that would see him break the British clean-sheet record. It was a run that encompassed games against every other team in the Premier League, including Hamilton Accies twice, which would prove ironic as it was the team at the foot of the Premier Division table that would bring the glorious run to a grinding halt when they visited fortress Ibrox in a Scottish Cup tie.

But all good things must come to an end, and for Woods, keeping the ball out of his net for just short of 1,200 minutes is right up there with everything else he achieved in a glittering 22-year career.

He said, 'I was very proud of that record because it was a fantastic run. As a goalkeeper it's all about keeping the ball out of the net, a bit like outfield players scoring goals, so to keep so many clean sheets – and in a row – was a big thing for me. But it was something that just materialised, to be honest. About seven games into the record, people were talking about how close we were getting, and that was when it first started to register. I will always remember Walter Smith coming up and saying to me, "Don't worry Chris, I'll let you know when you're getting close." And then he didn't speak to me for about another four or five weeks, so I realised then that maybe I hadn't been as close as I had first thought.

'But it's definitely an achievement I will always treasure, even though I think they tried to say it had been overtaken by Edwin van der Sar. The thing is, his run didn't come in consecutive games. In fact, I even spoke to commentator Martin Tyler – who is known for being one of the best in the business at keeping all the stats – just to ask if the record still stands, and apparently it does.'

Something else which sticks out in Woods's mind from his time north of the border is the afternoon when all hell broke loose – and he ended up in jail.

It was 17 October 1987 and definitely one of the most emotive Old Firm games of the period to take place at Ibrox. We hadn't even reached the 20th minute when fussy referee Jim Duncan red-carded both Woods and Celtic striker Frank McAvennie for nothing more than a 'handbags' confrontation.

From that moment on, the atmosphere remained at fever pitch – with both sides (on and off the pitch) – going at it hammer and tongs for the remainder of the game. Rangers came back from two goals down that afternoon to rescue a point thanks to strikes by McCoist and Richard Gough – with Graham Roberts going in goal, conducting the Ibrox choir, and Terry Butcher also seeing red.

Looking back, it has to be one of the craziest games in Scottish football history, but was perhaps symptomatic of a time when jealousy ruled, and Rangers appeared to be the favoured item of choice for those in the game desiring target practice.

Woods might have played for England, been on the bench for a winning European Cup team, amassed a list of honours to rival the best, coached at three Premier League clubs – including Manchester United – and enjoyed a career spanning more than 600 first-team appearances, but he will never forget *that* Old Firm game.

He said, 'Yes, it was a little bit different, to say the least. To have to go to the police station the next day and actually have your rights read to you was all a bit surreal. Obviously they were trying to make a point about things like that happening on the pitch but I just thought it was much ado about nothing.

'The referee and the police etc made so much of it in court, you know, the fact that it was going to make the crowd more violent. To be honest, I was actually staggered when the referee sent Frank [McAvennie] off to start with, because I knew straight away that I was going as well, and the upshot was that we missed the League Cup Final because of the suspension, which was a great shame. Looking back, it was all just a bit bizarre.'

Woods was Souness's second capture and admits he wasn't really aware of the scale of the changes taking place at Ibrox when he signed his contract.

He said, 'The only thing we focussed on was getting out on the pitch and playing football. We didn't really get to know an awful lot about what was going on off the pitch, and the way it was being run commercially.

'What I do remember clearly is that we didn't start the season particularly well and there were a few moans and groans coming from the stands. I think we were about nine points behind Celtic at Christmas, in the days when it was only two points for a win, but we ended up winning the league by quite a few points so it was a phenomenal run we managed to go on and sustain, and I think it ended up making everybody happy. At least all the Rangers supporters, that is!'

But throughout the four years he spent at Ibrox, Woods insists he quickly grew to love the club – and it's a passion that has never left him.

He said, 'Rangers genuinely is the type of club that becomes a big part of your life. And when I talk about Norwich being a really friendly club, even with the vastness of Rangers it was exactly the same. You got to know all the people that worked at the stadium, and any time I've gone back up there, those same people have still been working for the club, and if they weren't it was only because they had sadly passed away. I can say with hand on heart that Rangers are definitely a club that will always remain part of me.'

It was a shock to most when it was announced in the summer of 1991 that Woods was leaving Rangers and joining Sheffield Wednesday. The Light Blues had signed Andy Goram from Hibs and it appeared the club simply wasn't big enough for two world-class keepers.

Woods recalled, 'It wasn't a great time for me. I'd had viral labyrinthitis and hadn't played for a couple of months, and I remember coming back into the fold for the first time since getting the bug, and going out for a run round the Ibrox track. I was trying to run down the touchline and I couldn't even focus on the line. It was jumping all over the place and even when I came back to play, if I wanted to come out for a cross, and was running to go and collect the ball, it would have been juddering about and I couldn't focus on it properly, so I had to overcome that as well. After a period of time it cleared itself, but it was a frightening time to be honest.

'But despite moving on to pastures new, I will always look back on my time at Ibrox with great fondness. Not just at Rangers, but the time I spent in Scotland will always be dear to me. At the beginning it was a whole new experience but it was one I absolutely embraced and loved. It is something I am so glad I got the chance to do. I made some great friends and played for a great football club and won trophies as well so it is a part of my life that I will always treasure, that's for sure.'

17

Season Starts With A Bang

AUGUST 1986 signalled the dawning of a bright new era at Ibrox. Rangers were ready for the start of their 97th league campaign and the buzz surrounding the club was at fever pitch.

And that expectation cranked up a notch when Graeme Souness and David Holmes introduced their latest signing to the waiting press pack – England World Cup star Terry Butcher. With the swish of a pen, the Light Blues had just signalled their intention to be contenders. The minor league placings weren't an option!

In the process of signing for Souness, Butcher became Scottish football's most expensive player and the new captain of Rangers.

There was relief as well as delight for the genial England giant as a transfer saga which began with the relegation of his beloved Ipswich Town in May was finally brought to an end. And that was good news for Rangers fans as their club beat off the challenge of the likes of Manchester United and Spurs to capture the player many people believed to be the best centre-half in the world. In fact, the move left some supporters north and south of the border rubbing their eyes in disbelief. Had Rangers really just signed Terry Butcher – one of the best central defenders on the planet?

That view was confirmed when FIFA selected Butcher to play in a special UNICEF match in Pasadena for the Rest of the World against the Americas – and as well as being a superb defender, the player showed he could score goals too with the opener that day.

But all Butcher could think about was the start of a new challenge in Scottish football, beginning in just a few days at Easter Road, where Rangers would kick off their Premier League campaign against Hibs.

At the time he said, 'This is a terrific move for me. Rangers put their cards on the table when other clubs didn't and very attractive cards they were too. Everything is right about the set-up here and the warmth shown to me in Scotland since I arrived from the people – both Rangers AND Celtic fans – has been absolutely incredible.

'I've got no doubts this will work out well for me and I hope for Rangers. Anyone who doubts the wisdom of playing in Scotland and leaving English football – well, I would just point out a European tie a few years ago for Ipswich when we were stuffed by Aberdeen.

'I know the quality of football is good up here and I want to play against Aberdeen again and in an Old Firm match, which I have heard so much about. Playing in Europe again will be a great bonus too but that was only a minor consideration in me coming here. The club is ambitious, as ambitious as I am and that will do for me.

'Rangers have been straight and honest with me, have given my wife and family a super welcome and now I can say that the next four years look very good indeed.'

When Souness took the microphone at the press conference to unveil Butcher, he had a pop at Scottish clubs for being unwilling to part with their prized assets. He said, 'It's sad for Scottish football that this money has gone outside the country when it could have stayed in the game up here. However, we met with obstacles to doing that and it wasn't our fault that we had to go and outbid the biggest teams in England. But that's what we have done and I'm delighted that Terry Butcher will captain Rangers FC this season.'

Perhaps Souness was referring in particular to Dundee United, who refused to sell Richard Gough to Rangers but seemed to have little problem with punting him to Tottenham Hotspur.

David Holmes returned from holiday to tie up the deal, and said, 'Graeme Souness was the start and we have progressed from there and now Terry Butcher completes the picture. We are now ready to give the Rangers supporters what they have been waiting for and what they deserve.'

And what the fans got when they travelled down to London – in their thousands – for the Paul Miller testimonial match against Tottenham was a fantastic fighting display by their favourites, which ended in a well-deserved 1-1 draw. It might have been a friendly but Rangers and Spurs put on a show that suggested both could win their respective leagues.

Rangers were without Chris Woods (injured) and Butcher, but the influence of Souness in a light blue shirt was tremendous and already it was rubbing off on those around him – with certain individuals promising great things.

Star of the show was Cammy Fraser who had a terrific game playing in a wider role on the right of midfield. He seemed to have slotted into the Souness style perfectly and it was highly appropriate that he should score the goal which gave Rangers a 14th-minute lead.

A crisp move saw the ball worked on the left from Durrant to Souness on to McCoist and then to Cooper, who mesmerised England full-back Danny Thomas with a fantastic piece of skill. Coop – who had a great game – then swung over a perfect cross to the back post where Fraser stole in to head powerfully past Ray Clemence from eight yards.

Nicky Walker posted a warning to Woods as he made outstanding saves from Clive Allen, Ossie Ardiles, Gary Mabbutt and Paul Miller, but the former scored for Spurs and a draw was probably a fair result.

The Rangers team was: Walker, Dawson, Munro, Souness, McPherson, Cohen, Fraser, West, McCoist, Durrant, Cooper. Subs: Burns for Cohen (29); Fleck for West (46); Derek

Ferguson for Durrant (46); McMinn for Fleck (67) and Russell (not used).

After the game, player-manager Souness spelled out just how he wanted his team to face the challenge of the 1986/87 league title race – but didn't give too much away. He said, 'It's going to be a long haul and I can't make any comments on it until the final day of the season, when the title will have been won and lost. I have never played in Scotland and, as well as management being a new challenge to me, playing in the Premier League will be a brand new experience too. For now, I am only looking as far ahead as Easter Road on Saturday. There are two points to be won and I want both – that will be my attitude in every game.'

The forthcoming match with the Edinburgh side was a complete sell-out with almost 25,000 fans set to pack out Easter Road. Both sets of supporters were looking for something special from sides crammed with new signings.

Souness said, 'I'm very happy with how the players have responded to training and the warm-up matches. I just want to keep things ticking over when the real thing kicks off. I am doing this job my way and I will stand or fall by it – I'm looking forward to Saturday very much.'

But perhaps the Light Blues' gaffer had been looking forward to the match just a wee bit too much, as it was his foul on Hibs striker George McCluskey which set off some of the most astonishing scenes witnessed at a top flight game in Scotland for many a year.

Hibs won the game 2-1 but very few people were talking about the result afterwards. It was perhaps predictable that Souness would attract maximum attention wherever he went, but such a level of exposure had obviously rattled the normally unflappable midfield general.

And for the third time inside a year, Rangers were party to an incident which did little for the good of the game in Scotland. The repercussions for the Light Blues after the dismissal of Souness on his Premier League debut were sure to be severe – one red card and nine yellows hardly made for nice reading. It was accepted within the corridors of Ibrox that Rangers would receive a huge fine from the SFA following the unsavoury and regrettable scenes at Easter Road.

But while the Ibrox boss held up his hands and apologised for his rash actions afterwards, he acknowledged it was perhaps time for some sort of change in the way football matches were controlled in Scotland. The number of bookings and sending-offs had increased dramatically in recent years as the desire to win amongst professional players had become ever stronger. Certainly, the possibility of full-time referees, or some other major restructuring in officialdom, had to be considered.

Whatever was to come out of the Easter Road debacle, Rangers had certainly learnt that the Premier League had just become harder than ever before. The big money the club had spent on big-name players had made them even more of a target, and the team the rest wanted to beat – and that was going to mean a lot of bruises and tough action over the coming months.

Souness had been sent off by Cleland referee Mike Delaney in the first half for kicking out at former Celtic player McCluskey, after earlier being shown a yellow card, and in a chaotic match, eight other players – four from each side – were booked amid the on-field fury.

The previous season, the SFA had taken action against Rangers and Hearts after a match in which Ally McCoist, Sandy Clark and Walter Kidd had been sent off. One month later, Rangers and Aberdeen were fined by the SFA after another Ibrox fixture which saw Craig Paterson and Hugh Burns red-carded.

But the latest debacle was the kind of start to the season no one at Ibrox expected or wanted and Souness was quick to apologise for his part in the scenes. He said, 'I would like to say sorry for the incident which led to my sending off – it's something nobody could be proud of. But a lot went on before and a lot went on after. I regret it and the only person I am annoyed at is myself.

'I knew I was going to be a marked man in the Premier League and that was how it turned out. But I was disappointed in myself as I was suckered into it. I would just like to compliment the fans on their behaviour. Sometimes trouble on the field can spread to the terracing and I would hate to think I was responsible for that.

'I certainly learnt something from the game and if things continue as they are, we are going to end up with reserve teams playing each other in league games. It is something that has to be looked at both by the players and managers as well as the people who look after referees.'

Meanwhile, Souness moved to strengthen his team by signing experienced full-back Jimmy Nicholl. It was the second time the Northern Irishman had joined Rangers and it was a move he said had taken him from hell to heaven.

The 29-year-old defender had been contemplating a risky move back to the North American Indoor Soccer League to complete his career when Rangers came calling. He was with West Bromwich Albion as the club prepared to get back to the English First Division but Nicholl wasn't really part of Hawthorns boss Ron Saunders's plans. Then on the Wednesday night, he received a call from Souness and the Ibrox boss asked him if he would like a move back to Glasgow.

Nicholl said, 'I couldn't get to Ibrox quickly enough and I'm absolutely delighted to be a Rangers player again. The six months I spent here in my first spell were among the best in my career and now I've got a new two-year contract.

'I'm tremendously lucky to be getting this opportunity because when I came back from Canada just over a year ago I was offered terms by Jock Wallace but turned them down in favour of West Brom.

'I've regretted that for a while and everything went wrong for me at The Hawthorns. I was signed by Johnny Giles but he left and the new manager, Ron Saunders, clearly had no intention of playing me in the first team.

'I was unlucky with injuries too, and it wasn't much fun being at West Brom last season as it was pretty clear we were going down to the Second Division from an early stage. I had just about decided to go back to North America and try my luck in the indoor game which seems to have taken off in a big way there.

'Reading the papers over the past few weeks, I have been looking at lads like Chris Woods, Colin West and Terry Butcher going up to Ibrox and thinking how lucky they were. Now I have joined them and I'm just delighted to be part of the set-up here again. The place is clearly buzzing and I think the optimism is justified.

'In my first spell at the club, we won the League Cup which was a big thrill for me – but now I'd like to think I can be part of a team winning honours regularly.'

He added, 'Although I was only here for six months the first time, the Rangers fans really took to me. In fact, one of the highlights of my career was the farewell party a group of supporters put on for me before I left.

'I have played for Manchester United, probably the only club with a support anything like Rangers, but the Ibrox punters are something special.'

And with Ibrox set to house bigger crowds, Rangers were ready to experiment with new segregation measures for visiting fans. The aim of the new crowd control plans was to give more room to Rangers fans. Instead of the rear of the Broomloan Road stand being reserved for visiting fans, away supporters were to be housed in the front of that stand.

Campbell Ogilvie said, 'The way ticket sales have been going, we are anticipating much bigger crowds at Ibrox this season. So for games against opposition who don't carry a large travelling support, we want to provide as much space as possible for our own fans. The front of the Broomloan holds only 3,200 while the rear section accommodates 4,300.'

The Rangers players were facing a far busier schedule than normal, and were hopeful it would continue for the remainder of the season. But just so his men were doing no more than necessary, Graeme Souness slapped a ban on activities outside the club such as golf, squash and tennis.

He wanted the players to protect their feet, but promised, 'If we get a break later in the season perhaps we will have a day at the golf course and I will gladly join the players.'

Meanwhile, the Gers fans were quick to honour Terry Butcher, who had been a Rangers player for just over a week, when they named a supporters' club after him. Ibrox fans in

Blantyre adopted the new skipper to create the Terry Butcher (Blantyre) RSC.

And although Butcher had made his debut in exalted company, with Rangers losing 2-0 to Bayern Munich, it was said that Souness had learnt more from 90 superb minutes of football than the club had done in all of their recent European campaigns put together.

The Light Blues showed they were ready to live with the best the continent had to offer – but Bayern Munich showed Souness's men just what the finished Ibrox article must look like. The Rangers boss simply couldn't have chosen better opposition for his team, and the West German champions and cup winners confirmed their position as one of the favourites for the forthcoming European Cup.

They had players like Eder, Augenthaler, Brehme, Matthaus, Hoeness and Rummenigge, but Rangers had Butcher, although he emerged from his Rangers debut with a lump in his throat and a black eye for his troubles – but declared himself ready for the biggest challenge of his career.

The new captain enjoyed a superb first match in a light blue shirt and came close to scoring against Bayern, and despite the defeat at the hands of the German giants, the 27-year-old centre-half said, 'The response from the supporters as I led the team out of the tunnel was something else – I had to choke back a lump in my throat and it is a memory I will always cherish.

'They gave me every encouragement during the match and the only disappointment was that we couldn't give them a victory. However, I'm sure the fans can take a lot of encouragement from our performance.

'In the first half, I thought we played some terrific football and Davie Cooper was quite brilliant. There are such a lot of good players at the club that I'm sure we will be giving the fans trophies sooner rather than later. This is one of the best moves I could have made.'

He added, 'Pressure is what I have had at Ipswich for the last three years, struggling against relegation and for your future. That's the kind of pressure any player can do without. But going for trophies with a top club like Rangers is the kind of pressure I'll take any time.'

One battle Rangers did win before the Bayern Munich game was the race to get their flagship hospitality suite finished in time for their corporate guests. Work on the Thornton Suite, named after Gers legend Willie Thornton – who was the guest of honour on the night – had been going on round the clock right up until opening time. It was the first time, on such a grand scale, that we had seen workers from the Lawrence Construction company involved in building work within the ground. Next up was the Waddell Suite.

Meanwhile, Robert Fleck celebrated his 21st birthday still thanking his lucky stars about one happy return he never expected. The young striker had been placed on the transfer list by Souness during the close season following an unfortunate misdemeanour at Parkhead the previous Boxing Day, which eventually saw him fined in court.

Fleck's future at Ibrox, it seemed, was over – but at the end of July he was taken off the transfer list and restored to the first-team squad. It was a dramatic turnaround for the player, whose gratitude to Souness was matched only by his determination to make the most of his second chance.

He said, 'When I dropped my shorts at Parkhead, I let myself and Rangers down. It's something I regret and since it happened, right through to the court case and being put up for sale, I was pretty depressed.

'When the gaffer told me I was being made available for transfer, it was one of the worst moments of my life. I have been a Rangers player since I was at school and I just can't imagine leaving the club.

'I could have given in at that point, but I knuckled down in training and kept hoping all the time that I might get the chance to stay. The only club I was aware of who were interested in me was Dundee, who made an offer, but I really wasn't interested and told the boss I wanted to stay at Ibrox.

'Then he watched the friendly match at Brockville and in the first half I felt I played as well as I had for a long time. However, when the manager took me aside the following morning and asked me if I wanted to come off the transfer list, I could hardly believe it – and couldn't say yes quickly enough.

'I have been given a second chance which some people might think I don't deserve. But I know I have learnt my lesson and now I intend to prove to people that I am good enough to score goals in Rangers' first team. I have been given a great opportunity by Graeme Souness and I don't intend to let him down.'

It was a timely reprieve as Souness took the opportunity to spell out to his players the cost of getting into trouble with referees. The player-manager had been suspended after the Hibs–Rangers clash at Easter Road but he was determined to avoid any more disciplinary trouble.

He said, 'Before the season began I warned the players that we were going to be the team that everyone wanted to shoot down and that they had to stay out of bother. Then on the first day of the season, I fell foul of exactly what I had been preaching to the players. It was a big disappointment but it's something that I, and everyone at the club, has learned a valuable lesson from.

'The subsequent ban was the worst punishment I could have received as I was very much looking forward to playing in my first Old Firm game. But I have made it clear to the players that this is the biggest threat to their place in the side.

'At Liverpool, everyone was scared to miss a game for the first team as they knew it would be so hard to get back in. That's why there are so few injuries or suspensions at Anfield, and that's the type of situation I want to create at Ibrox.'

The Ibrox exit door sprung open again when strikers Bobby Williamson and Iain Ferguson joined new clubs. Williamson signed for English Second Division side West Brom as part of a straight swap for Jimmy Nicholl, while Dundee United paid £145,000 for Ferguson, who had initially knocked back the chance to return to Tayside.

Williamson was signed from Clydebank for £100,000 in December 1983 and made 70 first-team appearances, scoring 27 goals, while Fergie joined Rangers in May 1984 for £200,000 from Dundee and had notched 23 goals in 70 games.

Also on the move was transfer-listed midfielder Dougie Bell, who signed for St Mirren on loan in a bid to put himself in the shop window. And the news that three players had moved on to pastures new came just before the Light Blues played their first home league match of the season. Mind you, it took a McCoist penalty to gun down Falkirk in the midweek fixture.

The 'under new management' signs at Ibrox read slightly better after the final whistle sounded, as it was the first competitive win under Souness. Rangers won by virtue of a soft penalty award, although the mayhem that was Easter Road just four days previously was nowhere to be seen. A good crowd of 27,362 – plus the sidelined Souness – watched a mediocre match.

For Rangers, the result was all important after that 2-1 defeat by Hibs – but they could take little comfort from this performance. The penalty was awarded by referee Louis Thow when Bryan Purdie was adjudged to have pulled down Derek Ferguson. The official was well in line with play, but his decision seemed harsh as the Rangers player was actually veering away from goal and appeared to anticipate the tackle.

Ferguson wore the number four jersey vacated by Souness in a game that saw Nicholl return for a second stint. The win was tempered by the news that Souness was in line for an extra SFA ban. Souness was forced to sit out the win over Falkirk after his sensational ordering off against Hibs, but the authorities announced they were to hold a full-scale investigation into the trouble-torn Easter Road match.

The chairmen and managers of both clubs had been summoned to the special meeting of the SFA disciplinary committee. As well as the Souness red card, eight other players were booked at Easter Road by referee Mike Delaney and it was decided to hold an investigation after officials studied written reports from the referee, linesmen and the two match supervisors.

However, the committee wouldn't be using TV evidence, which meant McCoist, clearly seen to get involved in the mayhem but not warned by the referee, would escape censure.

And there was more controversy between the clubs when a row flared up over an alleged approach by Rangers for

Hibernian's youth-team coach Gordon Neely, and following an afternoon meeting between Neely and Hibs chairman Kenny Waugh it was announced that Neely had been suspended by the Edinburgh side.

An angry Waugh insisted Rangers had made an approach to his man without consulting Hibs, and said, 'We are very upset that we have heard nothing from Rangers over this approach to a member of our staff who is under contract until next May. Our fans have given Neely and the youth team policy great support, and I'm sure they will be disappointed that he now wants to leave.'

Rangers refused to discuss any possible move for the former Dundee United scout.

But there were more woes on the field when Souness's men contrived to blow a two-goal lead against Dundee United at Ibrox. McCoist had struck twice in the first-half and Rangers were on Easy Street, but the defence collapsed like a pack of cards after the break and allowed Kevin Gallacher to score twice before former Ger Ian Redford struck late on.

And quite what Souness made of it all was anyone's guess as he failed to show up to face the media for the customary after-match talk-in, which spawned the famous 'Walter will do the post-match press conference' line.

Smith was indeed left to make the apologies as 43,995 Bears made their way home furious with the way the second half had panned out. He said, 'I can understand completely people thinking we were content to sit on our lead, but that wasn't the case. As soon as we lost the first goal the complexion of the game changed. All credit to United, because they played the right kind of game, even if all their goals were the result of defensive blunders.'

Just a couple of days after the devastating defeat, one national paper had the audacity to suggest Souness was facing up to the worst 48 hours of his career. The line read, 'Today, Souness has to talk Rangers out of believing the spectator judgement that they are "expensive rubbish," and tomorrow he faces the SFA disciplinary committee with a strong chance that both he and the club will be severely punished for the Easter Road match.

Can Souness handle such pressure so soon after being given the important supplementary role of manager?'

It was trash talk at its worst, especially as the journalist continued down the road of suggesting Souness had 'walked off Ibrox after Rangers' 3-2 surrender to United, looking like a man who had just been told his house had burned down.'

Souness was three competitive games into his first ever job as a manager and already he was being termed a dead man walking; someone who was having to learn quickly how to deal with a crisis! Welcome to the whacky world of football in Glasgow.

Another newspaper columnist wrote, 'Not for the first time it is being demonstrated that money does not insure against failure in football. Football must hope this happens because a 44,000 Ibrox crowd, with others locked out, certified that Rangers' buying moves are not commercial insanity.

'Rangers must wonder, though, if there is a curse on them. Two English World Cup players, Butcher and Woods, and Colin West, didn't look tuppence worth, far less £1,525,000 at specific times in Rangers' collapse to United.'

Moving on and next up for Rangers was the proverbial Skol Cup banana skin tie. Stenhousemuir, with 103 season ticket holders and their £15-a-week players, provided the opposition. In reality they had little hope of eclipsing Rangers. Mind you, with the Light Blues in the middle of a 'crisis', anything was possible.

The clash was switched from Ochilview to the larger Brockville and Stenny manager Archie Rose said, 'Our players were watching Terry Butcher on the telly at the World Cup. Now they're not only on the same pitch – but playing against him. It's a big step. Realistically, we don't have a chance, but football is funny and if we can hold them early in the game – you never know.'

But Rangers afforded themselves some light relief from the negative headlines of the past few days by strolling to a 4-1 victory thanks to goals from Souness, West, Cooper and McCoist, who scored for the fourth game in a row.

But the result was far more pleasing than the outcome of a specially-convened meeting of the SFA's disciplinary committee, which found 21 of the 22 players involved in the fracas at Easter Road guilty of bringing the game into disrepute. Rather unsurprisingly, the heaviest sentence was handed down to Souness, who copped an additional three-match ban as well as a £5,000 fine for his club.

The only player not branded a hooligan when violence erupted on opening day was Hibs keeper Alan Rough. But his team was fined £1,000, and the 21 guilty men had two penalty points added to their disciplinary records.

SFA president David Will said, 'Actions by players would have led to arrests had they occurred on the terracing.'

Rangers were fined £5,000 because 'it was the third major incident in which players of this club have been involved in the past two seasons'.

The Light Blues decided to accept their punishment but Hibs manager John Blackley said, 'We're very disappointed with the fines and the bookings. We will be appealing.'

And while football's top brass held the inquiry in the comfort of their plush Park Gardens offices, outside police were called to sort out traffic congestion as groups of concerned Rangers fans gathered to await the verdict.

But Rangers were soon back doing what they did best and a rocket by Cammy Fraser and a bullet from Colin West were enough to gun down Hamilton Accies at Douglas Park as the Light Blues began to move up through the gears.

Rangers had threatened to swamp the Premier League new boys at times and, on the amount of scoring chances created, should have given their goal difference a considerable boost. As it turned out, the Rangers fans in the capacity 11,000 crowd were given visions of Ibrox seven days before when Hamilton scored 20 minutes from time – but thankfully there was no repeat of the Dundee United nightmare.

The two points were well deserved and most welcome for Rangers and provided the perfect springboard for moving up the Premier League table. Rangers were playing some classy football and once they managed to find the killer touch, they were sure to be a real force to be reckoned with wherever they played.

But there was agony and ecstasy for Souness and his men – one in particular – the following midweek when they headed for Methil to face East Fife in a Skol Cup tie. After a goalless 120 minutes, the Ibrox side won 5-4 on penalties – but lost West to injury after he was the victim of a crude challenge.

And it was the man with the ability to keep his head while all around were going crazy who fired Rangers into the quarter-finals. Davie Cooper produced probably the biggest collective sigh of relief heard in a football ground when he coolly slotted the ball home from the spot at Bayview Park to end a night of high drama and tension.

Rangers had been through two hours of gritty, no-quarter-given football against East Fife in which they applied almost constant pressure only to see themselves thwarted by a combination of a superb goalkeeper, stout defending, lacklustre finishing and the woodwork.

The First Division club gave everything they had in an effort to create their own piece of football history and, in the end, any sort of victory was welcome. As it was, it took a penalty shoot-out to put Rangers into the last eight, where they were drawn to face Dundee at Ibrox.

It had been an eventful month for Souness and his players but the final day of August saw Rangers emerge from one of the most one-sided Old Firm clashes of the decade with just a single-goal victory to show for their dominance.

But you would be hard pressed to find a dissenting bluenose complaining about the result, the performance or the two points which was set to signal the start of a genuine claim for dominance in the football-mad city of Glasgow.

The Light Blues' supremacy over Celtic was unquestionable. Rangers simply overran and outplayed the Parkhead men who had no answer to the determination and pace of the home side. Magnificently commanded from the back by Butcher, who looked every inch a golden buy and a wonderful captain, Rangers were never prepared to settle for anything less than victory. The Gers team did not contain a single failure and it would have been wholly unfair to single individuals out for praise, but along with

Butcher, the contributions of Cammy Fraser, Ted McMinn and Ian Durrant were immense.

Right from the start, that trio ensured Rangers had a grip on the game – and held on to it until the final whistle. For the magnificent Rangers supporters, though, there was the anxiety of consistent domination – especially in the first half – without finding a way past Pat Bonner.

One incident in the 37th minute had many fans wondering if it was going to be another one of those days, when a Derek Ferguson shot cannoned off Bonner's right-hand post before the Celtic keeper dived full length to block McCoist's effort from the rebound. Rangers maintained the pressure after the break and Bonner made another fine stop, this time from a low 20-yard Fraser free kick.

But the goal just had to come and when it did arrive in the 74th minute, it was well worth the wait. McMinn, who was perpetual motion personified, played the ball out to Cooper, whose lovely through pass into the Celtic area split the defence wide open. The ever-alert Durrant took the ball in his stride, steadied himself and then calmly tucked a low shot past Bonner into the corner of the net.

Rangers deserved more than one goal and did have another chalked off by referee Kenny Hope, but when the final whistle sounded, victory itself was enough reward for a fine performance.

And it was a double cause for celebration for Canadian starlet Colin Miller, who was given an extended new contract. The 21-year-old was on an initial three-month deal under Souness but was handed another opportunity until at least the end of the season.

He said, 'It's fantastic. The gaffer has given me a chance to prove myself. I have told him I intend to be a first-team player here and he has assured me that if I produce the goods I will get that opportunity.'

The tide was finally turning.

18

Derek Ferguson

TALENTED midfielder Derek Ferguson was just 15 years old when he made his first-team debut for Rangers, against Swansea City in the Tom Forsyth Testimonial match at Ibrox. His first competitive start arrived at the beginning of the following season, 1983/84, when he came on as a substitute against Queen of the South in a Scottish League Cup tie, and his European debut was just three weeks away – home and away ties against Valletta in the European Cup Winners' Cup.

But the impressionable teenager could have been forgiven for thinking he had signed up for some sort of footballing circus as the Light Blues scored an astonishing 28 goals in the four matches, and although the gifted youngster failed to get his name on the scoresheet he certainly made the right impression on his manager, the legendary John Greig.

Mind you, Ferguson would never actually become known for his prowess in front of goal – although his talent in the middle of the park was never in question.

He said, 'John Greig signed me for Rangers when I was 16, but he had actually been coaching me since just before my teens. Back then, it was a schoolboy form you were recruited on, which you signed at 12, and that covered you for about four years. About six months before your 16th birthday, the club made a decision as to whether or not they were going to take you on full time, and fortunately for me John Greig was the manager of Rangers at that time so I landed my first professional contract.

'John also gave me my debut, so he was a massive influence on me. And he remained a huge influence even when he left the manager's job, because when I got into one or two scrapes – while Graeme Souness was the gaffer – John was always about the place, and he always had time for me, so he was someone I definitely looked up to. He is obviously a Rangers legend, but if you can look past that, he is also a lovely guy.

'But he was one of my first coaches, which I suppose is unimaginable in this day and age. Mind you, I was also taken for coaching sessions by the likes of Tommy McLean and Alex Miller, so I was very fortunate. It was amazing for a young lad to be working with guys like them, but it was something I appreciated.

'But John Greig ticked all the boxes. He was as hard as nails but he could also play the game, a bit like Ian Ferguson. A lot of people only remember Fergie's tackling and aggression, but he was far more than that, he was a terrific football player. I played with him and against him and he was top drawer.'

Ferguson reckons the team-building efforts of managers such as Greig and Jock Wallace may have suffered because of the construction of a new stadium – although he insisted it was music to the ears of the up-and-coming youngsters of his era at Ibrox.

He explained, 'If you look back at 1986, I think a lot of money had been spent on the refurbishment of the stadium, which was fantastic, but it meant there wasn't an awful lot of cash left to bring in top players, and I think that's where the likes of myself and quite a few others benefitted.

'Some of the younger players on the staff – including Ian Durrant, Hugh Burns, Robert Fleck and Davie McFarlane – were fortunate to get an opportunity to play in the first team because there wasn't a lot of money swirling about. If that money had been available we might not have been given the same chance.

'If you even fast forward three or four years, when Graeme Souness was there, that certainly wouldn't have happened, because if you look at the team by then it was full of top international players. Sometimes, though, that's what it's like in football. You're in the right place at the right time and you get that wee bit of luck that we certainly got and I think that's important.'

But changes were afoot, and Fergie reckons the appointment of David Holmes as chief executive was a defining moment in the modern day history of Rangers Football Club.

He said, 'David Holmes was fantastic for Rangers. He was also such a lovely man, a top guy. Throughout my career I played with 15 different clubs and if we're talking chairmen, none were nicer than David, and he always had time for you. Some chairmen were perhaps too busy to stop and have a conversation but David would always stop and have a wee chat with you, ask how you were, ask about your family. That's the type of guy he was. Sometimes in football you get guys who won't give you the time of day, and that's why I mentioned John Greig, who would always have time for a cup of tea and a chat, and I think that's really important. Players really appreciate little things like that. Good people skills are so important.'

And one of David Holmes's first major tasks was to find a manager who could transform the club on the field – just like he was doing off it. But Ferguson recalls the day he discovered that Souness was the new player-manager of Rangers.

He said, 'When Graeme Souness arrived at Rangers, I found out just like everyone else. It was all over the TV and papers, and I'll tell you something, I was so excited about the appointment. I loved him as a player – he was one of the best. In fact, he was one of the top midfielders in Europe so to find out he was coming to my club, Glasgow Rangers, and that he was going to be my manager, was unbelievable. I was as high as a kite.

'It's hard to imagine, but here was a guy of his calibre coming to Ibrox, and it wasn't just that he was going to be my manager, he was also going to be playing as well – perhaps alongside me. It was a brilliant moment for Rangers – and a teenage Derek Ferguson!

'I think Graeme had done his homework before he came into the club and knew that myself and Ian [Durrant] were decent players, and perhaps he came to Ibrox with the vision that Ian and I would be the mainstay of his midfield for a long time to come, but mistakes were made on my part.

'Mind you, when you're young and playing for the team you supported, the club you loved, and earning okay money, I was having the time of my life although maybe enjoying my life a wee bit too much. But I can now look back on those days with a different perspective on life.'

But Ferguson reckons mistakes were made on both sides, and said, 'Perhaps Graeme's man-management skills could have been a wee bit better. I think if he looks back and reflects on when he was 18 or 19, and what he was like as a person, then it might all have been different, but he did what he thought was right for Rangers at the time.

'He might have thought a lot of me at the start, but he did try to change me a wee bit, in terms of the way I played the game, and it didn't go down too well with me at times. But again it's like everything else, it would have been far better managed with the benefit of hindsight.

'When you get a wee bit older and wiser you look back and think, "I realise why he was doing that," but it has to be the same with Graeme. I reckon he might look back and think he could have dealt with me a bit better, but I suppose it was a learning curve for both of us.

'When Graeme made his mind up about something he wouldn't change it. He was hard but you have to respect that. When you're at a huge club like Rangers then you have to respect what the manager is doing. He felt he was right, but it's about managing it and making the right decisions. I found out the hard way, but I wasn't alone. He thought it was the right way to do things and maybe that's the way he had been treated, but things have changed and even the way you handle football players is so different nowadays.'

Ferguson, who would go on to play for Scotland, reckons he was like a wee boy in a sweet shop when Souness was appointed, and he insisted the former Liverpool midfield lynchpin lived up to expectations, and some.

He said, 'I was so excited when Graeme came in and his appointment was definitely everything I had hoped for. The first time he walked into the dressing room he was magnificent.

Mind you, he didn't so much as walk in, he strutted in, but he was brilliant. Even the way he took training, it was all so professional. He changed loads of things, but mostly just small things, like making us wear flip-flops, and having Jacuzzis and saunas installed.

'And whereas we had previously worn suits from Slater's the Glasgow tailor, that soon changed to Armani, which made us all feel that bit more professional. But we had always enjoyed that tradition at Rangers where we were smart all the time. Even as a 12-year-old I would turn up for training in a shirt and tie!

'But training under Graeme surprised me a bit. It was very good, but it was also quite relaxed and not as intense as I thought it might be. I think it was a lot of stuff he enjoyed, and that he had brought over from Italy.'

Having initially played under Greig, and then Jock Wallace during the big man's second spell at Rangers, Ferguson realised there was a need for change as the club he had grown up supporting was in grave danger of falling even further behind in the Scottish Premier Division pecking order.

The 'New Firm' of Aberdeen and Dundee United were fully established, while old rivals Celtic, as well as Hearts, had all made rapid headway and laid genuine claims on the title. Suddenly, Rangers were left playing catch-up.

Ferguson said, 'When the changes at Ibrox eventually happened in 1986, they really were necessary. I grew up a Rangers fan, and supported the club all my days, whether that was going to the games with my dad or my mates. Rangers was everything, and Graeme Souness was the right choice at the right time, and he changed everything. He changed the philosophy at the club because he was a winner and you could see that in absolutely everything he did.

'And then there was Walter Smith. I think it was a really shrewd move by Graeme to bring Walter in as his assistant, as his time at Dundee United meant he knew the Scottish football scene inside out, plus he also knew that Walter was a Rangers man, which was really important. When you look back at some of the players Graeme signed, all these internationals such as Ray

Wilkins, Trevor Francis, Terry Butcher etc, Walter was probably his best signing.

'But there was no doubt we needed to change. Guys like David Holmes obviously had a vision for the club and knew exactly the direction they wanted it to travel in and Graeme Souness was no doubt a big part of that plan. Everything had to be first class, or I don't think he would have signed as manager, but everyone bought into it. Even things like staying in good hotels the night before matches. Everything was planned, right down to what we ate.'

Ferguson made 30 appearances for the Light Blues in Souness's first campaign and played an integral part in bringing the league title back to Ibrox. And when he clocked up more than 30 league matches the following season, and started to add goals to his game, his earlier prediction of Ferguson and Durrant becoming the mainstay of the Gers' midfield for many years to come looked set to bear fruit.

But nothing lasts forever and season 1989/90 saw him drift so far out of the first-team picture that a move seemed inevitable.

Ferguson said, 'When I left in 1990 it was because Graeme had made his mind up that I was leaving. I hadn't been behaving myself properly off the park, and he wasn't very patient with me. I was enjoying myself a bit too much and his patience was wearing thin. He decided three or four months before I actually left that I was going.

'It was a sore one for me, and it took a while for me to leave because I still had another year left on my contract and I wasn't going to budge, but when you're told that you will be training at certain times, and you won't be included in the first-team squad, and you won't even be playing for the reserves, that you'll be sitting on a bench, it made my mind up for me.

'For me, it was a lesson learned the hard way and I try to pass on that experience to the younger guys I coach, because I don't want it to happen to anyone else. Hopefully, most of them take it on board.

'I went on to play for Hearts for three years and absolutely loved my time there. There were a lot of ex-Rangers players at

Tynecastle at the time, including the manager Alex MacDonald, and Iain Ferguson, Nicky Walker and Davie Kirkwood, so that transition was quite easy. The only reason I left was because I lost a wee girl just seven weeks after she was born, and my wife and I made the decision to try and get away from everything so we headed down south and I signed for Sunderland.

'After everything that had gone on at Ibrox, I reckon Hearts was probably the perfect fit for me. I had all my ex-colleagues from Rangers, it was a brilliant family club and was only 40-odd miles along the M8, so I enjoyed playing with the Jambos. But whereas the destination of my Rangers career was out of my hands, my situation at Hearts was my decision to make, although I wish I had stayed there. But when things happen in your private life you make certain decisions and you have to stick by them.'

He added, 'Looking back, I think the introduction of Souness in 1986 was a good thing not just for Rangers but for the whole of Scottish football, as it helped raise the standards in this country. As far as Rangers is concerned, I don't think it was just the money that attracted some of the best players in the country to Ibrox. Rangers have always been a massive club, but I'm sure many of the top players came to the club because the manager was Graeme Souness.

'I reckon many of them could've earned a similar wage down south but they bought into Graeme's philosophy that they could be successful in Scotland and win leagues, cups and even trebles. Sometimes it isn't just about cash, but about the aura of the person that wants you, and that's what Graeme Souness had.

'I'm just glad I got to experience what was a fantastic time to be a Rangers player. Perhaps I could have made more of it, but we are all a little wiser with the benefit of hindsight.'

19

Second Chance For Fleck

RANGERS started off the month of September with a solid victory over Dundee, which took them into the semi-finals of the Skol Cup. Once again the Light Blues were taken to extra time, although on this occasion they managed to win 3-1 – and avoid a nerve-shredding penalty shoot-out.

Ten-man Dundee, who had central defender Jim Duffy sent off after only 20 minutes, had shocked Rangers with a last-gasp goal in regulation time. But Souness, back after his SFA ban, took control and in the 19th minute of extra time, from a pass by Ian Durrant, blasted a superb 18-yard shot past Bobby Geddes. Six minutes later, Ted McMinn headed in a Cammy Fraser cross.

England international Terry Butcher was booked and it was felt by the Ibrox side that he was being unfairly picked on by referees. The yellow card pushed him over the ten-point disciplinary mark and saw him land a suspension.

But as one player prepared to miss some match action, three others won a unique reprieve when they beat the SFA system. George McCluskey, Mark Fulton and Mickey Weir all had their appeals against respective cautions – dished out in the opening game of the season between Hibs and Rangers – upheld by a three-man tribunal at the SFA HQ in Glasgow.

Following a marathon two-and-a-half-hour meeting, the Easter Road trio emerged smiling and relieved. The Scottish Professional Footballers' Association had contested the decision to dish out blanket two-match cautions. Originally ten Hibs players had intended taking on the SFA, but the players' union decided on just three appeals, and after much deliberation won its case.

Meanwhile, it was turning into the autumn of discontent for one player who was threatening to quit football if he couldn't get a move to Rangers. Davie Dodds, the 27-year-old former Dundee United striker who was with Swiss side Neuchatel Xamax, had made it clear he wanted a move to Ibrox.

He said, 'I won't play for anyone except Rangers. The club can try to transfer me where they like but unless it's to Ibrox I'm not interested.'

Aberdeen as well as Rangers had made bids for him, and Hearts were also interested. The striker had been accused by the Swiss club of lacking the basic skills to fit into their plans, and a spokesman said about Dodds, who cost Neuchatel £180,000, 'He's not the player he was when we bought him.'

A couple of days later, Rangers were given a second chance to land the player. Aberdeen had tabled the highest offer – around £200,000 – to Neuchatel, for whom Dodds had yet to make an appearance that season.

Yves Deterrot, of Neuchatel, said, 'There isn't much between the bids so we have asked Rangers if they wish to increase their offer. The player has already said he wants to go to Ibrox, and we want to do the best for him because we know he is unhappy with us. We have told him if Rangers match the Aberdeen offer he can go to Glasgow.'

Neuchatel, ordered by a European tribunal to pay £180,000 for Dodds the previous May, denied they were holding clubs to ransom by asking for more money. The Swiss club claimed the pound had since slipped, hence the reason the buying club would have to pay more than the original fee.

Meanwhile, Rangers carried on their good form in the league by strolling to a 2-0 win over Motherwell at Fir Park.

Souness ran the show in the middle of the park and stamped his class and quality on an intriguing tussle as he coolly sent the match beyond the reach of the Steelmen. Indeed, had Ally McCoist and one or two others remembered their shooting boots, the end result might have been considerably greater.

Motherwell, with Stevie Kirk battling in the midfield, gave as good as they got until right on the sound of the half-time whistle. Souness's long throw looked innocent enough, but it totally foxed the Fir Park defence who stood stock still to allow Davie Cooper to stab the ball past John Gardiner.

The goal and timing clearly sickened Motherwell. That really was the last we saw of them as an attacking force, although Rangers were quite fortunate in the events leading up to their second goal.

Cooper, brilliant and not so great in equal measure, seemed to run into full-back Fraser Wishart. With the home defence still fuming, Coop hit the resultant free kick with pinpoint accuracy for Davie McPherson to side-foot it into the net.

If Souness, prompting and prodding his players, was the star, then Jimmy Nicholl wasn't too far behind. The Irish international relished his raids down the right flank and was a constant threat as Motherwell tried to swamp the middle of the park.

Souness's plan – the slow, patient build-up from defence – was the way Liverpool did it, and there was also more than a hint of some tactics picked up in Italy. The second-half performance at Fir Park was the best of the season to date with Terry Butcher and Souness in exceptional form.

And the good news just kept on coming as starlet Robert Fleck received a welcome request from the Scotland under-21 side. A phonecall the day after the win at Motherwell from Craig Brown told Fleck he was being called into the squad to replace Aberdeen's Joe Miller. The delighted youngster joined the squad and there was more good news in store when he came on as a 59th-minute substitute for Steve Gray and looked very sharp, ensuring the excellent German defence weren't given a minute's peace.

He said, 'It's a terrific boost for me to get involved with the under-21 squad. I was delighted just to get a late call-up and be involved but to play and do quite well was a great bonus for me. Now I just hope I made enough of an impression to be included from the start in the next squad.

'It's just another high point for me after a season which was looking really bad. I have gone from being up for sale to being involved in the first team with Rangers and playing for my country at under-21 level.'

Scotland beat West Germany 1-0 thanks to a Kevin Gallacher goal. Derek Ferguson and Ian Durrant both played from the start.

Rangers chalked up their seventh successive win – since losing to Dundee United on 16 August – with a 4-0 rout of Clydebank, and it was yet another highlight for Fleck. The striker stepped into the gap left by injured star Colin West and the rested Ted McMinn and capped a marvellous start to the season by grabbing a hat-trick.

In fact, Fleck might have doubled his tally had luck been on his side but a combination of the woodwork and terrific goalkeeping from the evergreen Jim Gallacher prevented that.

In the past, Rangers might have slipped up against the likes of Clydebank – but not now. And the fans were also onside, with a crowd of 26,334 testament to the way Souness and co were going about their business.

But as Rangers piled on the pressure, they suffered a blow in the 37th minute when McCoist was hurt in a clash with Gallacher. He had to be carried from the field but his replacement McMinn filled the gap admirably and grabbed the other goal.

After seven league matches, Dundee United were top with 12 points. Hearts were just one behind while Rangers and Celtic had ten. It was shaping up to be an interesting title race.

Days after the victory, Souness appointed former Liverpool team-mate Phil Boersma as Rangers' new physiotherapist/trainer. Boersma left Doncaster Rovers to take up the post, replacing Bob Findlay, who had been the Ibrox physio since joining from Raith Rovers in 1981.

But the person everyone was talking about was the unorthodox, but incredibly talented McMinn. He had taken

Scottish football by storm, and done so while carrying injuries to both feet.

The Dumfries man said, 'I first picked up the knock on my left ankle during the Stenhousemuir game and since then it has taken an infection which I haven't yet been able to get rid of. And for the last couple of weeks I have had what I thought was a chipped bone in my right foot which was quite painful. Thanks to the wonders of modern science, though, it hasn't stopped me playing so far.

'I haven't been able to train full out and it really caught up on me during the Dundee United game – I was absolutely knackered when I came off the park. But the way things are going for me at the moment, I can shrug off all the knocks a lot more easily.'

Surprisingly, McMinn didn't feel he was playing as well as he could and that all the headlines he had been attracting were a bit unfair.

He added, 'It's not fair on the other players at the club that I have got so much praise. Everyone has been playing well and as far as I'm concerned I haven't been consistent enough. I have had three or four very good games in which I have played as well as I ever have. I'm also scoring goals, which is unheard of for me, and something I hope I can keep up. But there is still a long way to go this season and I haven't proved myself as a regular first-team player yet although I'll obviously be very disappointed if I can't establish myself this time around.

'The difference in my form this season is down to the freedom I am getting from the gaffer. Previously I was told to stay in the one position all the time, but now I am being given the chance to move about more and it's paying off. But my feet are staying firmly on the ground – the gaffer makes sure you don't get carried away. When I hit a spell of good form last season and the press started giving me a lot of coverage, I got carried away. That won't happen this time.

'This is going to be a really exciting season for Rangers and I'm just so happy to be a part of it. We have all got our eyes on that Premier League flag and are determined to win it, especially for our fans. They have been out of this world so far this season and in my case, when they chant my name, it gives me a tremendous lift.'

But once again it was Fleck writing the headlines when Rangers swept aside Finns Ilves Tampere at a wet and windy Ibrox. Rangers comfortably and confidently allayed any pre-match worries about the tie and all but booked their place in the second round of the UEFA Cup, the tournament they had exited at the first hurdle the previous season. Taking centre stage was Fleck, the hat-trick hero against Clydebank. He came up with a European action replay – another treble to surely put the tie beyond the Finns.

It was no fault of Rangers that they were helped by a vital decision in their favour by Danish referee Jan Damgaard. He showed a red card on 20 minutes to Pekka Heino for a tackle on McCoist, who had recovered from the knock against Clydebank. It was a harsh decision, for although Heino had been involved in earlier fouls none of them had earned a caution.

The goal of the game – Fleck's third – arrived in 51 minutes and although he was the scorer the man who rightly earned an ovation from the 27,000 crowd was Davie Cooper. He conjured up a dazzling dribble through almost the entire Tampere defence to give the young striker the simplest of tap-ins.

The night wasn't a complete success, though, as the new Ibrox electronic scoreboard went on the blink. But it was the only part of Rangers' set-up which failed to function in another impressive victory for the team.

Mind you, there were red faces all round 48 hours later when ruffled Rangers chiefs were left frantically searching for a replay venue. NOT for a big cup tie…but for the club's AGM. The hunt was launched after the scheduled meeting was abandoned after half an hour – because there wasn't nearly enough room for the massive crowd. More than 400 shareholders had crammed into the Mitchell Theatre in Glasgow, with 160 others locked out.

Chief executive David Holmes said, 'I'm embarrassed and sorry. The level of interest in the meeting took us completely by surprise. The session was predicted to be the quietest and least contentious for many years.'

Virtually every Rangers fan and shareholder seemed delighted by the summer spate of big-name signings, but when chairman John Paton set the ball rolling, he had no idea of the chaos in a tea room downstairs. It was 25 minutes before a note was passed to secretary Campbell Ogilvie, saying that locked-out shareholders were demanding the meeting be halted.

One bellowed, 'We are shareholders and by law we should get in.'

A few minutes later the final whistle was blown. The Ibrox board agreed to meet ASAP to make plans for a replay meeting, the first in the club's 114-year history.

The business that did go ahead included a scathing attack on the players' behaviour in the infamous battle of Easter Road. Mr Holmes said remorsefully, 'I was embarrassed and ashamed.' And he promised the scenes at the Hibs match would never be repeated, adding that Souness had since been told 'in no uncertain terms' of the board's disciplinary requirements.

There were also issues with Rangers' methods of selling match tickets, and Campbell Ogilvie was forced to apologise to supporters who had been experiencing problems getting to see their team.

He said, 'There have been faults, and we're very sorry it has caused problems for the fans.'

The new-look Rangers' success had sparked off Scottish football's most amazing box-office boom.

And just as Ogilvie was apologising, fans had been queueing outside Ibrox since 7am as tickets went on sale for the home game against Aberdeen. Such was the demand to see Rangers that their next five games in Scotland were made all-ticket.

Ogilvie added, 'We have to make it easier for fans to buy tickets by cutting out queues as much as possible.'

Meanwhile, Rangers recalled Dougie Bell from his loan spell at St Mirren for the match at Dundee due to a spate of injuries, which saw them without the services of Souness, Butcher and McMinn.

But the move didn't pay off as a John Brown goal put Rangers to the sword at a packed Dens Park.

Rangers were sloppy, but as sucker punches go, Bomber Brown's winner was a classic of its kind. And for the stunned Gers fans it meant a long journey back home to Glasgow.

If ever a game – and not an especially good one at that – was heading for a 0-0 draw, this was it.

Then suddenly Dundee picked up a corner on the left with McKinlay flighting the ball in to Ray Stephen. He in turn edged it to Brown whose spectacular shot curled high past Chris Woods.

But if the defeat on Tayside was a hammer blow to legions of Ibrox supporters, it was nothing compared to the personal anguish felt by striker John MacDonald when he was given news of his impending departure.

It spelled the end of a dream story which had turned into a bit of a nightmare, because the 25-year-old was once described by former Ibrox boss John Greig as 'a Rangers fan first, a Rangers player second' and that was pretty accurate.

Not that MacDonald ever accepted second best when he was playing in a light blue jersey and his goalscoring record for the first team would bear comparison with most.

After signing on for the club as a schoolboy from Clydebank Strollers, John realised a personal dream when he was called up full-time by John Greig in 1978. Within weeks, he was playing in the first team and went on to notch up more than 100 goals for the club before his release in the last week of September.

After all his initial success which saw him win Scotland under-21 caps and be tipped for full international honours, things turned sour for him. Under Jock Wallace he was never a regular in the first team and he was also unlucky with injuries, particularly to his back. Dumbarton, Partick Thistle, Norwich, Charlton, Barnsley, Stockport and Chesterfield were just some of the clubs chasing his signature.

But despite his personal disappointment, MacDonald was still delighted to see Rangers reach the Skol Cup Final when they edged form side Dundee United at Hampden in a semi-final thriller. And victory set up a final showdown with Celtic, with Sunday 26 October quickly crossed off in diaries up and down the country – especially by the legions of fans who were watching the exciting development of a Rangers team equipped to challenge for honours on a consistent basis.

There was hardly ever any doubt that the Skol Cup Final date would be for an Old Firm clash as the Light Blues produced a high-class, professional performance against a United side who could have no complaints about their first domestic defeat of the season.

As Jim McLean was the first to concede afterwards, Souness and his merry men simply outclassed United on the night.

The writing was on the wall early for United and after Billy Thomson had made a fine save from a McCoist header, then watched as Cooper ended a superb piece of skill with a 20-yard shot which went inches wide, Rangers opened the scoring in the 19th minute. It was a magnificent goal for McCoist, celebrating his 24th birthday, and as the fastest strike of the semi-finals it won him a special barrel of lager from the sponsors.

But McMinn deserved a pint or two from the keg as he danced down the wing, slipping past a bemused Dave Beaumont not once but twice before crossing low to the near post, where McCoist stepped in and whipped the ball over Thomson and into the net. It was his 17th League Cup goal since joining Rangers.

In the 58th minute, Cooper and Stuart Munro combined to play in McMinn. He completely baffled United skipper Paul Hegarty before squeezing a 12-yard shot in at the post. Former Rangers striker Iain Ferguson scored a consolation in front of 45,000.

But if ever a day proved the Rangers revival was at long last underway, it was on the last day of September. One victory over a strong Aberdeen side may not have won any trophies but it was a clear signal to the Ibrox faithful that Souness was steering Rangers on a path to glory.

There was still a lot of work to be done and plenty of football to be played but if Rangers were to maintain such a high standard, there was little doubt that silverware at Ibrox would become the rule rather than the exception once again.

A full-strength Aberdeen were beaten 2-0 by a Rangers team that looked a million miles away from the one that had failed so woefully against the Dons in the recent past. Rangers picked up two well-deserved points by playing football in a controlled, composed and confident fashion, which had the fans turning up in numbers wherever they played. It was exactly what the supporters had been waiting for – and their patience was finally being rewarded.

For much of a fine game, Rangers held the initiative against the Pittodrie men and when they were forced to defend for a nerve-jangling spell in the second half they coped superbly. But while it was a team effort in which Rangers yet again had no failures, Terry Butcher stood out throughout – but particularly during a hectic spell of Aberdeen pressure in which he cleared five corner kicks in quick succession.

By that time, Rangers had already taken the lead with a magnificent goal from Souness which clearly gave the Ibrox boss a lot of pleasure – as it did for around 40,000 Rangers fans. Souness strode on to a clever McMinn pass and from 20 yards, struck a left-foot shot of awesome power. It beat Jim Leighton, struck the right-hand post then rolled agonisingly along the line for what seemed an eternity before trickling into the net.

Rangers' second goal caused Aberdeen a lot of anguish but whatever its merits or otherwise, no one could doubt that Souness's men were well worth their advantage as McCoist and Fleck broke clear and played a clever one-two before McCoist knocked the ball over the line from four yards.

Sure, it was a simple tap-in, but it signalled Rangers' intent. Aberdeen might have been one of the top dogs in the country but the Light Blues were coming for them, and the others who had dominated the domestic scene in recent years. It was game on.

20

Ian Ferguson

TRUE Blue Ian Ferguson is one of just three players to have taken part in Rangers' entire record-equalling feat of nine championships in a row. He will always be remembered as the tough-as-teak Gers supporter who patrolled the midfield area with an iron fist during the Souness years – but there was far more to Fergie than crunching tackles and toe-to-toe confrontations.

The vision he possessed which allowed him to pick out a killer pass, or the lung-bursting runs from the edge of his own penalty box deep into the heart of opposition territory, were also used to great effect by the former Clyde and St Mirren midfielder.

Fergie shot to prominence when he scored the only goal of the game – a trademark rocket from just inside the box – to win the Scottish Cup for unfashionable St Mirren over Dundee United at Hampden Park in May 1987.

Despite being just 20, he had also given Souness's Rangers enough problems during matches against the Paisley side that the former Liverpool and Sampdoria star had more than just a keen eye trained on the combative midfielder with the blonde streaks.

But the truth is Ferguson could have been a Rangers player long before Souness was handed the keys to the manager's office at the top of the marble staircase.

He explained, 'I believe the story is told that Peter McCloy came to watch me while I was playing for Clyde, and there was also someone watching from St Mirren. I was told the feedback

Rangers got was that I wasn't quite ready for that level yet, but then St Mirren moved to sign me.

'The good thing for me was that I didn't hear anything about this story until much later on, probably about five or six years down the line. That was the perfect scenario. I think had I heard it at the time I would have been very disappointed, and it might have seriously affected my game.'

Ferguson spent two happy years at Love Street, mostly under the managerial guidance of Alex Smith, with the Scottish Cup success an obvious highlight. After a third-round win over Inverness Caley the Buddies edged a five-goal thriller against rivals Morton, before beating Raith Rovers in the last eight.

That set up a semi-final clash with Hearts at Hampden and Ferguson grabbed the first goal in a 2-1 win. He then scored the winner in the final in front of almost 52,000 fans. Perhaps it was written in the stars that afternoon that he would go on to have a medal-laden career in the game.

Meanwhile, just a few miles down the M8, Souness had been causing something of a stir himself. Mind you, Rangers' Scottish Cup campaign of 1986/87 is certainly best consigned to the annals of history, as Hamilton Accies pulled off an upset at Ibrox in the third round.

Naturally, Fergie had been looking on with great interest as events unfolded at Ibrox over the spring of 1986, and beyond.

He said, 'The signing of Graeme Souness was a huge thing as he turned Scottish football on its head. He also took Rangers to another level because he came to the club and set the standards that he wanted.

'He started bringing English international players to Scotland, reversing the trend of the annual exodus which saw our top guys head over the border to further their careers. At that time, the English clubs thought nothing of cherry-picking the best talent up in Scotland, so Souness was massive for Scottish football and did a fantastic job at Rangers.

'Rangers weren't exactly enjoying a lot of success at that time and the crowds were dwindling, but when Graeme was announced as the next manager, the level of interest in Rangers shot up again. It was just the shot in the arm the club desperately required.'

Despite enjoying two good years in Paisley, Ferguson insisted it wasn't a difficult decision to leave when he learned of Rangers' interest.

He said, 'It really wasn't an issue because it was Rangers who came in for me. Had it been another club, then it would probably have been more of a trauma because I was enjoying being at St Mirren and was in no hurry to leave. The truth is my boyhood heroes wanted to sign me; the team I supported and went to watch through the late 70s and early 80s, until I started playing football myself, so it certainly wasn't a problem.'

Ferguson added, 'I remember reading in one of the papers that Rangers were showing an interest in me, and I was flattered. Then it was on the radio and TV and the rumour started gathering momentum and getting stronger. It just kept coming and coming and eventually St Mirren decided to tell me that the move was on – but there was a snag. They wanted me to go down south and speak to Manchester United, who were also interested.

'I decided to do as they asked and headed down the M6 to Manchester to speak to Sir Alex Ferguson but I felt I was travelling down there with a heavy heart. It just didn't feel right. I'm a person who works a lot on gut instinct and nine times out of ten that feeling is right. As far as I was concerned, once I knew Rangers were interested there was only one team I wanted to play for.

'Manchester United are a massive club but that didn't matter too much because they weren't *my* club. To this day, people ask if I have any regrets, but how can you possibly have regrets when you've won ten championships, Scottish Cups, League Cups, two trebles, you've had a testimonial and you're in the Rangers Hall of Fame? How on earth could you regret that?

'When I put pen to paper for Glasgow Rangers I felt very emotional, for both myself and my family, because we were all brought up in the Rangers tradition and we followed in our father's footsteps, so it was a great moment for them as well.'

Ferguson admits that as a boyhood supporter, playing for the club he loved was everything he had ever dreamed of – and more.

He said, 'It certainly was. Winning titles and cups is unbelievable but, don't get me wrong, it wasn't all plain sailing. There were lots of difficult times as well, but you have to get through them. For every time you get knocked over, you must dust yourself down and get back up again. That was my attitude rather than spitting the dummy out the pram.

'You have to be quite thick-skinned to play for a club like Rangers because there are many, many challenges. Thankfully, I was thick-skinned and didn't let things affect me too much. It also helped immensely that I was the sort of person who didn't get too star-struck; I was quite humble and didn't ever let fame go to my head. I was there to do a job and didn't let all the other stuff get in the way.'

Ferguson reckons the timing of Souness's introduction to Rangers was priceless. He said, 'We definitely needed something at that time because neither the performances nor results were great and we weren't winning much, apart from the odd cup here and there.

'So Graeme Souness was great for Rangers and, of course, Scottish football. The man had a fantastic aura, a presence, and the way he swept through Ibrox and brought English internationals to Ibrox just turned Scottish football on its head. It's a time in the game I will never forget, even though I was playing for St Mirren at the time.'

Ferguson is one of the most decorated players to pull on a light blue jersey, a fact that makes him proud and humble in equal measure.

He said, 'Naturally I am very proud that a wee boy from the east end of Glasgow managed to accumulate all these medals. I think I have 23 in all, and 19 of them are winner's medals, which is a good percentage, so of course I'm very proud.

'But no matter what I've achieved in life or football, I've always tried to remain very humble. I don't let things go to my head or listen too much to what people are calling you. Sometimes you get branded a legend, but that's just not me. As far as I'm concerned, if I didn't play for Rangers I would have been on the terracing beside the other supporters. I was simply very fortunate.'

Many folk could have been forgiven for thinking that two such full-blooded personalities like Ferguson and Souness would have clashed on more occasions than both might care to remember – and to a certain extent they may just be right – but Fergie insists he still has nothing but respect for the man who transformed Rangers, and took him to Ibrox.

He said, 'I loved Graeme and couldn't say a bad word against him. I thought he was excellent. He brought me to Ibrox and to be honest we had our ups and downs. He's said a couple of things, as have I, but I sussed him out pretty early on that if you wanted to speak to him, you had to do it behind closed doors, rather than doing it in front of people because that way there was only ever going to be one winner, so I knew from early on how to treat him.

'What I really liked about him, though, was that he was very hard but equally as fair. He was a good man and definitely someone I was glad to have in my corner.'

Just as Ferguson can remember clearly the day he walked through the front door at Ibrox for the first time as a Rangers player, he will never ever forget the day he left.

He recalled, 'It was a very sad day when I left Rangers, more so because I never got an opportunity to say goodbye to the fans. I was with the club for more than 11 years and I would love to have been given the chance to say goodbye to our supporters at Ibrox before I left, but it didn't happen.

'To be fair, I got one of the best receptions I ever had at Ibrox when I moved away! I had signed for Dunfermline Athletic and we were due to play Rangers at Ibrox which, as you can imagine, was quite an occasion for me. Jimmy Nicholl was the manager and he took me off after about 75 minutes and the whole place erupted. The ovation I got was outstanding and I got really emotional – in fact, I get goosebumps thinking about it even now. I remember seeing David Murray standing in the tunnel and that just set me off. It was a nice touch because he had been at Ibrox almost as long as me. Yes, it was very emotional.'

But Ferguson revealed how he felt a totally different type of emotion in 2012, when Rangers hit their financial problems and the club went into meltdown. And what made it harder, he said, was that he was 12,000 miles away in Australia.

He explained, 'That was very difficult, especially when I saw all the turmoil at the club I had supported and played for, and the shape the club was in. But more importantly, I was very disappointed at how the whole of Scottish football and the SFA treated Rangers when they were down. I think they should hang their heads in shame because what they did was take the game in this country to a new low, where they were missing the likes of Rangers, Hearts and Hibs from the top league, and to me that was the biggest blunder in the history of the game in this country.

'And do you know what, the people responsible for this dreadful act never even had the courage to implement it themselves. They used people from other clubs to do their dirty work, and I don't think they were the right people – with the right credentials – to make that decision with regards to a club like Rangers. It was done through others and that was shameful.'

But to finish on a positive note, Ferguson summed up his time at arguably the most successful football club in the world by insisting his journey throughout his stay at Ibrox had been akin to the most wonderful dream imaginable.

He said, 'The best way I can describe my time at Rangers is to say that I lived the dream. I did what every Rangers fan would love to do and I was just privileged, proud and honoured to get that opportunity. I had a great career and there isn't one thing I would change. I enjoyed every day and didn't take a single one for granted because I knew one day it would all end and I would be out the door, so I always had the view that today was my last day and I made the most of it – and thankfully that "day" lasted for 11 years. It was quite a journey!'

21

Cup Glory For Gers

I T was a fine start to October for the Light Blues as Graeme Souness and Terry Butcher scooped an Ibrox double in the monthly Scottish Brewers football awards. The player-manager was named Manager of the Month while Butcher took the Personality Player of the Month for September. Both men received a cheque for £250 and commemorative plaques.

But there was bad news looming for four members of the Ibrox groundstaff – including young Alex Rae – as they were released from their contracts.

And it was a bittersweet night for the Gers in Finland as they lost 2-0 to Ilves Tampere in the second leg of their first-round tie but still progressed on a 4-2 aggregate. Tampere shocked Souness and co with a battling performance but in the end their victory merely restored lost pride. From the gaffer's point of view, though, the defeat was justification of the warnings he had been handing out to his players in the run up to the match.

Souness sat out the second leg with a calf strain but his desperate urgings from the touchline showed that his team's display in the Tampereen Stadium was just as big a strain on him.

In the first half, Rangers probably just had the edge and might have added to their 4-0 first-leg advantage, but one plus point was the performance of Colin Miller on his European debut. Scott Nisbet, who was just 18, was another to take to the European stage for the first time.

It was back to league business for Rangers a few days later as a capacity crowd of 29,000 watched Scotland's pre-billed match of the day at Tynecastle, although the game against Hearts turned out to be a damp squib in terms of entertainment.

Thankfully, though, the glorious sunny afternoon was graced with a piece of magic worth travelling to the capital for by thousands of Rangers fans. Davie Cooper displayed his genius at a crucial moment and grabbed a magnificent goal which earned the Ibrox men a point they were well satisfied with in the circumstances.

Rangers were minus Souness, McMinn and Derek Ferguson, while Cammy Fraser hobbled off after just four minutes and was replaced by Dougie Bell. The draw left Rangers trailing leaders Dundee United by four points with Celtic and Hearts also above the fourth-placed Light Blues.

But things were looking slightly better for Rangers the following midweek when they carved out a 1-0 win over St Mirren in Paisley. Mind you, it took a late injection of Souness sparkle to earn two very valuable points at Love Street. The player-boss had relegated himself to the subs' bench but at the end of the night had to disregard his calf injury and enter the fray.

When he joined the action in the 84th minute the game was locked at 0-0, but two minutes after his grand entrance he struck a sweet through ball into Saints' penalty area which deceived the unfortunate Tommy Wilson. Davie Cooper strode on to the pass, steadied himself and looked up before lashing a low shot past Campbell Money into the corner of the net from a tight angle.

That was enough to give the Light Blues both points, despite the earlier heroics of Money, which had looked likely to frustrate the Gers. A draw would probably have been a fair result but a touch of Souness–Cooper class at the end was enough to grab a vital win. It was Rangers' first win at Love Street for three years.

The wins just kept on coming and once again the sublime talents of Super Cooper proved the undoing of Hibs. A near-40,000 crowd saw Rangers cruise to their most comfortable Premier League win of the season – with the magical skills of Coop glistening in the October sunshine.

It really was a walk in the park and the performance never had to be anything other than just good to pick up the points. The Easter Road men were never seriously in the game and had Rangers stepped up a gear, they might have won even more handsomely. However, there could be no complaints about such a victory and the home supporters left the ground believing Souness had Rangers on course for a genuine tilt at the title.

The home side scored through McPherson, Fleck and Bell. The latter, who had replaced Souness, had worked his way back into the manager's thoughts after appearing surplus to requirements earlier in the season.

One topic of conversation that just wouldn't go away was the state of the Ibrox pitch. But far from being the butt of criticism, the playing surface had come in for some lofty praise. In fact, wing king Cooper reckoned it was just 'pitch perfect' and added considerable weight to the discussion when he declared the lush Ibrox turf as being 'better than at any other time since I joined the club'.

There were many times in the first couple of months of his tenure that Souness had expressed disappointment at the way his team had played in certain matches. It quickly became obvious just how hard it would be for his players to please him.

But on Saturday 18 October at Brockville, the manager was as satisfied as he had been since taking over the reins at Ibrox as he watched his side tear Falkirk apart with a terrific display of attacking football. The Light Blues were in stunning form and when asked for a man of the match, Souness replied, 'All of them!'

He added, 'I could single out Davie Cooper for his world-class form, Robert Fleck for his hat-trick or Chris Woods who made an amazing save when we were just 1-0 ahead, but it really was a super team display and one which sets us up very nicely for the big games against Boavista and the Skol Cup Final against Celtic. To make things even better for us, Cammy Fraser, Ted McMinn and myself are fully recovered from injury and available for selection.'

In the fourth minute, Jimmy Nicholl broke forward and played in McCoist, who slid a perfect through ball to Fleck, who turned and shot past Watson. Cooper then left two players in his wake and his cross was headed home by the on-form Fleck.

However, McCoist was then fouled in the box by Manley and Fleck was about to step up and take the kick, to try and secure his hat-trick, when the instruction came from the stand to give it to Cooper, who duly scored!

Four minutes after Manley had been sent off for a bad foul on Cooper, the winger carried out his own form of retribution with an incredible run inside the Falkirk penalty box, beating four defenders before squaring for McCoist to score.

Six minutes from time, Fleck completed his third hat-trick of the season by scoring easily from the spot after McCoist had been upended in the box by Purdie. It was a satisfactory day at the office for Souness and co, and one was given the impression that great things were just around the corner.

And one of those 'great things' arrived in the shape of the first Old Firm cup final under the watch of the new boss. Entering the Hampden showdown, Rangers had won the cup 13 times – but there was nothing like bad luck on show and goals from Durrant and Cooper ensured a party at Ibrox for the returning heroes.

It was Souness's first trophy win as boss and he said, 'It's great to win a major trophy so early on – although the pressure was such that I didn't particularly enjoy the match. But it's only a start for this club and the priority for me is still the championship – and it always will be as long as I'm in charge. We still have a long, long way to go.'

It was the fourth time Rangers had won the League Cup in six seasons, and despite being separated by a decade in terms of experience, Durrant and Cooper both showed the kind of calmness and precision in front of goal which proved enough to overcome Celtic's powerful challenge.

The Hampden showpiece turned out to be something well short of the Sunday best hoped for by both clubs. It was distinctly untidy at times and while Souness was delighted with his first major triumph as manager, he recognised that his team didn't turn in one of their better displays.

But the fact they were able to overcome a team like Celtic in such circumstances spoke volumes for the new kind of professionalism Souness had installed into the players under his command. Years of being a winner were slowly but surely being transferred over to everyone at Ibrox, and the supporters were reaping the rewards.

The 90 minutes, in which Celtic were just about the better side overall, were lifted by three examples of classic finishing – with two of them thankfully coming from Rangers. After a first half in which the closest things to goals were shots by Fraser and Mo Johnston, both of which hit the woodwork, Rangers broke the deadlock in the 63rd minute – and right in front of their own fans.

Fraser's free kick was nodded down by Butcher into the path of Durrant. He killed the ball before picking his spot past Bonner from around eight yards. The way the match had been progressing, it seemed that one goal might win it – but Celtic hit back in stunning fashion, with Brian McClair shooting home from 16 yards.

Extra time loomed until six minutes from the end when Derek Ferguson floated over a free kick. Butcher was pulled down by Roy Aitken and referee Syme pointed immediately to the spot. After furious protests from the Celtic players, Cooper stepped up to calmly drive the ball past Bonner.

The final had an unsavoury ending when Johnston was sent off for a rather unnecessary off-the-ball incident with Stuart Munro, but no one could deny Rangers the victory and it was one to savour for everyone of a light blue persuasion.

The big games were coming thick and fast and next up for Souness and Rangers was a UEFA Cup tie against Portuguese side Boavista at Ibrox.

But things didn't quite go according to plan and despite finishing the game with a narrow 2-1 win, the away goal would leave the Ibrox men walking a qualification tightrope in the return game at the Bessa Stadium.

However, there was a confident message coming out of Ibrox after the game – and Souness was adamant his side could still reach the third round. It was a well-below-par performance and the fact they had emerged from the game with any kind of victory was some form of consolation.

Souness was at great pains before the game to stress the importance of not conceding an away goal, but Rangers did make up for their lack of usual cohesion with bags of fighting spirit to equalise, and then go ahead before half-time.

One incident that had the Light Blues fuming with disbelief and annoyance came in the 71st minute when McMinn was blatantly fouled inside the area, but instead of giving a penalty, the Swedish referee gave an indirect free kick. A third goal would have given Rangers far more of an advantage ahead of the second leg in Portugal.

Boavista had taken the lead against the run of play in the 33rd minute when Brazilian striker Antonio Nelson split the Rangers defence with a low cross which Joao Tonanha slammed past Woods from 16 yards.

Within three minutes, Rangers were level. Cooper swung over a corner kick and McPherson powered home a header. However, Souness was forced to leave the field moments later with a recurrence of his calf injury.

McMinn replaced him and his first touch was a back-heel which nutmegged two Boavista players in one movement.

However, the goal that gave Rangers the lead arrived right on the stroke of half-time when an intelligent lob forward by Jimmy Nicholl beat the offside trap and Butcher headed down for McCoist to score at the second attempt, much to the delight of the 38,772 looking on.

A couple of days after the tie, Boavista coach Joao Alves launched a scathing attack on Rangers, complaining bitterly that the Light Blues had refused to let his players train on the Ibrox pitch the night before the match.

He said, 'We were directed to Tinto Park, home of Benburg (sic) Juniors, and the pitch there was of use only for planting potatoes. We will be making a protest to UEFA.'

However, the protest was certain to be dismissed by the European Union as Rangers were only working to UEFA rules, which clearly stated that a visiting team must be allowed 20 minutes of training on the home club's pitch before a game – weather permitting. As there was torrential rain the night before, Rangers were completely within their rights to keep Boavista off the Ibrox pitch to prevent any further damage.

Walter Smith said, 'This is part and parcel of European competition and you don't go making a song and dance of it.'

Teenager Derek Ferguson was enjoying an extended run in Graeme Souness's all-conquering side, and hadn't been short of people in the game to help and advise him during his fledgling career. But the 19-year-old midfielder suddenly found he was taking more stick after games from someone who had been in football for an even shorter time – his nine-year-old brother Barry.

Barry was already making his own progress as one of the star players with Mill United Boys Club under-10s and was keen to follow in his brother's footsteps and become a Rangers player.

Big brother Derek said, 'The wee man's doing well and looks like a fair player but we'll just have to wait and see. He's certainly one of my biggest fans as well as one of my biggest critics. He's Rangers daft and hates it when we lose – and naturally he takes it all out on me.'

22

Mixed Fortunes For Rangers

THE first day of November started off with a bang for the Old Firm as the great rivals served up a cracking match at Celtic Park. Both sides put in a tremendous amount of effort and the result was 90 minutes packed with entertainment and edge-of-the-seat stuff, which was a credit to the game.

Sure, there weren't too many white doves or olive branches around, but this was one of the better Old Firm matches played with plenty of pride by both sides. The troubles of the Skol Cup Final were safely consigned to the history books and the players looked like they were enjoying themselves as they moved heaven and earth to grab the win.

There was little space – or time – offered for quality front players like Davie Cooper and Ally McCoist, or Mo Johnston and Brian McClair, as defenders dominated and directed the manner in which the game was to be played, but it certainly didn't detract from the quality or effort. But no matter how much defences are on top, the game lasts an hour and a half and there is always room for a forward with a predator's eye, like McCoist, and he sniffed out a great goal for Rangers to ensure a share of the spoils.

Next up for the Light Blues was a trip to the Bessa Stadium, and the second-leg tie with Boavista. The big question on the lips of Rangers fans was whether or not Graeme Souness would be fit to take his place in the side for the crunch second-round game.

He trained at Ibrox the day after the Old Firm match to try to improve his chances of making an appearance, and after a punishing 30-minute session, Souness, who had been suffering from a calf muscle injury which needed a specialist's examination, said, 'I was reasonably pleased, but now I have to wait and see if there is any reaction.'

It was the first time he had trained since being forced off after only 37 minutes of the first game against the Portuguese, which Rangers won 2-1. Since then, in two of the three games they had played, teenager Derek Ferguson had taken his place and performed admirably, but the vast European experience of Souness would be a big boost.

Meanwhile, Ferguson, who had required a 'piggy back' out of Parkhead from team-mate McCoist because of an ankle injury, had recovered and was available for selection. And boy how he was needed. Despite the injury, young gun Fergie was leaping in the air when he scored the only goal of the match in Portugal to see Rangers safely through to the third round of the UEFA Cup. It was the kind of hurdle they had fallen at so often in the past, but an injection of steel by Souness ensured his men had the grit and determination to get through a tricky tie.

In a packed Bessa Stadium, Ferguson's marvellous 72nd-minute goal gave Rangers a well-deserved victory. The Ibrox side had reached the third round just once since winning the European Cup Winners' Cup in 1972, but marched proudly – with wins against Boavista in both legs – into the draw.

Ferguson's goal couldn't have come at a better time, for it arrived during the one stage in the game when Rangers looked rocky. A superb save from Chris Woods ten minutes before the goal had kept them in the match. Somehow he managed to touch over a rocket shot from striker Jose Augusto.

And only a minute before Rangers scored, Cammy Fraser was another defensive hero when he popped up on the line to nod away a well-placed strike from Boavista's English midfielder Phil Walker.

But on 72 minutes, Davie Cooper, an injury doubt, suddenly sprinkled his special kind of magic over the game. Like he had done so often in the past, he weaved his way past a number of defenders and almost casually stroked the ball forward to Ferguson. The teenager, who was watched by Scotland boss Andy Roxburgh, fired in a glorious right-foot shot.

The Ibrox bench, Souness and his backroom team, plus the subs, jumped up to hail the goal, but were forced to dive for cover and rush for the safety of the dug-out as they were pelted with missiles – and a police guard surrounded them for the rest of the game.

However, long before the end, the black and white flags of Boavista had been lowered, and just like their team the home fans headed for the exits. By contrast, the 1,000 Rangers fans waved their banners joyfully in a tribute to the team's marvellous achievement.

Souness said, 'It was a wonderful result, especially as we have had such a tough programme and so many injuries recently.'

But the news emanating from Ibrox the day after the victory in Portugal wasn't so good. It was announced that the influential player-manager would be missing from the team for the next month. He needed an operation on the damaged Achilles tendon which ran up to the calf muscle. It had kept him out of action for four successive games.

Meanwhile, the measure of Rangers' achievement in their 1-0 win over Boavista became even more impressive when another injury was disclosed. Derek Ferguson had been so doubtful he'd had extra strapping put on his injured leg after picking up a knock in the pre-match warm-up.

In the event, the only loss was Davie McPherson's moustache as he had promised to shave it off if they won – and the big man kept his pledge.

When the third-round draw was made Rangers were paired with German side Borussia Munchengladbach. They were drawn to play the first match away from home, before being told they would have to switch dates with the Germans. Scotland's other UEFA Cup representatives, Dundee United, were also drawn to play the first leg of their third-round tie at home against Yugoslav side Hajduk Split.

Campbell Ogilvie clarified the reason behind the switch, 'It was explained to the clubs before the draw that if there were two matches within 50km of each other there would be a change and not just a shuffle of dates to the Tuesday. The priority would go to the home side who finished ahead in their own league.'

West German team Bayer Uerdingen, who were drawn against tournament favourites Barcelona, were near neighbours of Borussia so they were given permission to play at home in the first leg while Munchengladbach were ordered to travel to Ibrox.

One of the first things Rangers did after the draw was to contact British Army top brass in West Germany to make sure soldier supporters didn't cause any bother. Rangers were keen to eliminate the risk of trouble as the last time they had played in Munchengladbach they were fined by UEFA after a fan threw a bottle on to the park.

But after the highs of European success, the Light Blues were brought crashing back to earth with a bump – courtesy of a legendary Barcelona Bear. Motherwell boss Tommy McLean brought his side to Ibrox for a league fixture; they came, defended and scampered off into the night with both points.

It was easily the most frustrating match of the season for the high-flying Gers as they fell to a sucker-punch goal three minutes from time. Call it smash-and-grab if you like, but it was a superb tactical victory for McLean – as patience was his virtue.

He deliberately set out to frustrate Rangers with a man-for-man defensive system which gave Butcher and his mates constant possession but, astonishingly, Rangers had only one effort on target in the entire match – a header from Butcher on 79 minutes.

Too often the Ibrox men dallied on the ball. Too often they were content to knock it wide when the game was crying out for the incisive one-touch pass forward. Well sucked them into their web of defence and on the only occasion they looked like scoring – they did. John Reilly pushed the ball out to the hard-working Andy Walker with the Rangers defence looking sluggish. Through the middle ran Ray Farningham and when

Walker's cross came over, he headed the ball out of the reach of Woods and into the net.

For the first time in months there was a chorus of boos from the Ibrox terracing, but the bitter lesson for Rangers, badly missing the midfield influence and tenacity of Souness, was that possession football is only useful with penetrating passes.

But while McLean exposed the fact that Rangers weren't yet invincible, he did reveal that his side had been hit by a sickness virus prior to the game – hence the need for 'parking the bus'. But he apologised for styling his team so unattractively, while Rangers' assistant boss Walter Smith seethed about his team's inability to cope and remain unbeaten for a 13th successive game.

McLean said, 'I don't suppose we made many friends with the way we had to play. Steve Kirk had to be sent home and three others who played were also troubled by the virus. So we simply had to be cautious. There was no other way and I know it didn't help the entertainment.'

Rangers had full control of the match but simply didn't make it happen on the day, which led Smith to say, 'We will need to work on this – and fast. It's happened to us before when we met a side set out so defensively. This was the kind of match in which we should have been going round defenders on the outside and getting the ball in behind them. Too much is being left to Davie Cooper and Ted McMinn. It will be sorted out.'

Six weeks after suffering a horror injury at East Fife, Gers hitman Colin West, the forgotten face of Ibrox, was on his way back. While fellow countrymen Butcher and Woods had been enjoying the fruits of the Rangers revival, West had endured a long slog back to fitness, courtesy of the FA and its state-of-the-art rehabilitation centre at Lilleshall, near Shrewsbury.

It was back in August that West's world had crashed around him just 12 minutes into the Skol Cup tie at East Fife. A ferocious tackle saw him limp off with damaged knee ligaments followed by an op and the long haul back. The injury to the ligaments in the right knee put him in plaster for several weeks before his three-week stint at Lilleshall.

But he said, 'I'm having a couple of days' break over the weekend with my family and in-laws at Whitley Bay. I'll be back in at Ibrox on Monday morning and once I get the all-clear from the doctors, the hard work will begin again. I've got a lot of catching up to do but hope to be challenging for a place by the start of December.'

It was the 'English' connection of Souness, physio Phil Boersma and coach Donald Mackay who had come up with the idea of Lilleshall. Mackay said, 'The treatment is expensive but first class, and if at the end of the day we get a fully fit Colin back in business two or three weeks ahead of schedule, then it has been worth every penny.'

For 23-year-old West it had meant a combination of a luxury country club tucked away in the heart of the English countryside, combined with the kind of regime that would do credit to Colditz!

He smiled, 'The place is under the control of head physio Graham Smith and when he says jump, that's exactly what you do – injury permitting, of course. Life consists of a round of swimming, running, weight training, circuits, massage and gymnastics. I'm considering entering for the next Olympics!'

West, who had played just six matches and scored two goals before the injury blow, suddenly found himself down the pecking order for a jersey, behind the likes of McCoist, Robert Fleck and McMinn.

And there was more good news for Rangers supporters when Souness shelled out around £150,000 for Israel skipper Avi Cohen. He had finally got his man four months after first trying to sign the experienced defender. Cohen played in pre-season matches against Spurs and Bayern Munich and talks went on with Souness keen to sign him, but Rangers and Maccabi, Cohen's Israeli club, could not agree on a fee.

However the deadlock was finally broken and, as a result, Rangers took their spending for the year to around the £2m mark. Souness and Smith had earlier taken a secret flight to Israel with the Rangers manager later appearing on television in Tel Aviv.

One Wednesday in November, David Holmes became indisputably the most powerful man in Scottish football when he was appointed chairman of Rangers – to go with his title as chief executive. His elevation to the Ibrox chair – albeit accepted with great reluctance – was announced after a quick board meeting.

Four hours earlier, John Paton, 62, had quit as Rangers chairman – and also of Taggarts, the car sales company which was a subsidiary of the John Lawrence Group. Holmes insisted Paton's resignation came 'out of the blue'. But Paton admitted he had spoken to Marlborough when he was in Glasgow on a flying visit from America the previous week.

Paton, a lifelong Rangers fan, said he was about to become involved in a new family business and wanted to lend his full weight to it. 'The parting was amicable,' he added. 'We're still friends. David Holmes walked with me down the marble stairway and said he was sorry I was going.'

Paton's departure left Holmes as chairman and chief executive, and Jack Gillespie as vice-chairman, along with directors Freddie Fletcher and Hugh Adam.

Holmes said, 'With the help of the gentlemen around me we'll continue the job at Ibrox which was started nearly a year ago. There are no plans to add to the board.'

It was indeed exactly a year to the day since the Rangers board of directors had received a new addition with the appointment of David Holmes, and 12 months on, he had completely transformed the fortunes of the Ibrox club and dragged them into the 20th century.

The achievements and changes had been remarkable with huge crowds following Rangers all over the country – and Souness leading the Light Blues into a thrilling new era.

Mr Holmes said, 'The last year has just flashed past and it has been the most exciting and at the same time most traumatic of my life. It has been a completely new experience for me and has added a whole new dimension to all the other tasks my job involves.

'There can be times in any job when you start to take things for granted and I was in that kind of rut – but taking on the challenge Rangers presented has brought a spark back into everything I do.

'But that challenge has hardly even started and there is still a lot of work to be done. The challenge fascinates me and I'll be more interested to look back on what we have achieved a further year from now.'

And the day after his appointment, Holmes awoke to read that he had become Scottish football's most influential figure. 'It just confirmed what I had feared when I accepted the chairman's role – that I would be left exposed and with even less privacy than I have had.

'I was, to be truthful, reluctant to become chairman but it's a great honour and I couldn't turn it down. I have to lead from the front to achieve the ambitions this club now has. I am not the most powerful man in Scottish football, I don't think I am and that is where it starts and ends.

'I am not participating in the game anywhere outside Rangers. Football for me is all about Rangers Football Club. That in itself can benefit the Scottish game as a whole, of course, and I want to see the game flourish here.

'Power is something I'm just not interested in. Yes, I want to be attached to success and be a top businessman, but that's it. Power can be a destructive thing and I am trying to create something with Rangers. The intrusion into my private life over the past year is something I have been forced to accept but it's something I could've done without. I am giving 100 per cent to Rangers and I will live with whatever is or isn't achieved.

'Rangers get my time as a person but as a businessman my priority is for all UK operations of the Lawrence Group and that involves the building and motor side. Eventually I would like to step out of the limelight and let Graeme Souness and Walter Smith be more in the public eye – but right now the priority for them is to get the right team on the park.'

And Holmes insisted Rangers had never tried to buy success, claiming they didn't have to. He explained, 'The first thing any business needs is a backbone. Rangers didn't have it and by bringing in Woods, Butcher, Souness and West the spine of the side was there. That was money well spent but in itself it hasn't changed the team. It has made lads like McPherson, Durrant and Munro all different players and the Skol Cup win has been an early justification.

'But the team is still being assembled and while the cup win was great for the fans and nice for the players, we have to temper our happiness with a responsible outlook. The team must sustain a high level of performance and achieve the kind of consistency necessary to win the Premier League. Nothing less will be satisfactory. Progress is being made but the Motherwell game showed we still have a lot to learn. If Graeme wants to bring more quality players to the club, the money is there for him. In recent years, teams were coming to Ibrox with the attitude that they were going to whip Rangers – now they sit back and do everything to avoid getting whipped.

'The Boavista match in Portugal was a big bonus for the club as will be anything we achieve in Europe this season. But it was certainly a great sight to see Rangers dominating a match away from home in a European tie.

'And the match against Munchengladbach will be another new experience for our players and education is a great thing no matter what you do. Win or lose this tie, Rangers will still be winners.'

But Holmes also insisted there was an important role at the club for its supporters, and said, 'I want Rangers to be a team with a million players. The supporters are as much a part of this club as the employees and that's the way I want it to stay.

'It's my ambition to stay in touch with the punters and in no way will I be aloof from them. I have had nothing but support and encouragement from them all along and I greatly appreciate it. I made a point of talking to the fans in Finland and Portugal this season after our matches. They were a credit to Rangers and I hope those that go to Germany will be similarly good ambassadors.

'We are re-educating the fans, too, and they are taking it very well. Their patience has been amazing and that Skol Cup win was for them more than anyone else. They are what the club is all about and that's why a year from now I want Rangers to be more influential in the top echelons of football.'

Midway through November, Ally McCoist travelled to Paris for one of Europe's top sporting ceremonies, *France Football*'s Golden Boot awards. It had been a busy couple of days for McCoist, as he had come on as a substitute during Scotland's European Championship clash with Luxembourg at Hampden – before jetting out to the continent for the prestigious ceremony.

He was in Paris to collect his prize for being the Premier League's top scorer in the 1985/86 season with 24 goals, but he would go on to win the main prize – the Golden Boot – in 1992 and 1993, the first Scot to win the coveted award.

Also at the Paris ceremony was Diego Maradona and West German keeper Harald Schumacher. Maradona was awarded the Golden Ball for the best player in the World Cup, and runner-up Schumacher got the Silver Ball.

As McCoist was heading home from the French capital, a new face was checking in to Ibrox. And if the Cheshire Cat had been at the stadium, he would have looked positively grumpy compared to Lyndsay Hamilton.

The 24-year-old goalkeeper, signed for £25,000 from Stenhousemuir, was taking part in his first training session with Rangers and was clearly loving every minute. The following day, Hamilton was back at his work with British Steel in Bellshill where his friends gave him a rousing send-off on his final day after seven years in the job.

He said, 'It's a little sad to leave so many friends behind but I just can't believe my luck in being signed by Rangers. Full-time football has always been my ambition and there have been times when I wondered if I would ever achieve it. It could hardly have happened with a bigger or better club.'

Hamilton's career had seen him on the verge of making the big time on several occasions and the way he arrived at Ibrox was somewhat ironic.

After leaving school, the 6ft 2in keeper played in junior football for two years with Thorniewood United before Stenhousemuir snapped him up in 1982. Rangers were among several senior clubs watching his progress in the junior ranks, with St Mirren and Falkirk also interested, but the Larbert side were the only ones to make a concrete offer and Lyndsay went to Ochilview.

At the end of the 1985/86 campaign he took advantage of freedom of contract to put himself in the shop window but was alarmed when no one came in for him.

He said, 'It was worrying and at that stage I wondered if I would ever get to the top. Then Hearts came in for me last season and I seemed set to sign for them. I was all ready to put pen to paper but the deal broke down between the clubs and I was back to square one again.'

The close season had seen Rangers lose goalkeeper Andy Bruce on a free transfer to Hearts and with Nicky Walker asking for a move, it meant Souness needed cover for Chris Woods.

Goalkeeping coach Peter McCloy said, 'I watched Lyndsay four times and he has the right material for us to work on at the training ground. It will take me a month or so to get him to the level of fitness required by a keeper at the top level – and if he doesn't shape up, I'll just have to make another comeback!'

Ironically, Hamilton was set to make his first appearance in a Rangers jersey at Tynecastle, while at the opposite end in the Hearts reserve-team goal would be Bruce.

Hamilton said, 'It's a whole new world coming from Stenhousemuir to Rangers but I'm confident I can make the transition after lots of hard work. It's going to be marvellous – I've got a two-year contract and I intend to make the most of it.'

Meanwhile, Rangers made Clydebank pay heavily for seven days of frustration. All week the Ibrox men had been desperate to get the defeat by Motherwell out of their systems, to the point that you could almost sense the players straining at the leash as they waited for the referee to start the game.

And just eight minutes in, a double from McCoist had Rangers two ahead, and it was a case of some clinical execution ensuring there would be only one winner. Rangers added another couple before the break but the goals dried up in the second half and it was job done before the players stepped down the gears.

But the poor Bankies didn't know what had hit them in the opening period. McCoist should have had another three after the break, and Fleck a couple, while Cammy Fraser was the man of the match.

And there was more positive news when it was revealed that Souness was to have his leg plaster taken off after a successful operation. He was expecting to begin light training the week after, and was aiming to be fit for the Euro match against Borussia Munchengladbach on 3 December.

And Colin West was also one step closer to a top-team return – after being out of action for three months with severe ligament injuries. He watched Rangers thump Clydebank – only the second time he had seen the team in three months – and said, 'This is really my big test over the next few days.

'I'll be playing in my first practice game and hopefully a reserve match on Saturday. It was a bad injury, but I never thought it would have any permanent effect on my career. I've just been too busy trying to get fit again.'

But while Rangers were working hard to clear the decks in the Ibrox treatment room, arguably their finest player was making noises aimed at reducing the number of walking wounded heading for the physio in the first place. Davie Cooper spoke about the season's tough fixture list as the Premier League lined up for yet another midweek card in the intense 44-game schedule. Coop said, 'Part of the reason for Rangers' continuous matches is our success in Europe and obviously I'm not complaining about that, but the programme is so heavy just now there is no time for players to recover from injuries. If you get a knock on a Wednesday it obviously cuts down the time to recover by Saturday.

'That's why every top team has had three or four players injured at the same time and sometimes it can lead to strange results. It's something the authorities are going to have to look at closely. The demands on top players are very heavy this season, especially those playing for Scotland as well.'

He added, 'I'm sure Graeme Souness played only half the number of games in Italy compared to a top name in Scotland during the current season.'

And in their latest midweek fixture, Rangers ran up against another version of the 'Ibrox Wall' – although this time they managed to dislodge a brick or two and grab the win. But if the eventual 2-1 win over Dundee was late, it was no less welcome after the Light Blues had emerged empty-handed from a similar contest against Motherwell ten days previous.

After the match, Souness insisted his men would have to learn quickly how to cope with sides playing defensively when they came to Ibrox. It was sound advice because with very few exceptions, Rangers would find themselves up against defensive tactics more or less every time they were at home.

To their credit, though, they were wholly persistent in their efforts to overcome a Dundee side who had clearly left their attacking boots at home. Woods was all but a spectator and Rangers were miles ahead, and should have won by a bigger margin.

McCoist was a constant threat to the Dark Blues' defence but he certainly wouldn't have been applying for membership of the Bill Crombie fan club in a hurry. The Edinburgh ref was less than sympathetic to the rough treatment handed out to McCoist and the Rangers striker could hardly believe it when, in the 19th minute, no penalty was awarded when Jim Smith tripped him from behind as he was set to score.

Another penalty claim was knocked back when Jim Duffy appeared to foul Dougie Bell, but Crombie eventually pointed to the spot in the 39th minute when McCoist was brought down by Ian Angus – but it certainly wasn't a case of third time lucky as Cooper's spot kick, hit well enough, was saved by Bobby Geddes.

Happily, Rangers made the breakthrough a minute before half-time when McCoist was rewarded for his hard work with a goal. Fraser's free kick deceived the Dundee defence and Terry Butcher nodded on for McCoist to slam home his 16th of the season.

But eight minutes from time, Ian Angus sent Ross Jack clear and his cross was smashed past Woods by Rab Shannon. It was hard to take but Rangers simply resumed on the attack and after McPherson had hit the post, the well-deserved winning goal arrived.

Rangers' outstanding player, Jimmy Nicholl, found McPherson with a great through ball and with the subtlety of a top striker, the big defender turned and fired in a 20-yard shot which flew past Geddes. It was no more than Rangers – and their 22,000 fans – deserved.

But Rangers – and Souness – were left seeing red a couple of days later when they travelled up to Pittodrie to play Aberdeen. The Ibrox player-manager was greatly disappointed by the way his team performed against Aberdeen and the dismissal right on half-time of McPherson didn't help.

McPherson, who was enjoying a first-class season, blotted his copybook when ref Tommy Muirhead showed him the red card for an off-the-ball incident with Davie Dodds, who had chosen to join the Dons over Rangers. McPherson had earlier been booked for a foul on Dodds but this was never an over-physical game with Alex McLeish and Dougie Bell cautioned for fouls which might have gone unpunished in matches between other clubs.

Ironically, Rangers looked the more likely to take something from the match when they were reduced to ten men and were often the more dangerous of the two. By that time, though, the damage had been done in the space of just seven first-half minutes.

First of all, Rangers were denied a penalty kick when, following a terrific run which took him into the heart of the Dons' penalty area, Davie Cooper was fouled by Stewart McKimmie. The ref waved play on and in the 19th minute Aberdeen scored what turned out to be the only goal of the game. Fraser, one of Rangers' better players, was woefully short with a pass back to Woods and John Hewitt pounced on the loose ball. Woods did well to block his shot but as the ball spun in the air, Dodds bundled it over the line.

And there was more disappointment in store for Souness and his players when they failed to beat Borussia Munchengladbach at Ibrox in the third round of the UEFA Cup. The Light Blues left themselves a mountain to climb in the return in Germany. Mind you, they had come up against supremely well-organised opponents and so nearly got the kind of result which would have given them a better chance in the second leg.

However, the goal scored by the Bundesliga men right on the stroke of half-time at a packed Ibrox was a deadly blow. Rangers had done everything right up until that point, taking the game to the Germans and enjoying so much possession that Woods was a virtual spectator.

A 14th-minute goal from Ian Durrant, the player with an uncanny knack of hitting the target on the big occasion, had set the Light Blues up for the kind of result they craved. However, the threat of Uwe Rahn, subdued for the rest of the 90 minutes by the impressive McPherson, was enough to ensure that Rangers were forced to settle for a draw.

Losing the goal was a bitter blow for Gers after all their good work in the first half, highlighted by Durrant's strike. A superb six-man move started on the right with the ball moving sweetly from Nicholl to Cooper and then to Fraser, who spread it out to Munro. The full-back's fine through ball was flicked on by McCoist, and Durrant ran on to smash a rising left-foot shot past Kamps, which went in off the underside of the bar.

But there was better news on the final weekend of the month when Rangers signalled their clear intention of catching up with Celtic at the top of the Premier League. They turned on the style at Ibrox and were much too good for a surprisingly weak-willed Hearts side, eventually triumphing 3-0.

The result was never in doubt and Souness's men could have won the match by a clear six or seven goals, such was their superiority. It was a pleasing afternoon for more than just the two points, as two players missing from the first-team scene for some time returned to action and did very well.

Hugh Burns, playing in midfield, had a tremendous first half, while Craig Paterson kept Sandy Clark quiet all afternoon. Sadly, though, a small section of the massive Rangers support took it upon themselves to boo Paterson every time he touched the ball. It was grossly undeserved and the kind of behaviour that the club – and player – could have done without.

That, though, was the only sour point in a fine afternoon's work by Rangers in which a certain Mr Cooper reminded us once again of his very special talent. He constantly teased and tormented the Hearts defence, taking one goal brilliantly and setting up another in equally stylish fashion.

The opening goal arrived in the 18th minute when Fleck played in McCoist and the potent goalscorer first-timed it past Henry Smith. It was McCoist's 17th of the season and ten minutes from half-time came Rangers' second of the day. McCoist and Burns combined to set Cooper off on a run. He bemused Whittaker and Berry, before leaving Smith equally bewildered as he drove the ball low through the keeper's legs and into the net.

Fleck hit the woodwork twice in the second half although a third goal did arrive when Durrant scored with six minutes to go. It was a fitting end to something of a roller-coaster month, but it had nothing on December, which would see the Light Blues emerge unbeaten, with the only blot on the landscape an unfortunate exit from Europe.

Jock Wallace and Alex Totten were in charge until April, 1986

Rangers' main goal threat Ally McCoist in action

Cammy Fraser took a bit of time to settle at Ibrox

John 'Bomber' Brown enjoyed a good record against Rangers while at Dundee

Ian Ferguson scored the Scottish Cup winner for St Mirren

John MacDonald bagged over 100 goals for the Light Blues

Bobby Russell was one of the classiest players at Ibrox

Aberdeen and Rangers players square up to one another

Ally Dawson achieved so much at Rangers

Hugh Burns can't hide his delight at scoring for the Gers

Manager Jock Wallace with new signing Dougie Bell

Skipper Craig Paterson shows off the League Cup

Peter McCloy in action, as Alex Miller looks on

John Spencer – pictured with Ally McCoist – came through the Ibrox ranks

Ted McMinn runs the Dundee United defence ragged

*David
Holmes was
hard at work
long before
Graeme
Souness
arrived at
Ibrox*

*New boss
in town –
Graeme
Souness with
the Rangers
directors*

Graeme Souness – the shirt fits!

The opening day match against Hibs didn't quite go according to plan!

Robert Fleck was given a second chance by Graeme Souness

Scott Nisbet in action against Dundee – and future Ger Cammy Fraser!

Ally Dawson and Graeme Souness enjoy a few laps of the track

David Holmes
and director
Freddie Fletcher,
right, beside a
painting of John
Lawrence

Derek Ferguson
and Ian Durrant
were 'capped' for
Scotland under-21s

Souness gets his man – World Cup star Terry Butcher

Ally McCoist tries his luck against Hibs

The Rangers players celebrate another goal

The English connection – Terry McButcher and Chris McWoods!

Derek Ferguson and Robert Fleck in action for the Light Blues

Graeme Souness celebrates with Colin West

Colin West and Ally McCoist – together again at Rangers

Chris Woods pictured with Davie Cooper

Former vice-chairman of Rangers Donald Findlay

Cammy Fraser, Chris Woods and Ally Dawson celebrate winning the League Cup

David Holmes promised the supporters silverware – and he delivered

Ted McMinn and Colin West relax off the park

Alex Totten and Davie Cooper show off individual trophies

Graeme Souness delivered Graham Roberts to Gers supporters at Christmas

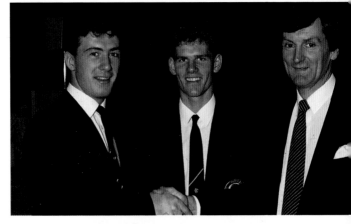

Derek Ferguson and Ian Durrant with Scotland under-21 boss Andy Roxburgh

Graeme Souness didn't so much walk, as strut!

Walter Smith, Phil Boersma and Graeme Souness have a secret pow-wow on the Ibrox turf

23

Scott Nisbet

F ANS' favourite Scott Nisbet absolutely loved his time at Rangers and insists he was very fortunate to play under so many club legends; managers such as John Greig, Jock Wallace, Graeme Souness and Walter Smith.

The downside to his Ibrox career, if there is one, is that it hit the skids far too soon, at the age of 25, just as he was holding down a regular first-team place – but the forward-turned-defender said he has no regrets.

Nisbet won four league titles and two Scottish Cups while a Ranger and also enjoyed playing in the Champions League, with his 'fortuitous' goal against Bruges at Ibrox one that many supporters will never forget.

But his journey to the promised land of Edmiston Drive started many years beforehand, on the mean streets of a tough Edinburgh housing scheme, as he explained, 'John Greig signed me initially and he was fantastic, but I will never forget the day he came to my house with Davie Provan, another ex-Ranger, to speak to me about joining Rangers.

'I lived in Muirhouse at the time, which was one of the toughest schemes in the capital. It certainly wasn't the best place for a beautiful Jaguar car to turn up unannounced! Mind you, everyone was out in the street playing football after school and couldn't believe it when John Greig stepped out of this flashy car.

'It was 1982 and I was just into my teens. John Greig was a huge name throughout the country, as he had played for

Rangers and Scotland for years. Everyone knew who he was – but I was probably the only one who knew WHY he was there. The moment I saw him I completely bottled it and ran away. He was there for talks with me and my mum but I didn't actually get to speak to him. I got off my mark and left mum to deal with everything. She apparently waited on me for ages to come in, and when I didn't, she sorted everything out and signed the papers.

'But she said he was a lovely guy and when I eventually plucked up the courage to speak to him he couldn't have been nicer. What I also liked about him was the way he treated my mum with the utmost respect. I was gutted when he left Rangers, but thankfully Jock Wallace took over, and he was also a joy to work for.'

As a promising and talented youngster, Nisbet knuckled down and worked hard. He was a prolific centre-forward with a real eye for goal, and those in the know were tipping him to achieve big things in the game.

But his apprenticeship was still in full swing when he received the biggest shock of his young life one morning. He explained, 'I will never forget the day the club announced we were going over to Malta to play a couple of games. We were out of the Scottish Cup and had a free week, and the gaffer decided to make the most of it.

'When the sheet of paper went up on the notice board with the names of those making the trip, I couldn't believe my name was on it. I was only 16 years of age at the time, so it was a big deal for me, and I was so excited.

'On the morning of the game against Hibernians of Malta, we were all relaxing by the pool when big Jock [Wallace] suddenly appeared on one of the balconies upstairs and shouted, "Nisbet, up in my room, now!"

'Right away, all the other players started ribbing me and saying I was in big trouble. I'll be honest, I was a bag of nerves as I made my way up the stairs. I stood outside the door, plucked up the courage to go in and knocked before entering. Standing there was Jock and two of the directors, Mr Dawson and Mr

Gillespie. I asked what was up, and Jock said, "You better phone your mum, son."

'I panicked and asked what was wrong. "Nothing," came the reply. "Just tell her you're making your debut for Glasgow Rangers tonight." It was an unbelievable moment and I just sat there for a few moments, drinking it all in. I was about to make my Rangers debut!

'I had grown a few feet taller by the time we arrived at the Hibernians ground and I couldn't wait to get out there. It was an incredible feeling and I even scored a couple of goals to mark the occasion. I also played in our second tour game, and scored in that one as well, so it was a great start for me.

'When we got back to Scotland, I made my competitive debut against Hibs, and I managed to score in that as well, so the whole thing completely blew me away. I had started out as a centre-forward and was so happy that big Jock had given me my debut for the club, so you can imagine how disappointed I was when he eventually left the club.

'John Greig and Jock Wallace were genuine legends, so to have worked under both of these guys was something else, but now it was time for me to start impressing a new manager all over again.'

Graeme Souness replaced Wallace – but Nisbet admitted he had a rather bizarre way of finding out when something important was going down on Edmiston Drive.

He explained, 'The big change happened and the club brought Graeme Souness in. It was strange the way it all came about, though. We had a commissionaire called Stan, who used to work at the front door at Ibrox, and he would normally be dressed smartly in a shirt and black trousers, but when he had his full commissionaire's outfit on you knew something big was in the offing – and he had the full uniform on the day Souness arrived. That was how I found out.

'But I got on well with Souness although like everyone else, I had my barneys with him. He was just a young manager as well and that was the way he operated. He was good with me though, and I'll never forget the day he told me he wanted a word about a reserve game in Dundee, and asked me to play because the second team was short of bodies. I had no problem with it at all, but he asked me to play centre-half, which wasn't my usual position, but I agreed and off we went.

'Even though I say so myself, I had one of my best games ever. I knew that when the gaffer walked into the dressing room after the game, although he never actually said as much. Mind you, he did turn to me and say, "That's it Nissy, you will never play centre-forward again. From now on, you're a centre-half." And that was it.

'That was the moment I knew I'd had a good game – and I never did play up front again. From then on in I was either a centre-half or a right-back, and that was just fine by me. I would have played anywhere for Rangers.

'Souness also put me out on loan for a short spell to East Fife because he wanted to toughen me up, so I played a couple of games there. It was probably the best thing for me at the time. I enjoyed it but it also toughened me up like he had initially said it would.'

But Nisbet reckons that as long as he lives, he will never forget the player-manager's competitive debut, against Hibs at Easter Road. It was the stuff of legend, and nightmares, as he soon found himself alone in the dressing room with Souness – just seconds after the gaffer had been sent off.

He explained, 'That is one memory I'm sure will live with me forever. I was in the squad that day but it was the time when you were only allowed to name two substitutes, and I was like the 14th man so I didn't get stripped. There was the big fight on the pitch and the gaffer got sent off. He was walking up the tunnel and Walter Smith turned to me and said, "Nissy, go and make sure the gaffer is okay."

'So I walked up to the changing room and waited for a moment before opening the door and going in. He was absolutely furious and was shouting and bawling and throwing his strip and shin pads about, but he stopped when I entered the room. He gave me that Souness look and said, "Nissy, what do you think, front page or back page tomorrow?" I said to him straight away,

"Gaffer, I reckon it will be on BOTH!" He looked at me and gave me a wry smirk.

'On the Sunday morning I went down to get the papers and sure enough, he got absolutely slaughtered on both the front and back. It was in every paper – they were all full of the goings-on at Easter Road.'

But despite this 'close encounter', Nisbet was delighted with the appointment of Souness and reckons the Scotland star was just the man Rangers needed in their hour of need.

He said, 'At the time, Souness coming in was fantastic for Rangers, because the club was a sleeping giant and was in the doldrums. It was a bit like where Rangers have been recently. It was, and still is, an absolute disgrace. A massive stadium and a massive worldwide support. Rangers are up there with the top clubs in Britain so it has been tough to see them struggle.

'I was still there when Souness left the club, and Walter Smith took over. He was also a fantastic manager to play under. He was brilliant for me and for Rangers. But I will always remember when Souness left to take over at Liverpool and Walter was left to try and guide the team to the league title. There was only a few weeks left of the season and it soon came down to the last match of the campaign against Aberdeen at Ibrox to see if we could win the league.

'We had a depleted squad and John Brown took an injection to help him through the match. I remember during the game he went to clear a ball, and you could actually hear his Achilles snap, and down went Bomber in mortal agony. As he was lying there, Phil Boersma, our physio, ran on to the park to treat him. Mark Walters then trotted over to Phil and said to him calmly, "Phil, you'll need to take me off, I think I've pulled my hamstring." Bomber, who had just snapped his Achilles, looked at Mark, and said, "Are you taking the fucking piss Mark?" Bomber ended up getting stretchered off, and Tom Cowan broke his leg, it was a horrendous day for injuries – but we won the game and the title.'

Nisbet added, 'Before that game, Mark Hateley had pulled me aside and said, "Launch the ball into the box as high as you can and I'll give the Aberdeen keeper Michael Watt a wee reminder of just how important today's game is" – and he done exactly that. It was one of the best tactics of the day – and the remainder of nine in a row was history!'

But sadly for Nisbet, a cruel twist of fate decreed that his career would end prematurely. It was a dreadful blow for the young player who simply loved being a Ranger.

He recalled, 'The bottom line is I had a bad hip and groin injury and that was that for me, but I have absolutely no regrets because I had a great time with Rangers. That was the year we went 44 games undefeated and reached what was effectively the semi-finals of the Champions League. We were only allowed three foreign players at the time and the rest had to be home-grown.

'But I've always been a great believer that the Champions League should only be for the teams who win their respective leagues, so for me that season was the genuine Champions League. Not teams that come second, third or fourth. Champions League should mean what it says on the tin.

'That year, though, we were only a whisker away from being kings of Europe, which would have been a remarkable feat. We went through that campaign and never lost a game, and then it transpired that eventual winners Marseille were stripped of their title for cheating. That was such a hard one to take, knowing we had gone so close.'

But despite his cruel luck with injuries, Nisbet put his experience to good use and jetted out to the Canary Islands to carve out a new career.

He explained, 'I started a soccer school in Lanzarote – and it has been very successful – but when I get back home I always try and get to a game at Ibrox. I love going back there and seeing the team and all the old faces. Thankfully, though, the soccer school has been going really well for me and I've now been running it for more than a decade.

'In 2015 it was voted one of the top ten sporting activities in the world by the *Sunday Times*. We were voted into sixth place and were right up there beside Venus Williams's tennis academy in Barbados, so that was an amazing achievement and something I am very proud of.

'In the first ten years we had around 11,000 kids taking part. It's something I am thoroughly enjoying and to be up there with Venus Williams is something special. But playing for Rangers was also something very special, and it's a part of my life that I will always cherish.'

24

Euro Heartache
For Gers

RANGERS went into their home match with St Mirren at the beginning of December trailing league leaders Celtic by nine points, but with the Parkhead men treading dangerous ground at Tynecastle there was a good chance of that total being reduced by the end of the Wednesday night.

And that proved to be the case as Rangers duly collected a couple of vital point thanks to a 2-0 win – and Celtic lost by the only goal in the capital. It was a minor turning point in the season.

But this was definitely a game which tested the patience of the 23,110 crowd – for Rangers really only played in fits and starts. As it happened, the starts eventually fitted – just before and after half-time – when Rangers grabbed the two goals that mattered.

On 33 minutes, Davie McPherson, back in the side following suspension, headed the opening goal from a Davie Cooper free kick. And on 53 Rangers were two up with Cooper again the architect. This time his wicked cross was turned past Campbell Money and into his own goal by young Saints midfielder Ian Ferguson.

A few days later, Graeme Souness announced he would make his comeback before a handful of fans on a Monday night at Dumbarton's less-than-fashionable Boghead. Walter Smith confirmed the game had been arranged with Souness – and Borussia Munchengladbach – specifically in mind.

Smith said, 'That's not to say he will definitely play from the start, but we're hopeful Graeme will be involved at some stage.'

Souness's last appearance came against Boavista, when he made a self-confessed mistake by turning out and aggravating his calf injury. In fact, since joining Rangers, Souness had played only six of 22 matches.

But the gaffer was presented with an unforeseen problem when he awoke to discover that two of his first-team players had been arrested after a late-night brawl and alleged assault in East Kilbride town centre.

Ian Durrant and Ally McCoist were the players being questioned in East Kilbride police office, and Strathclyde Police confirmed a report had been sent to the Procurator Fiscal. Durrant, 20, and 24-year-old McCoist were released pending a possible appearance in court at a later date. The investigation started after a youth aged 18, who had not been named, alleged he was attacked in the early hours of the Friday morning.

George Moore, present when the players were interviewed, said, 'Both have been charged, but I can't give details. They deny the charges.' A few days later, police refused to confirm reports that a third Rangers player – Ted McMinn – was to be interviewed over the same incident.

Almost a year later, in September 1987, McCoist was convicted of assault and fined £150 at Hamilton Sheriff Court. A verdict of not proven was returned against McMinn and Durrant, although it was later reported that McCoist and Durrant were each fined £1,500 by Rangers.

Meanwhile, Souness announced a same-again line-up for the clash against Hibs at Easter Road – because they had no players left to make changes. Revealing the massive injury list, Walter Smith said, 'We are down to the bare bones. We have only 13 fit players with first-team experience. Seven others are sidelined at the moment.'

It also meant a giant headache for Souness and Smith ahead of the second leg of the UEFA Cup tie in Germany the following

Wednesday night. Monday's pre-arranged friendly game against Dumbarton was also rated doubtful, and Smith said, 'If Graeme doesn't play before we leave for Germany it's most unlikely he will be in the team over there.'

Rangers were in action at Easter Road, and while they drew a blank, they still managed to come away with a point. In fact, two spectacular saves from Chris Woods denied recently-installed Hibs manager Alex Miller the perfect start to his new job.

Rangers, looking for a good performance ahead of Munchengladbach, struggled throughout. They lacked quality, control and co-ordination in the attacking areas and in the end survived only because of the ability of the stylish England keeper.

After picking up a point at Easter Road, all thoughts switched to Europe, and the second-leg tie in Munchengladbach. Rangers had asked their fans not to travel, but around 2,000 were still determined to 'follow follow' their favourites to the Bokelberg Stadium. It was the third time in the season that Gers bosses had urged their fans not to follow them to the continent, and on the previous two occasions, supporters had been warmly welcomed in Finland and Portugal. However, the club was still determined to go to any lengths to ensure there was no trouble. Secretary Campbell Ogilvie flew to Munchengladbach with SFA security adviser Alistair Hood and returned with some very firm dos and don'ts for the travelling support.

Ogilvie said, 'We had discussions with the local police, the Munchengladbach chairman and the liaising officer for the British Consul in Dusseldorf. Everyone at the club was very proud of the good conduct displayed by our fans in Finland and Portugal and we would like to see their reputation enhanced even further in Germany.'

Hood added, 'The police in West Germany are very tough, professional and firm. They will not tolerate misconduct in any shape or form. If the fans follow the guidelines we have issued them with, there should be no trouble at all.'

The main points were, 'No drunkenness will be tolerated and fans will not be allowed to disembark from ferries or leave aircraft in a state of drunkenness,' and, 'Supporters will be searched entering the stadium – and will not be allowed to carry alcohol inside, or fireworks, metal poles, or offensive weapons.'

Whether it was simply rhetoric designed to scare fans into behaving in Germany, or the Rangers board ticking boxes in an exercise, was unclear, but the reality was that following your team abroad wasn't always as easy as ABC, and check boxes weren't always followed by foreign police officers, much to the chagrin of good-natured and enthusiastic fans.

Military police were on red alert for Rangers' visit to Germany. About 800 soldiers were expected at the match to support the Gers, and the redcaps were given permission to patrol the stadium.

There were three Scottish regiments serving in Germany at the time – the Gordon Highlanders, the Royal Scots and the Royal Scots Dragoon Guards, and an Army spokesman said, 'We will assist the German civil police in the event of any trouble. Because all the fans will be in civilian clothes there could be identification problems. We will only be called in if the local police want our help.'

The previous time Rangers had played in Munchengladbach, in 1973, the club was fined £4,000 after a bottle was thrown on to the pitch, and drunken squaddies were blamed for the incident.

Before heading off to the continent, though, Souness made a valiant attempt to bring Tottenham's experienced defender Graham Roberts to Ibrox. He made the London club an offer for the 27-year-old but the figure was deemed unacceptable by Spurs boss David Pleat.

Souness said, 'We made what we feel was a more than adequate offer for the player and we will not be improving on it.'

So it appeared Spurs would have to lower their £500,000 valuation if the player was to join Rangers.

Meanwhile, Roberts said, 'It's tremendous that a club like Rangers want me and I would have no hesitation in going to play in Scotland.'

On the week of the Euro match, the *Daily Record*'s Alex Cameron decided the time was right for a mid-term report, which he 'addressed' to club owner Lawrence Marlborough.

It read… 'Dear Lawrence, Graeme Souness has just reached the halfway stage in his first Premier League race, but Rangers – eight points behind Celtic – are far from favourites to be first. Souness never said they would be, of course. Only that the championship was his target. Celtic are not uncatchable but, playing the way they did at Easter Road on Saturday, the title seems out of Rangers' reach.

'The performance of both Rangers and Hibs in a goalless game wavered between rotten and really rotten. It was all fire and fury in the midfield and then a stuttering full-stop. However, at the midway point of the season, here is the report on Souness to you as boss of the Lawrence dynasty which controls Rangers. You authorised the expensive new deal at Ibrox from Lake Tahoe, Nevada, where you mysteriously continue to live.

'Personal performance – above average. Team showing – good but needing consistency, must do better. Entertainment value – generally good. Spectator reaction – unbelievable. Future prediction – promising on all fronts.

'With almost half the season gone, Rangers have been watched by approaching a million fans at Ibrox, with all other 11 Premier Division clubs reporting better attendances. David Holmes is adamant that it is up to the team to ensure they sustain this incredible spectator enthusiasm, which he describes as 'participation', and he is right.

'The business enterprise of Rangers is envied even at Old Trafford and at a time when football worldwide is on a downswing, the Light Blues are reversing that trend. Since Graeme Souness has arrived at Ibrox, players such as Cammy Fraser have shown improved form, and youngsters like Derek Ferguson and Ian Durrant have won, and held down, first team places, so there is much to be excited about.'

The day before the tie against the Germans, Borussia's Uwe Rahn predicted Souness would make a Euro comeback – even though the player hadn't decided himself. The West German international, a scorer in the first leg, said, 'We're certain he will play, and we know he can make a big difference to Rangers.'

It was a tribute to the reputation the Rangers boss held in Europe that Rahn, who had forecast that he would score in the first match, didn't sound as confident this time round. 'We know it won't be an easy tie. We have to be very careful they don't score or all the good we got from the first game will be wiped out.'

On the morning of the game, Souness announced exactly what Rahn had already told us – that he would indeed take his place in the starting line-up. It was good news for Rangers supporters. Souness, who hadn't kicked a ball in earnest for seven weeks, said, 'I've had no reaction from my two practice matches. I just hope I don't have a nightmare.'

Terry Butcher added, 'There can be no half measures now.' Butcher, Woods and West had attracted a posse of Fleet Street reporters to Germany, and he continued, 'We know we have to make up for not scoring the goals at Ibrox, and it won't be easy. But it never is by this stage of the competition, although we will give it our best shot. British teams have a pretty good record against German sides.

'I suppose the worst result for us would be a no-scoring draw. Normally that's a good result away from home but it would put us out this time.'

Sadly Butcher was right, and the match did indeed finish goalless, but everyone connected with the club felt a real sense of injustice at the manner in which they exited Europe – and it left a sour taste in the mouth long after the final whistle had sounded.

The Light Blues produced a fine team performance, which stood head and shoulders above any managed by a Rangers side in Europe in the first half of the 1980s, and at times they simply outclassed Borussia who resorted to over-physical tactics and were unjustly rewarded with a place in the quarter-finals.

In the cold light of day, it was the goal lost at Ibrox which ultimately put Rangers out of Europe, but had there been any justice in Germany, then Graeme Souness and his men would have been looking forward to another European tie in the New Year.

Instead, the facts and figures showed that Rangers had three men booked and two sent off by bungling Belgian referee Alex

Ponnet, but the villains in Munchengladbach were certainly not wearing blue jerseys – as the stud marks on the legs of Ted McMinn and co would clearly testify.

Ponnet was by reputation one of Europe's best referees, but he certainly didn't enhance that reputation in this match. It was particularly difficult to understand why Stuart Munro was shown a red card in the 74th minute after being all but physically assaulted while lying on the turf by defender Andrew Winkhold.

Winkhold was one of the evening's chief sinners, and was also responsible for bad fouls on Cooper and McMinn, yet he wasn't even booked.

It was all so hard for Rangers to accept – over the two matches it was clear they were a better side than Borussia but lacked a killer touch in front of goal. Rangers created all the best attacking situations in Germany and yet goalkeeper Uwe Kamps was virtually untroubled.

The closest the Ibrox men came to grabbing the goal they so richly deserved as reward for their dominance was in the eighth minute. McCoist outpaced the home defence when he ran on to a Butcher through ball and from 20 yards he struck a dipping shot with plenty of power. To the agony of the large Gers support, the ball hit the bar and was cleared by the Borussia defence.

Rangers were also denied one of the most blatant penalties seen when Butcher was pulled down inside the box by Hans-Jorg Criens as he ran to meet a Souness free kick. But Ponnet was nothing if not consistent and true to the rest of his display, he waved away claims for a penalty.

No Ranger suffered more on the night than the magnificent Butcher whose tears of anger, frustration and disappointment at the end of the match summed up the evening. Rangers had outplayed a side that had employed cynical tactics in an effort to get their 'rewards'. If there was comfort for Rangers to take, and it was difficult, they seemed equipped to at long last compete in Europe with credibility. That improvement alone meant their gallant efforts were not wholly in vain.

The morning after the night before did little to dull the agony of Munchengladbach for Butcher, with the captain still bitterly upset and angry at the way his side had so unjustly made their UEFA Cup exit.

Butcher did find a moment, though, to contemplate the performance of the 3,500 Rangers fans in the Bokelberg Stadium, which was just as impressive as the one put on by the players themselves.

He said, 'The punters were simply unbelievable and I know they all feel just as gutted as the team do about the way we went out of the competition. The backing they gave us was magnificent and for long periods you could hear them above the German fans. It was a very emotional moment at the end of the match when we saluted the fans. They deserved a win to celebrate but they gave us a great ovation nonetheless.'

David Holmes added, 'The behaviour of our fans was exemplary and I was very, very proud of them. The local chief of police spoke to me personally and said our supporters were the best he had ever come across. That was a fine tribute to them.

'They must have been as disappointed as anyone at the way we went out but I must stress to them that defeat doesn't change a thing. Yes, the club could have made a fortune from the quarter-finals but that would have been a bonus. The money is there to buy and I saw plenty in Germany to convince me we are heading in the right direction. We have a lot to be happy about.'

Meanwhile, it was announced by Rangers that Munro and Cooper would not be punished for their red cards in Germany. Souness made this clear after the controversial match, and said, 'As far as I am concerned, the players will not be disciplined. I was close enough to the incidents to know exactly what went on and it's not my players I blame.'

Butcher had to be physically held back by Souness at the end of the match as the captain's disappointment channelled itself into sheer anger – but the manager had only sympathy for his skipper. He said, 'The important thing is that nothing came of the incident. I fully understand how Terry felt and it reflected the way he has quickly come to feel about Rangers. It proves he is a winner and that's what I want at Ibrox – he will do for me.

'I was far from disappointed with the team in the Bokelberg. At half-time I was convinced we were going through but at the end of the day our final ball let us down.'

Rangers got back on track with a crushing 4-0 win over Falkirk, and after their valiant midweek exertions in Munchengladbach this was a Saturday afternoon stroll in the park. They never had to stretch themselves in taking two points from the tough-tackling Bairns, although Souness would not be pleased with the way his men eased off after the break.

Souness missed the game through a bout of flu, but even without his huge influence Rangers were never going to take anything less than maximum points. With Davie Cooper in stunning form, Rangers might have doubled their tally but the commendable crowd of over 24,000 went home happy enough.

They also experienced the joy of Butcher scoring his first goal for the club – although most people weren't quite sure when he actually got it. When Cooper's 15th-minute corner swung in viciously towards the near post, it appeared Butcher got the slightest of touches to the ball before it went past George Watson and into the net. However, the Ibrox skipper admitted afterwards he hadn't touched the ball and Cooper was credited with his eighth goal of the season.

But there was no doubt about the big man's contribution to the second Rangers goal. Another Cooper corner caught out the Falkirk rearguard and Cammy Fraser sent the ball across the face of the goal, where Butcher diverted it into the net with the outside of his left boot.

Five minutes from the break, Robert Fleck grabbed the third when he turned and shot home from the edge of the box after fine work by McCoist, and the young striker scored his second with a neat flick from another Cooper corner.

They say every cloud has a silver lining, and no one could begrudge the players a holiday in the sun after the disappointment of Munchengladbach. Five days after the game, a squad of 18 jetted off to Majorca for a well-earned break. It was ideal timing for the trip, coming halfway through the season, and gave Souness and co a chance to recharge the batteries for the gruelling run-in.

Souness said, 'It's the first chance we've had of a clear midweek and it presents a good opportunity to try and clear our injury list. Going out of Europe the way we did against Borussia was the most frustrating experience of my career but my job as a manager is to look forward, not back.

'The Premier League has always been my number one target and now we can concentrate solely on that objective. There is a long way to go in this championship and although Celtic have built up a useful lead, there's no way our challenge is over. There is still a lot of football to be played.'

Rangers didn't arrange any matches in Spain, with Souness insisting the priority was to help the likes of Jimmy Nicholl, Ian Durrant and Cammy Fraser back to full fitness.

There was mixed news for two of the young players at Ibrox just after the squad arrived back from their midweek break. Derek Ferguson was on top of the world when he did the double – and a historic presentation was made to him at Ibrox. For the first time ever, the same player won both major players' awards available within the Scottish game. Rangers' 19-year-old midfield star lifted the Fine Fare Young Player of the Month and Scottish Brewers' Personality Player of the Month prizes for October. As well as receiving commemorative plaques from both sponsors, Ferguson also received a cheque for £250 from Scottish Brewers together with grocery vouchers to the value of £50 from Fine Fare.

The young midfielder was also presented with a set of strips for a boys' club, and chose Blairhall United under-12s in Coatbridge, as his dad was involved with them.

However, a career which had promised so much for young defender Hugh Burns looked like grinding to a halt when the 20-year-old slapped in a transfer request. Rangers agreed to listen to offers for the player, who hadn't been happy at losing his place in the first team.

But as one Rangers player looked to be heading for the exit, another moved in. Neil Woods, the 20-year-old Doncaster

Rovers striker, joined the Light Blues after being watched by Walter Smith. Dundee United, Liverpool, Manchester United and Everton had also been tracking Woods, who cost £100,000.

But the topsy-turvy Rangers career of Colin Miller came to an end when Woods arrived in Govan. The Canadian international signed for Rovers as part of the deal that brought the young Englishman to Rangers.

The 22-year-old World Cup player had joined Rangers in August 1985 and despite making a handful of first-team appearances, he failed to establish himself in the side. He managed only one game under Souness, against Ilves Tampere in Finland.

Miller signed a contract to keep him at Belle Vue until the end of the 1987/88 season and insisted he was happy with the deal, although he was disappointed at having to leave Rangers. He said, 'I'm desperately disappointed I didn't win a regular place at Ibrox and anywhere after playing for Rangers is going to be a step down the ladder. But I'll always be proud to say I played for Rangers Football Club and I will listen out for their result every Saturday night. It has been great to be part of the club.

'Doncaster made me a very good offer and they really impressed me. The club are confident of going up to the Second Division at the end of this season and I know this is a place where I will be noticed by bigger clubs and am guaranteed regular football.'

With just eight days until Christmas, Rangers gave their fans an early present with a 2-0 win at Hamilton – and it was gift-wrapped by a youngster given a reprieve by Souness.

Robert Fleck, who scored one and made the other for McCoist, had a great game and reminded his manager of his claim to be Rangers' top goal-grabber with an impressive display at Douglas Park. Fleck looked equally at ease in partnership with McCoist in the first half and Colin West in the second, when McCoist dropped back to midfield to fill in for the unwell Derek Ferguson.

Despite Hamilton's 7-0 drubbing at the hands of Hearts seven days previous, Rangers were on a hiding to nothing but led coolly by boss Souness, they did a professional if unspectacular job to strengthen their championship challenge.

Chris Woods had a few great saves and was the mainstay of the best defensive record in the league.

Rangers took the lead in the 13th minute when Souness beautifully chipped the ball over the Accies defence for McCoist to run on to. His looping header beat Dave McKellar only to rebound off the crossbar, but the ever-alert Fleck dived in to power a header home.

Two minutes from time, Rangers confirmed their superiority by adding a second goal. It came after Cooper had watched McKellar save his 73rd-minute penalty. Fleck was again the man who did the damage when the Accies keeper could only parry his fierce 20-yard drive and McCoist pounced to net his 18th of the season. Colin West was unlucky not to add to Rangers' tally.

And if the 2-0 win was an early Christmas present, then Souness had the perfect gift up his sleeve to put a big smile on the faces of supporters as they ploughed through the snow to get to work on a cold and dark Monday morning – because the persistent player-manager finally got his man when Graham Roberts signed from Tottenham Hotspur for a fee of £450,000.

The defender – who could also do a job in midfield – had been the subject of a £400,000 bid from the Light Blues a fortnight previous which had been rejected by Spurs boss David Pleat.

Roberts was delighted to move to Ibrox, and said, 'Rangers are a big club with the same kind of high ambitions that I have as a player. I'm also pleased to leave Spurs as I didn't really have a future there. I aim to prove my critics wrong by enjoying a lot of success with Rangers.'

Roberts was known as one of the game's 'hard men' but hit out at that image, saying, 'I've only been booked twice this season and was sent off for something I didn't do. I aim to show the Rangers fans I'm worth the trouble Graeme Souness took to sign me.'

Roberts began his career with Southampton before moving to Sholing (a non-league side from the Southampton area), Bournemouth, Portsmouth, Dorchester Town and Weymouth, before Spurs signed him in 1980. He won two English FA Cup winner's medals with the London giants and captained them to a UEFA Cup triumph over Anderlecht in 1984.

One Rangers player certain to have a great Christmas was Chris Woods. The England keeper celebrated the end of the year by keeping his seventh successive clean sheet. Woods was also unbeaten in Rangers' first five league games of 1987, and clocked up an astonishing 1,196 minutes without losing a goal – a record that still stands to this day.

A year which had started off in such turmoil was set to end on a different note altogether. It was set to be a good Christmas for Bears.

Epilogue

JANUARY 1987 was a carbon copy of the previous month with four wins and a draw ensuring Rangers kept tabs on league leaders Celtic. The sides met at Ibrox on New Year's Day and it would have been easier to get a seat on Apollo 11 – the first manned mission to land on the Moon – than a ticket for the big game, as there wasn't a brief to be had for love nor money. It was massive and Rangers supporters knew that victory would take them to within a point of Celtic, assuming, of course, they managed to see off Hamilton Accies in their game in hand.

As it turned out, goals by deadly duo Robert Fleck and Ally McCoist sealed a 2-0 win – but there was more. Celtic had rightly been lauded for being the better team in October's Skol Cup Final – even though Rangers won 2-1 – but on this occasion it was no contest. Rangers were superior in every department. In fact, so far were they in front that the biggest majority of the home support left the stadium with their fingernails still intact.

Was Graeme Souness the new Jim Baxter? If the answer was in the negative, then there really wasn't an awful lot between them, because the Scotland skipper showed his skills – and swagger – off to great effect, and Celtic simply couldn't cope with him. He was imperious. Just like Glasgow, Rangers were miles better, and one memory from that afternoon that flashes instantly to mind is Souness's early challenge on Roy Aitken, and the ensuing lecture the bossy player-manager gives to the referee before he is booked.

Davie Cooper was also at his brilliant best and it was his cross that Pat Bonner spilled, which allowed McCoist to tap home number two – and it was all played out to the magnificent backdrop of incessant falling snow, giving Ibrox the appearance of a wonderful winter wonderland.

The bookmakers agreed that Rangers were well ahead of their biggest rivals and the dominant team in the city – and immediately installed the Light Blues as favourites for the Premier Division title.

The winter months of December and January – favourites for any mid-term shutdown – saw Rangers excel. Unbeaten with seven wins in succession – and clean sheets in the lot – meant Souness and co had come alive at just the right time.

A midweek win at Motherwell – courtesy of a Graham Roberts goal – was followed up with a 5-0 demolition of Clydebank, although the significant thing about the match against the Bankies, the two points apart, was the size of the crowd. When the sides had met exactly a year earlier, just over 12,000 had paid to watch Rangers win 4-2. Fast forward 12 months and more than 36,000 were inside the ground to see Fleck and McCoist share the goals in the 5-0 win.

It was quite an amazing turnaround. Once again, the supporters proved they wanted to watch attractive football, and the stadium was rocking as each goal flew in. The apathy and greyscale of a Saturday afternoon in Govan had all but disappeared. The Light Blues were once again in vogue – and Souness had to take most of the credit.

Mind you, the supporters were still sad to see Ted McMinn leave, when the trailblazing winger decided to join old gaffer Jock Wallace at Seville. In his three years at Ibrox, McMinn had tormented many an opposition defence, although it's fair to say he had also done the same thing to the home fans at times. But as frustrating as he could be, he was also a real character, and they were in short supply in the Scottish game.

But there was a lot of anger about down Ibrox way when the results of a UEFA inquiry into the aftermath of the Borussia Munchengladbach v Rangers clash were made public. Rangers were fined more than £5,000 for their part in the ugly scenes that followed the full-time whistle, but the decision everyone found hardest to accept was the four-match ban handed out to Stuart

Munro, who had been sent off in Germany after being assaulted by a Borussia defender while lying on the ground. It was one of the most disgraceful decisions ever taken by UEFA, which merely sullied its already tarnished reputation by coming up with such joke punishments.

On the final day of January, Hamilton Accies arrived at Ibrox for a Scottish Cup third-round tie – and left victorious after one of the shock results of the season. Never before had Adrian Sprott – scorer of the only goal – gained so many column inches, but his Roy of the Rovers strike in the 70th minute was greeted with incredulity by the majority of the 36,000 crowd, as the entire match up until then had been played in or around the visitors' 18-yard box.

At the time, Souness said, 'Good luck to Hamilton, but their goalkeeper had one of those days. We played almost the entire game within touching distance of him but the ball just wouldn't go in. It is an unhappy part of our history now but we just have to put it behind us and concentrate on the league.'

David McKellar was a journeyman keeper who played for 16 different clubs – including the likes of Carlisle United and Brentford – before finally calling it a day after a spell at, you guessed it, Glasgow Rangers. He signed for the Light Blues in 1991 – the year Souness exited for Liverpool. The man who had put the shutters up on Rangers that fateful January day ended his 20-year career at Ibrox – and well deserved it was too!

But sadly it was also the day that saw Chris Woods's clean sheet record come to an end at 1,196 minutes without conceding a goal, which was a phenomenal run, but you know what they say about all good things.

Despite the shock defeat, Rangers were still moving in the right direction and if there were still folk doubting Souness and his team as genuine championship contenders they were surely converted on Saturday 7 February at Tynecastle, where they hadn't won a league match since April 1977. This time, though, it would be different; very different. Just a few punters short of 30,000 crammed into the Gorgie Road stadium and watched a rampant Rangers win 5-2.

St Mirren were next to fall, thanks to a McCoist hat-trick, but with no Scottish Cup tie the following weekend, Rangers invited French cracks Bordeaux to Ibrox for a friendly and the supporters were in raptures watching the sublime talents of French World Cup stars like Jean Tigana. They also had players such as Patrick Battiston and Bernard Lacombe, although Gers fans had a good old laugh when the name of their goalkeeper – Dominique Dropsy – was read out! The 30,000 who turned up for the Friday night match were treated to another fine exhibition from both teams, with goals by Fleck, Neil Woods and Souness ensuring a 3-2 win.

Perhaps that was the moment the supporters started to believe. Or maybe they waited until the following month – marvellous March – when Falkirk, Hamilton, Dundee, Dundee United and Motherwell were gunned down. Five victories on the trot, ten goals scored and just one conceded. McCoist was banging them in for fun and there wasn't a defender in the country who could live with him. Once again, it was fun being a Rangers supporter.

After McCoist had scored his 31st goal of the season against Motherwell, Rangers had six league games left to play and knew that victory in them all would secure their first title in a decade – but things didn't quite go according to plan at the start of April. Rangers had entered the Old Firm fixture with a four-point advantage – although that was halved as Celtic won 3-1 to throw their manager Davie Hay a title lifeline.

The match had plenty of talking points for the 60,000 crowd and the millions of armchair fans around the globe. The most hotly-disputed were the two penalty kicks awarded to Celtic by referee Bob Valentine, which were both converted by Brian McClair. There was also a perfectly good 'goal' scored by Cooper straight from a corner, but ruled out by the man in black for a phantom foul by Fleck on Bonner. The match was played a couple of days before Souness's first anniversary in charge at Ibrox – but there were no celebrations that night.

However, the next three matches – against Dundee, Hamilton and Hearts – proved the result at Celtic Park had been no more than a blip, with three wins, three clean sheets – and six goals from that man McCoist.

The second of these games, a 3-0 win at Clydebank's Kilbowie Park, saw Rangers edge three points clear of Celtic – who had dropped a point at home to Dundee United – with three games left to play. Victory over Hearts at Ibrox – in front of yet another full house – meant that just a point was required in the next game for the Light Blues to be crowned champions. And that game was against Aberdeen at Pittodrie.

And what a game, and afternoon, it turned out to be for the thousands of Rangers fans that descended upon the Granite City. It was quite a match, and threatened to explode early on when Souness went in late on Brian Irvine. If the referee hadn't been about to show Souness a yellow, then Aberdeen skipper Willie Miller made sure by badgering the match official until he produced the card. The player-manager was then red-carded for another bookable challenge on the same opponent and was sent packing, much to the delight of the home players and fans. Souness's season would ironically end the way it had started – with a red card.

But with five minutes remaining of the first half Davie Cooper was fouled by Stewart McKimmie close to the Aberdeen touchline, and a free kick was awarded. Coop took it and Terry Butcher bulleted home a header, leaving Jim Leighton stranded. Despite Aberdeen equalising, it was enough to give Rangers the title, with Falkirk's defeat of Celtic merely confirming the outcome.

When the referee blew the final whistle at Pittodrie it was the cue for the pitch invasion to begin, and on poured thousands of Rangers fans. The heavy burden of nine frustrating years without a title win had been lifted from their shoulders with one strain of the captain's neck.

The police appealed for the Rangers supporters to clear the field, and 25 minutes later, the players – led by Butcher – re-appeared for a dramatic lap of honour. More than 10,000 supporters were in the ground – many of whom had been ticketless, but were allowed in for the post-match celebrations –

and they lapped up the drama with all the pomp and ceremony of the Last Night of the Proms. It was unforgettable stuff.

As the goalposts were 'dismantled' Butcher described the day as 'the happiest of my life', adding that when he had arrived at Rangers, Cooper had told him the team had a great chance of winning the league. How right Coop was.

There was one more league game left to play, at home to St Mirren, and a Fleck goal ensured another sell-out crowd – who had come along mainly for the party – went home with a smile.

It had been quite a journey, and one that had started with the curved-ball appointment of the Scotland midfield star just over a year beforehand. That's how long it had taken Souness – and his Rangers Revolution – to completely transform a sleeping giant, and boy how we partied!

1986 Results Part One

Date	Opponent	Result	Competition	Venue	Scorers	Att
Jan 1	Celtic	0-2	League	Away		49,812
Jan 4	Dundee	5-0	League	Home	McCoist 3; W'son; Fleck	13,954
Jan 11	Clydebank	4-2	League	Home	Paterson; McPh; W'son; McCoist	12,731
Jan 18	St Mirren	2-0	League	Home	McCoist; McPherson	17,528
Jan 25	Hearts	2-3	Scottish Cup 3	Away	McCoist; Durrant	27,500
Feb 1	Aberdeen	1-1	League	Home	Burns	29,887
Feb 8	Motherwell	0-1	League	Away		11,619
Feb 14	Chelsea	3-2	Friendly	Home	Paterson; Bell; Burns	17,512
Feb 19	Aberdeen	0-1	League	Away		19,500
Feb 22	Dundee Utd	1-1	League	Away	McCoist	14,644
Mar 1	Hibernian	3-1	League	Home	McCoist 3	16,574
Mar 15	Dundee	1-2	League	Away	McCoist	10,965
Mar 22	Celtic	4-4	League	Home	Fraser 2; McCoist; Fleck	41,006
Mar 29	Hearts	1-3	League	Away	McCoist	24,735

Date	Opponent	Result	Competition	Venue	Scorers	Att
Apr 6	Tottenham	0-2	Friendly	Home		12,665
Apr 12	Clydebank	1-2	League	Away	Durrant	7,027
Apr 19	St Mirren	1-2	League	Away	Dawson	9,760
Apr 26	Aberdeen	1-1	League	Away	McMinn	17,000
May 3	Motherwell	2-0	League	Home	McPherson; McCoist pen	21,500
May 9	Celtic	3-2	Glw Cup final	Home	McCoist 3	40,741

1986 Results
Part Two

Date	Opponent	Result	Competition	Venue	Scorers	Att
Aug 9	Hibernian	1-2	League	Away	McCoist pen	24,576
Aug 13	**Falkirk**	**1-0**	**League**	**Home**	**McCoist pen**	**27,362**
Aug 16	**Dundee Utd**	**2-3**	**League**	**Home**	**McCoist 2**	**43,995**
Aug 20	Stenhousemuir	4-1	League Cup 2	Away	Souness; West; Cooper; McCoist	9,052
Aug 23	Hamilton Acc	2-1	League	Away	Fraser; West	10,000
Aug 27	East Fife	0-0	League Cup 3	Away	Won on penalties	8,835
Aug 31	**Celtic**	**1-0**	**League**	**Home**	**Durrant**	**43,502**
Sep 3	**Dundee**	**3-1**	**League Cup 4**	**Home**	**Fraser; Souness; McMinn**	**33,750**
Sep 6	Motherwell	2-0	League	Away	Cooper; McPherson	17,013
Sep 13	**Clydebank**	**4-0**	**League**	**Home**	**Fleck 3; McMinn**	**26,433**
Sep 17	**Ilves Tampere**	**4-0**	**UEFA Cup 1**	**Home**	**Fleck 3; McCoist**	**27,436**
Sep 20	Dundee	0-1	League	Away		17,132
Sep 24	Dundee Utd	2-1	League Cup S	Hden	McCoist; McMinn	45,249
Sep 27	**Aberdeen**	**2-0**	**League**	**Home**	**Souness; McCoist**	**40,155**

Date	Opponent	Result	Competition	Venue	Scorers	Att
Oct 1	Ilves Tampere	0-2	UEFA Cup 1	Away		2,109
Oct 4	Hearts	1-1	League	Away	Cooper	28,637
Oct 8	St Mirren	1-0	League	Away	Cooper	16,861
Oct 11	**Hibernian**	**3-0**	**League**	**Home**	**McPherson; Fleck; Bell**	**38,196**
Oct 18	Falkirk	5-1	League	Away	Fleck 3 (1p); Cooper pen; McCoist	16,800
Oct 23	**Boavista**	**2-1**	**UEFA Cup 2**	**Home**	**McPherson; McCoist**	**38,772**
Oct 26	Celtic	2-1	League Cup F	Hden	Durrant; Cooper pen	74,219
Oct 29	Dundee Utd	0-0	League	Away		20,179
Nov 1	Celtic	1-1	League	Away	McCoist	60,000
Nov 4	Boavista	1-0	UEFA Cup 2	Away	D. Ferguson	23,000
Nov 8	**Motherwell**	**0-1**	**League**	**Home**		**33,966**
Nov 15	Clydebank	4-1	League	Away	McCoist 2; McPherson; Durrant	9,906
Nov 19	**Dundee**	**2-1**	**League**	**Home**	**McCoist; McPherson**	**22,992**
Nov 22	Aberdeen	0-1	League	Away		21,733
Nov 26	**B Mon'bach**	**1-1**	**UEFA Cup 3**	**Home**	**Durrant**	**44,000**
Nov 29	**Hearts**	**3-0**	**League**	**Home**	**McCoist; Cooper; Durrant**	**38,733**

Date	Opponent	Result	Competition	Venue	Scorers	Att
Dec 3	St Mirren	2-0	League	Home	McPherson; Cooper	23,110
Dec 6	Hibernian	0-0	League	Away		18,536
Dec 10	B Mon'bach	0-0	UEFA Cup 3	Away		36,000
Dec 13	Falkirk	4-0	League	Home	Fleck 2; Cooper; Butcher	24,177
Dec 20	Hamilton Acc	2-0	League	Away	Fleck; McCoist	10,000
Dec 27	Dundee Utd	2-0	League	Home	McCoist; Fleck	42,165